James, Lawrence, 1943-
    The savage wars : British campaigns
in Africa, 1870-1920 / by Lawrence
James. -- 1st U.S. ed. -- New York :
St. Martin's Press, c1985.
    xvi, 297 p. : ill. ; 24 cm.

    Bibliography: p. 283-287.
    Includes index.
    ISBN 0-312-69987-5 : $19.95

(Cont'd on next card)

The Savage Wars

The
Savage Wars

British Campaigns in Africa, 1870–1920

by

LAWRENCE JAMES

St. Martin's Press
New York

To my wife, Mary

Library of Congress Catalog Card Number: 85–24388

Library of Congress Cataloging-in-Publication Data
James, Lawrence, 1943–
  The savage wars.

  1. Africa – Colonization.   2. British – Africa –
History – 19th century.   3. British – Africa – History –
20th century.   4. Africa – History, Military.   5. Great
Britain. Army – History.   I. Title.
DT32.5.J36 1986   960'.23   85-24388
ISBN 0-312-69987-5

First published in Great Britain by Robert Hale Ltd.
First U.S. Edition

10 9 8 7 6 5 4 3 2 1

Contents

Illustrations

Maps

Picture Credits

The following photographs are reproduced by kind permission of:
Colonial Office Library: 1, 6, 8, 9, 14, 15, 18, 24, 29, 30, 47, 48, 49, 52, 54, 55, 58, 59, 61, 62, 63, 69, 73, 74, 88, 91, 96, 98, 117; National Army Museum: 2, 11, 13, 16, 20, 33, 34, 35, 36, 37, 41, 42, 43, 44, 45, 46, 50, 51, 53, 67, 68, 70, 71, 72, 80, 81, 82, 84, 86, 87, 90, 94, 99, 102, 108, 109, 114, 115; Imperial War Museum: 10, 12, 26, 27, 28, 31, 40, 56, 57, 60, 64, 65, 66, 76, 77, 78, 79, 83, 103, 104, 105, 106, 107, 111, 112; Africana Museum, Johannesburg: 22, 23, 100, 101; Cape Archives: 17, 19, 21, 25, 93; National Film Archives and Stills Library: 3, 7; National Maritime Museum: 32; Private Collections: 4, 5, 38, 39, 75, 85, 89, 92, 95, 97, 110, 113, 116, 118, 119.

Acknowledgements

I would like to thank Captain Ewan Campbell, Colonel and Mrs Victor Collison, Martin Edmonds, Michael Ffinch, Dr John MacKenzie, Charles Mahon, Dr Jeffrey Richards, Dr Bill Sheils, Dr Martin Stephens, Andrew Williams, Vivian Williams and Percy Wood for their advice, suggestions and criticisms which together have helped greatly in the preparation of this book. Its errors and shortcomings are not of their making. I wish to express my thanks to Mrs Anne Simpson for her kind permission to use the diary and photographs of her father, Dr Richard Tooth, and to the Lord Chancellor's Department for allowing me to examine files concerning courts martial. Thanks are also due to the staff of the Public Record Office, the National Army Museum, the Imperial War Museum, the Africana Museum, Johannesburg, Rhodes House, Oxford, and the library of the Foreign and Commonwealth Office. The quotation from Thomas Hardy is from his *Collected Works*, published by Macmillan; the Newbolt quotation is from his *Collected Poems*, published by John Murray.

Introduction

With the exception of the Boer War of 1899–1902, the campaigns of the British conquest of Africa are little known today. This book is an attempt to describe the wars, small and large, waged by British forces in different parts of Africa between 1870 and 1920 which led to the final extension of Britain's global empire. The starting point is the growth of aggressive, imperialist sentiment in late Victorian Britain which, together with a changing political and economic climate provided the impetus for the acquisition of colonies in Africa. From here I have passed to the mechanics of conquest, the political decisions which sent the armies into battle and the strategic and tactical considerations which shaped the subsequent wars. In the hope of making these matters clear, I have looked at southern, northern, west and east Africa separately although at times regional distinctions mattered little in the eyes of imperialists who thought in continental terms. In the second part of the book I have examined the campaigns through the eyes of the men who had to fight them in order to create an impression of what it was like to have waged war for the Empire. I have looked at war against the black Africans and the Boers ('the white man's war') and how British forces adapted to fighting different foes in different regions. I have also considered the long periods of inactivity and mundane chores which marked out the fighting man's life in the field. Finally, since Britain's success in her African wars was in part the triumph of technology, I have described those artefacts of an industrial age which so frequently made the defeat of pre-industrial peoples so easy.

In re-telling and, at times, elaborating on this story, I realize that I am covering historical events which stirred up much passion, some of which is still very alive. Imperialism is still, for many, a dirty word which is widely used as a piece of political

Billingsgate between left and right, the West and the Third World. Along with 'colonialism' it has become synonymous with self-interested paternalism, economic exploitation, oppression and the domination of the strong over the weak. This is by no means a recent connection for it was recognized by critics of Empire over a hundred years ago. It was indeed true that many who left Britain for the tropics did not include ideals of individual liberty in their baggage nor were their consciences disturbed by the commonplace use of force to impose their will on those who resisted them. It is easy to feel sympathy for the casualties of imperial conquest like Cetshwayo and Sekukuni and feel disdain for their opponents, the shifty Shepstone and Frere and the callous Wolseley. Yet others who took part in the conquest of Africa did so in the belief that their actions would bring benefits to its people, not least the end of slavery, and their idealism cannot be dismissed out of hand as humbug.

Many Africans died in apparently one-sided and hopeless battles against forces possessed of overwhelming firepower but the trail of corpses produced by the many hundreds of tribal wars and raiding was also long. Europeans did not introduce war into Africa. They did however bring the warfare of modern technology to Africa but there were plenty of African rulers who were more than anxious to import it long before the era of partition. Nevertheless partition and the wars of conquest created lasting political grievances amongst African peoples which can still be manipulated by politicians. The repercussions of the wars of imperialism are still with us and will long remain so. Perhaps the most potent political consequence of the sudden and brief conquest of most of Africa by the European powers has been the question of what might have happened if there had been no conquest? History cannot be written in the subjunctive but this has not prevented speculation of an indulgent kind and the persistence with which many African leaders blame the 'colonial' period for all their people's present problems. In Britain there is often a different reaction, one of shame for the deeds of another generation's heroes.

I have tried to steer clear of both attitudes. During my childhood the Empire was still very real, Empire Day was celebrated at school and it was made clear that Britain's rule over distant lands was humane and beneficial. To me the Empire was the source of finely produced postage stamps which showed King George VI's firm features looking over small vignettes of cocoa farmers, tobacco plantations, native villages and the like. Names such as the Gold Coast, Nyasaland and Bechuanaland held a special romance. What I knew of the history of the Empire came from the reading of such authors of Henty and Brereton which had survived in school and public libraries. Since those days a little learning and scepticism have disabused me of this roseate view of the British Empire, although I am less than convinced that in many parts of Africa, the pre-colonial systems of government offered much in the way of happiness to their subjects. Cruelty, arbitrariness and aggression like courage and humanity are not the monopoly of any one nation or race.

SPANISH
MOROCCO

TUNISIA

IFNI

MOROCCO

RIO DE ORO

ALGERIA

LIBYA

EGYPT

MAP 3

FRENCH WEST AFRICA

GAMBIA

PORTUGUESE
GUINEA

MAP 4

EQUATORIAL AFRICA

ANGLO-
EGYPTIAN
SUDAN

ERITREA

FRENCH
SOMALILAND

SIERRA
LEONE

LIBERIA

GOLD
COAST

TOGO

NIGERIA

CAMEROONS

RIO MUNI

FRENCH

BELGIAN

CONGO

BRITISH
SOMALI-
LAND

ETHIOPIA

UGANDA

BRITISH
EAST AFRICA
(KENYA)

ITAL-
SOMALILAND

GERMAN
EAST
AFRICA

MAP 5

ANGOLA

NORTHERN RHODESIA

NYASALAND

MADAGASCAR

GERMAN
SOUTH
WEST
AFRICA

BECHU-
ANALAND

S.
RHOD-
ESIA

MOZAMBIQUE

SOUTH

AFRICA

SWAZILAND

BASUTOLAND

Miles   1000

0

km   2000

MAP 2

Africa 1914

xvi

I
THE NEW ROME

1. Imperial Visions, 1870–1914

It is said that our Empire is already large enough and does not need expansion. We shall have to consider not what we want now, but what we want in the future. We have to remember that it is part of our responsibility and heritage to take care that the world, so far as it can be moulded by us, should receive the Anglo-Saxon and not another character.

Lord Rosebery, 1893

The table was lit with huge many-branched candlesticks which commemorated the military history of the last century in silver palm trees and bowed silver savages.

Evelyn Waugh, *Sword of Honour*

In the priory church of Lanercost, not far from Hadrian's Wall, a stone monument commemorates two sons of the ninth earl of Carlisle who met their deaths in Africa. One, Hubert Howard, was a war correspondent for the *Times* and *New York Herald* attached to General Kitchener's army in the Sudan who died at the moment of victory during the battle of Omdurman in 1898. A few hours before he died, he had charged with the 21st Lancers, a passage of arms which had left him so exhilarated that he remarked to a fellow newspaperman, 'This is the best day of my life.' His brother Oliver, a soldier-administrator and veteran of the Boer War, died at his post in the newly annexed territory of Northern Nigeria in 1908. Both men lost their lives while they were helping the extension and consolidation of Britain's imperial frontiers, so it is nicely appropriate that they should share a memorial close to the frontier of the Roman Empire.

During their lifetimes comparisons between the British and Roman Empires had been frequent. In 1900 the former Liberal

3

Prime Minister, Lord Rosebery, had asked his audience of Edinburgh University students, 'Are we, like the Romans, not merely a brave but also persistent, business-like, alert governing people?' One such business-like and governing person, Cecil Rhodes, admired Roman civic virtues and fancied that his features closely resembled those of the Emperor Hadrian, a conceit which he expressed through the commission of carved busts of himself and the wish that his funeral should be based upon that of a Roman emperor. When Kitchener's victorious army paraded through the streets of Berber in 1898, an eye-witness compared the procession to 'a Roman triumph', a likeness made more vivid by the presence of the defeated Dervish emir, Mahmud, who trailed behind his conqueror, shackled, yoked and goaded forward by whips.

Hubert Howard no doubt watched this bizarre scene, and if he disapproved, he hid his feelings for he had won and kept Kitchener's admiration, which was unusual, since the commander normally disliked all war correspondents. Howard's duty, like that of his colleagues, was to describe the desert war for his readers, and they for the most part warmly approved of its purpose and shed no tears for a defeated foe. The conquest of the Sudan was a part of Britain's imperial destiny, a major undertaking which would bring order and civilization to a land which had hitherto known only anarchy, slavery and suffering. It was also an act of revenge for the humiliation of 1885 when General Gordon had died at Khartoum. At that time a faltering Prime Minister, Gladstone, had turned his back on Britain's honour, prevaricated and then taken her armies out of the Sudan. When he claimed that Britain had no real interest there, baulked at the cost of a war there and even thought that the Dervishes possessed the same rights of self-determination which he was soon to offer to the people of Ireland, Gladstone had misunderstood the mood of the British public.

That mood was better appreciated by Gladstone's fellow Liberal John Bright, who sensed and regretted a new spirit abroad in the Britain of the 1880s. The old, mid-Victorian certainties were under assault. Britain was no longer set fair on a course of moral and material progress, guided by the Christian faith and the principles of Free Trade between nations. Her future prosperity was in question as the old pattern of industrial paramountcy and burgeoning wealth was broken up by foreign competition and a gloomy cycle of alternate recessions and recoveries which had begun in the 1870s. When old certainties disintegrated, men cast around for replacements. As a consequence, Bright feared the spread of a new, unscrupulous and aggressive spirit which he knew would morally subvert his countrymen and send them chasing after the gods of conquest and empire. His misgivings were justified. The public enthusiasm for the conquest of Egypt in 1882 and the anger which exploded after the failure to rescue Gordon were manifestations of a new national mood. Britain was developing the will for imperial adventure and conquest.

The impulse which drove Britain's rulers to send armies into Africa to fight wars of conquest and consolidation was imperialism. This late-Victorian imperialism was an oddly hybrid ideology which affected its champions in different ways. At a popular level it took the form of a mindless and noisy reaction to wars and rumours of wars which came to be called 'jingoism'. Such a phenomenon was not new, since belligerent patriotism had flourished throughout the nineteenth century. It had revealed itself through the cartoons of Gillray during the Napoleonic wars and found a new, characteristically loud voice when the crowds had cheered the soldiers who embarked for the Crimea. It flared up again in 1877, when a crisis in south-eastern Europe seemed likely to lead to a war against Russia. Then the music-hall audiences had sung the chorus:

> We don't want to fight
> But by jingo if we do,
> We've got the men, we've got the ships,
> We've got the money too!

Thus the word 'jingoism' came into the English language, synonymous with all expressions of warlike, mass patriotism. It was a popular emotion and seldom sober. In 1900 a beery party of jingoes carried a wooden coffin filled with a mock corpse of President Kruger, the Boer leader, through the streets of the small Lancashire town of Ulverston and stopped at every public house they passed. Such behaviour was traditional, for when Kruger took his place as a national bogeyman in 1899, he was assuming the role that 'Boney' had played a hundred years earlier and which 'Kaiser Bill' would succeed to a few years later.*

Kruger's war did provide jingoism with its imperial climax in 1900 when the news broke that Mafeking had been relieved.

* Subsequent holders of this title have been Hitler, Nasser and most recently Galtieri.

Imperial celebration: Zanzibar street decorated for Queen Victoria's Diamond Jubilee, 1897.

Throughout the country there were wild and noisy celebrations. Private Frank Richards remembered the news reaching the small South Wales town of Blaina, where his Tory aunt 'was so overjoyed that late in the evening she made a huge bonfire with four old straw mattresses on some waste ground in front of the house'.[1] Neighbours quickly joined her, and a party was soon underway. Patriotic songs were sung and a partisan suggestion was made that the effigy of the pro-Boer politician Lloyd George should be placed on top of the blaze. In rural Suffolk the sons of labouring men had celebrated the war in South Africa with impromptu parades along village streets during which they sang:

> Lord Roberts and Kitchener, Generals Buller and White,
> All dressed in khaki, going out to fight . . .

One who watched this remembered that the singers' faces appeared sincere and their manner was self-important. It was all, he added, 'My country – country – country.'[2]

Jingoism of this kind flourished in a soil which had been well prepared. The 1890s saw the rapid expansion of the popular press, and the new newspapers, such as the *Daily Mail* (founded in 1896), aimed deliberately at the working and lower-middle

Dance to the tune of empire: Patriotic music-cover of the Boer War.

classes. This readership, which had been created as a result of the extension of education to all during the 1870s and 1880s, was offered a simple, pungent journalism which aimed to excite as well as inform. The *Mail*'s owner, Lord Harmsworth, remarked that the British people relished a 'good hate', and by presenting issues in stark terms of black and white he made sure that they were not deprived of this necessity. The 'new' press needed to keep and hold its readers, and to do this it naturally exploited the wars of imperial conquest. War correspondents and artists marched with the armies, and through their reports and on-the-spot sketches the public of all classes was able to follow the campaigns and share the tension and excitement of battle. Lists of wounded officers were published in exhaustive detail ('Major D. T. Cruikshank, face and eye, severe'), and there were fulsome obituaries of those who fell in action. One, from the *Evening News*, may stand as a fair sample not only of the prose but of the sentiments of such journalism:

> He [Captain Boyle, Imperial Yeomanry] stood for that enthusiasm of service which drove English gentlemen from their pleasure and business out here to help us. He was the first of the English Yeomanry to arrive in Africa, he is the first to leave it. And he came, not, as most of us, with a personal motive, neither from *ennui* nor for glory, but from love of his land.
>
> For him it was England only, and still England: the steadfastness of her valour, the strength of her purpose, the clearness of her fame.

When it came to describing the fighting, the newspaper style was graphic. Column headlines in the *Sun* during 1900 included 'Koorn Spruit Ambush', 'More Deeds of Derring Do', 'New VCs – shells that come in the Night' and 'The Banner-Cry of Hell'.

The master wordsmith of the new war journalism was George Steevens, who reported the Sudan War of 1898 for the *Daily Mail* and died whilst covering the Boer War. A colleague described him as 'the High Priest of Imperialism' whose plain, evocative style possessed the ability to have 'taken all England to South Africa'. In the same obituary Steevens's prose was called 'cinematographic' which was paradoxical since the journalist was already in competition with the moving film. Films, a novelty of the 1890s, were soon pressed into service to show the public the wars of imperial conquest. A cameraman stood on the deck of a gunboat and took pictures of the Dervish charge at Omdurman in 1898, but the blast from a cannon blew the back off his camera

Imperial conquest on film: Cavalrymen dismount and set up a Maxim machine-gun, South Africa, c. 1900.

and exposed what would have been some of the most remarkable newsreel footage of all time. A number of commercial films were made of operations in South Africa between 1899 and 1902, including shots of forces retiring from the battle of Spion Kop. So hungry did the public appear for actual moving pictures of these events that one company concocted bogus Boer War footage filmed on location close to London.

The extensive reporting of wars in Africa not only stimulated popular jingoism: it created public heroes. Soon after the dismayed British public heard how Colonel Fred Burnaby had died, 'sword in hand while resisting the desperate charge of Arabs', at Abu Klea in 1885, the *Illustrated London News* printed a full-page engraving of him in the splendid ceremonial uniform of his regiment, the Blues. A London firm offered for sale copies of the last photograph of this hero, and for those with more to spend, the Staffordshire Porcelain Company produced a brightly coloured equestrian figure of Burnaby which was twinned with one which depicted another heroic victim of the Sudan war, General Stewart. Poets hurried to commemorate the brave Burnaby, whom an anonymous scribbler in *Punch* set alongside the paladins of history:

9

But alas! for the spear thrust that ended a story,
Romantic as Roland's, as Lion Heart's brief!
Yet crowned with incident, gilded with glory,
And crowned by a laurel that's verdant of leaf.

Each imperial conflict produced its crop of such fustian. The Boer War, which was the largest in scale, was the most prolific in spawning mementoes of every kind. There were busts of the generals whose features also appeared on lapel badges, china-ware and cigarette- and postcards. There were verses and songs which commemorated fighting men and their deeds, and souvenir books which recounted their campaigns. Even advertisers seized the chance to promote their goods through war. Readers of *The Graphic* of 2 March 1901 were offered the 'Bovril War Picture' which showed the brave scene when Ladysmith was relieved, and a firm-jawed colonial cavalryman in a 'smasher' hat asserted his preference for Tortoise-Shell mixture pipe tobacco. A serving soldier attested to the value of Dr Collis Browne's Chlorodyne, a universal curative which had enabled him and his brothers-in-arms to recover from dysentery contracted whilst on active service in the Gold Coast. Elsewhere the makers of patent cure-alls and universal palliatives offered sheaves of similar statements from enteric victims in South Africa.

Imperial conflicts even penetrated the nursery. Ernest Shepherd, whose delightful drawings illustrated the first and many later editions of *The Wind in the Willows*, happily remembered a gift of toy soldiers in the 1880s which included European troops and 'black savages'. His figures were German-made but the London firm of Britains offered a wide range of imperial troops from British regulars in khaki to native askaris and Camel Corps troopers with all their paraphernalia of mules, machine-guns and war-rockets. These delighted the schoolboys of late Victorian and Edwardian Britain and enabled them to play out, in microcosm, the wars of empire. Such things may have passed through the mind of Flora Thompson when in *Lark Rise* she recalled her childhood in an Oxfordshire hamlet during the 1880s: 'Theirs had been the day of the bayonet and the Gatling gun, of horse-drawn gun-carriages and balloon observation, of soldiers fighting in tight-necked scarlet tunics.'

This was popular imperialism, garish, noisy, sentimental and above all celebratory. It was an intensely patriotic reaction to a series of wars in remote and exotic lands where gallant British soldiers overcame savage foes. If there were issues, they could

10

Technology tames the savage: Aerial warfare in North Africa, 1915 (from a boys' adventure story).

be either ignored or reduced to a simple chiaroscuro. In the film of Noël Coward's *Cavalcade*, the butler who is just about to leave with his master for the war in South Africa answers his wife's question about the need for that or any other war with the claim that it has to be fought so that the British can 'prove we're top dogs'. Although fictional, the comment was authentic of time and place. Yet as the opponents of imperialism repeatedly alleged, it was ideology which inevitably led to wars and fostered militarism. In the popular mind the heroes of empire were warriors whose virtues were those of courage, determination and patriotic self-sacrifice. War generated popular enthusiasm for empire and vested it with glamour.

The generation before 1914 dreaded a European war between the great industrial powers with their mass armies, and for those who survived the Great War, this dread became revulsion. Colonial wars were different. They were the means by which civilization was advanced and ignorant savagery tamed. They were testing grounds of the nation's virtue as represented by its fighting men, as Winston Churchill, then a young cavalry subaltern, recognized in the introduction to his *The Malakand Field Force* which first appeared in 1897. It was, he promised, a tale which embraced 'the stubbornness of the British soldier, and the jaunty daring of his officers', qualities which were shown on many 'occasions of devotion and self sacrifice, of cool cynicism

11

and stern resolve'. Those who followed imperial wars through the newspapers or campaign histories like Churchill's would share at second hand the suffering and heroism of war and find also testaments to the special qualities of the British race. Pluck, gallantry, selflessness and determination were the manly virtues prized by the Victorians, and they were truly mirrored in these wars. Here too was the modern apparatus of war: repeating rifles, machine-guns, gunboats and railway trains, each and all examples of the scientific and technical genius of Britain and its people. The wars were therefore a means by which national qualities and abilities were vindicated, and the victories achieved were tokens of national greatness.

Many, more thoughtful champions of imperialism, were unwilling to regard their creed as merely a bellicose expression of national superiority. Sir Ralph Furse drew more than patriotic self-satisfaction from his boyhood reading of the newspaper accounts of the Sudan War. He recollected how his father had stimulated his curiosity about the growing African empire: 'He led me from tales of Isandlwana and Rorke's Drift to Seeley's *Expansion of England* and Cromer and *England in Egypt*.' From admiring the flowers of imperialism, Furse passed to an examination of their roots. He discovered why the armies had marched and fought. To his youthful fascination with British Africa was added an admiration for the Elizabethans, with whom Furse closely identified himself, then and later. 'And as the typical Elizabethan lived to serve Gloriana, so I would wish to serve England.'[3] The winners and makers of Britain's new empire consciously looked back to find parallels for their ideas and tasks. Lord Rosebery imagined that the young men who would rule and serve the empire would have to possess the discipline and dedication of the 'militant orders of monasticism'. 'Empire', he proclaimed, 'represents to us our history, our tradition, our race. It is a matter of influence, of peace, of civilization, above all a question of faith.' The bishop of Grahamstown, Natal, expanded on this lofty theme when he preached in London in 1896. Britain had been given her colonies by 'the Prince of Kings of Earth' and were to be held in his name. 'To have him owned as King is the end for which our empire had been granted, wherever we go.'[4]

There are two complementary strands of thinking here, and each played an outstanding part in providing an impetus for imperial expansion in Africa. One singled out the British, or sometimes the Anglo-Saxon, race and made it an instrument of

Divine imperial mission by which civilization and Christianity would be brought to those who lacked them. The other called upon Britain's youth to rise to the demands of its birth, race and national destiny. Just as animals had evolved and survived thanks to special qualities, so, it was thought, nations developed, some emerging in a form which gave them a natural right to conquer and rule. This adaptation of Darwinian theories, transferred from the world of beasts to that of men, encouraged imperial thinkers to argue that Britain had achieved the highest possible state of civilization. In a *credo* first composed in 1877 Cecil Rhodes asserted 'that we are the first race in the world, and that the more of the world we inhabit, the better it is for the human race'. Lord Lugard, who was responsible for the extension of British control over Uganda and Northern Nigeria, would have concurred. He saw 'something fine in the sight of the Englishman standing up for the right and trying to conquer by their force of superiority the rooted customs of centuries, saying they would have no carrying off of slaves and women, and urging the wild passions of these savages to seek a nobler channel'. Pressed forward by such dedicated warrior-apostles, the power of civilization would advance and that of ignorance and brutishness fall back. This was inevitable in the view of another soldier-administrator, Rudolph von Slatin, an Austrian Jew who had commanded the Egyptian forces in the southern Sudan. Here he had witnessed 'Wild tribes, who in their modes of life are nearer to beast than to man' realize 'that there were beings mentally superior to themselves, and who, through the appliances of modern civilization, are unconquerable even in foreign lands.'[5]

Imperial wars in Africa were therefore being undertaken to overcome backwardness and savagery and were waged by a nation which saw itself as the banner-bearer of civilization. As part of this civilization, indeed at its heart, were the personal and political liberties of which the British were proud. Civilization was not just the ability to make and use a machine-gun, and the upholders of imperialism were quick to show that peace, justice, stability and the end of slavery were the results of imperial conquest and government. Lord Milner, High Commissioner in South Africa from 1897, was convinced that the art of giving good and fair government was peculiarly British and one in which the Englishman was as 'handy and adaptable as he is angular and clumsy in society'. Ten years after the British occupation of Egypt, Milner claimed that the country's moral

Youth leads the way: The jacket illustration for Captain Brereton's With Wolseley to Kumasi *(c. 1900).*

and material progress had been made possible only by the devotion of its British administrators. No doubt Milner would have applauded the opinions of J. E. Welldon, the Headmaster of Harrow, who in 1899 affirmed that his duty was one of instilling into each of his pupils 'a faith in the divinely ordained mission of their country and their race'. His mind filled with the great principles of 'truth, liberty, equality and religion', the Harrovian was then bound to take them to every corner of the world.

Many Harrovians, confident of their calling and charged with an awareness of their country's high moral authority, would have joined the ranks of the soldiers, sailors and administrators whose task it was to impose that authority. Like many other young men of other classes, these public school boys would have learnt a few of their imperial ideas from the writers of popular stories for lads, who like journalists, were a potent force in spreading the imperial gospel. From about 1870 to 1914 (and well beyond for that matter) a persuasive group of writers made the empire alive and exciting in the minds of the young.

Sir Arthur Conan Doyle deliberately invoked the past to stir

14

the imagination of his own generation and make it aware of its duties. (Doyle was an ardent imperialist who wrote a sympathetic account of the Boer War and later stood unsuccessfully for Parliament as a supporter of Chamberlain and imperial free trade.) His *The White Company* (1890) and *Sir Nigel* (1906) were tales of pluck and endurance set against the background of Edward III's French wars. In both these novels, he constantly reminds his readers of the honourable heritage of their race and its prowess in battle. The fourteenth-century warriors are bands of brothers in which noble knights led sturdy yeomen, just as gentlemen officers led stalwart rankers on the battlegrounds of empire. There were hints too of Britain's future imperial glories. In a powerful episode in *The White Company*, the wife of the French commander, Bertrand du Guesclin, crystal-gazes and foresees Britain's great empire:

> 'My God!' she cried, 'what is this that is shown me? Whence come they, these peoples, these lordly nations, these mighty countries which rise up before me? I look beyond, and others rise, and yet others, far and farther to the shores of the uttermost waters. They crowd! They swarm! the world is given to them, and it resounds with the clang of their hammers and the ringing of their church bells. They call them many names, and they rule them this way or

Empire and civilization: Teachers and pupils, mission school, Accra, Ghana, 1893.

that, but they are all English, for I can hear the voices of the people. On I go, and onwards over seas where man hath never yet sailed, and I see a great land under new stars and a stranger sky, and still the land is England. Where have her children not gone? Her banner is planted on ice. Her banner is scorched in the sun. She lies athwart the lands, and her shadow is over the seas.'

A nation which was marked out for such great enterprises required for inspiration examples drawn from the deeds of their warrior forebears. As Conan Doyle pointed out at the conclusion of *Sir Nigel*, 'Our strength may be greater and our faith firmer if we spare an hour from our present toils to look back upon the women who were gentle and strong, or the men who loved honour more than life.'

For those who could find the time, the literature of Britain's heroic past was plentiful. G. A. Henty, a journalist who had served in the Ashante War of 1873–4, turned out an amazing series of boys' adventure stories drawn from all periods of British history. In each he firmly emphasized themes of bravery, resourcefulness and personal honour. His message was straightforward and was laid out for his young readers as it was for the hero of *Through the Sikh War*:

> 'Think it over yourself, Percy. Can you thrash most fellows your own age? Can you run as far and as fast as most of them? Can you take a caning without whimpering over it? Do you feel, in fact, that you are able to go through fully as much as any of your companions? Are you good at planning a piece of mischief, and ready to take the lead in carrying it out? For though such gifts as these do not recommend a boy to the favour of his schoolmaster, they are worth more out here than a knowledge of all the dead languages. It is pluck and endurance, and a downright love of adventure and danger, that have made us the masters of the great part of India, and ere long make us the rulers of the whole of it.'

Needless to say, Percy soon showed that he possessed all these qualities, as did his fellows elsewhere in Henty's yarns when they found themselves fighting in the latest imperial wars on the North West Frontier, the deserts of the Sudan, the jungles of West Africa or the veldt of the Transvaal. The same Anglo-Saxon virtues which had stood the test at Crécy, Agincourt and Corunna were not found wanting during the wars of imperial expansion. Henty made the imperial wars part of a greater process by which the British triumphed because of their superior character. He did much more, for he shared with the newspaper reporters the burden of making the empire popular and its service attractive.

Henty also offered his impressionable audience models of the type of men most needed to build and rule the empire. When, in 1894, the *Times* correspondent in Rhodesia watched a race meeting at Bulawayo, he recognized the breed already familiar from the pages of Henty – 'Energetic, stalwart, bronzed, the pioneers of Matabeleland were the pick of Anglo-Saxon manhood.'[6] They were the living counterparts of the fictional heroes of imperial literature who might be found in any imperial army or on any imperial frontier. Writing of Robin Corfield, a young soldier-administrator in Somaliland, his friend Dr Drake-Brockman praised his 'characteristic pluck and cheerfulness' when recovering from an infected wound suffered whilst hunting lion. 'His nature could never have been capable of a mean act, and, whatever his faults, his greatest enemy could never say that he was not as fine a specimen of British manhood as it was possible to meet.'[7]

Writers like Henty were also at pains to give their readers something more than imperial archetypes. They also wrote thinly disguised political justifications for the wars of empire. In Captain F. S. Brereton's *In the Grip of the Mullah* (1904), the British consul in Berbera explained to the two heroes the purpose of British government in Somaliland: 'Britain has always been the one friend of the oppressed. It has been our policy for generations, and we are known the world over as a fighting race who love freedom and hate the oppressor. Look at the manner in which we subdued the Soudan at enormous cost to ourselves, and yet without benefit to our country. This is a sample of the work we do, and we are about to repeat the same process here.' Of course neither speaker nor listeners would have cavilled about the cost. As Englishmen they were moved by higher considerations of racial destiny, honour and imperial duty. They would have warmly endorsed the words of Joseph Chamberlain, Colonial Secretary in the Conservative and Unionist governments between 1895 and 1903, who, in November 1895, boasted, 'I believe in the British Empire, and in the second place I believe that the British race is the greatest of governing races that the world has ever seen.'

Chamberlain's trumpeting came towards the end of a swift and unprecedented burst of British colonial expansion in Africa. In the previous twenty years, Zululand (1879), Egypt (1882), Som-

17

Sons of the breed: Newsreel film of Australian horsemen riding through Cape Town, 1900.

aliland (1884), Bechuanaland (Botswana) (1884–5), Nigeria (1885–1900), Uganda, Kenya, Nyasaland (Malawi), Zanzibar (1885–94), Rhodesia (1889), the Sudan (1896–8), the Transvaal and the Orange Free State (1900) had all been added to the British Empire. The small colonies of the Gambia, Sierra Leone and the Gold Coast (Ghana) had all been enlarged to include their hinterlands. So, when Chamberlain and other imperial encomiasts created their image of Britain's imperial destiny and future duty, it was natural that they drew much of their evidence from what they had been witnessing. Yet the spate of imperial growth in the 1880s and 1890s was only the frantic culmination of a longer and older process which had had its beginnings over two hundred years before.

In 1870, on the eve of her inruption into Africa, Britain was already the possessor of the world's largest empire and a global power without equal. This empire owed its existence to the aggressive commercial expansion of the seventeenth, eighteenth and early nineteenth centuries, when the prizes had included a scattering of West Indian sugar islands, Canada, Australia, New Zealand and, most treasured of all, India. The safety of these possessions, the requirements of stable bases from which to conduct trade and the maintenance of unchallenged sea power, itself the foundation of world power, demanded further acquisitions. So Cape Colony, Mauritius, Singapore, Aden, the Falkland Islands and Hong Kong were obtained. All these territories, bound together by the warships of the Royal Navy, ensured Britain her unrivalled position as a world and imperial power. Spain and Portugal were moribund, hardly able to keep together the lands which they had inherited from the conquests of the sixteenth century; Russia was solely concerned with engorging herself on the khanates of Central Asia in an advance eastwards, and France clung on to isolated fragments of her earlier colonial empire together with the recently acquired extension of the motherland, Algeria, and a toehold in Indo-China. The United States was busy with subjugating the Plains Indians, industrial expansion and keeping a stern paternal eye on the republics of South America.

Two factors had underwritten the growth and maintenance of the British Empire and Britain's unique role as a world power. The first was sea-power, which had been established during the wars of the eighteenth century and those against Revolutionary and Napoleonic France. In a long series of battles, her fleets had destroyed those of her rivals, and Britain had made herself the

The sea lanes of empire: Gunboat (extreme right) keeps watch over merchantmen anchored off Freetown, 1871.

mistress of the oceans and made it impossible for her opponents to sustain and defend their colonies. At the same time sea-power determined that, whilst Britain participated in wars, she suffered none of their debilitating consequences for she was safe from invasion. So, in 1815, Britain had emerged from over a hundred years of world-wide conflicts relatively unharmed, possessed of a territorial empire across the world and supreme at sea. In the century which followed, she did everything within her power to uphold this supremacy and succeeded, for no other nation felt inclined to question, let alone test, the Royal Navy's mastery. Even when, in the mid-1880s, France offered a tentative challenge and in the early 1900s Germany a more forceful one, Britain was still able to hold her own with a growing and formidable battle fleet. Secure in home waters and unassailable on distant oceans, Britain could not only control and develop her empire but play the part of a global power.

The second factor which contributed to British world supremacy was her fast rise to the standing of the world's first industrial power, which, by 1850, meant that she was the foremost manufacturing and trading country. Twenty years later just under a third of the whole world's industrial capacity was concentrated in Britain, and her businessmen were advancing her position as the world's leading banker, shipper and marine insurer. Britain lay at the centre of the world's commerce, and her interests were international, but their welfare depended upon unhindered access to world markets and sources of raw materials. This was vouchsafed by the possession of the world's greatest navy, whose men o'war cruised on every sea and ocean, guardians of the peace and ever watchful of British interests. A system based upon prestige, bluff and menace enabled Britain's commerce to flourish and increase.

In 1870 those areas where Britain had managed to establish a political primacy and thereby assert backstairs influence were known as the 'unofficial' empire. Here British subjects and their property were treated with respect by local rulers who had come to learn that a failure to conform with the wishes of the British consul would lead to the summoning of gunboats. When, in 1874, a British explorer in East Africa, then under the nominal sovereignty of the Sultan of Zanzibar, was crossed by a troublesome Arab slaving chief, he 'threatened him with all the terrors of the Sultan and the English consul'[8] and so got his way. The Sultan was the puppet of the British consul-general, behind whom was the strength of the powerful naval squadron based at Simon's Bay near Cape Town. So it was with 'unofficial empire' elsewhere, whether on the China coast, in the Persian Gulf or in South America.

So, before 1870, Britain possessed two 'empires', the one territorial and controlled by the Crown and the other 'unofficial', resting on the biddableness of local rulers who could be coerced by the Royal Navy's warships. In Africa the extent of Britain's territorial empire was small and confined to the coastal fringes of the continent. There was the inheritance of the old days of slaving, the tiny enclaves of the Gambia, Sierra Leone and the Gold Coast, together with Lagos, which had been acquired by force in 1861 as a base for anti-slavery patrols and a stable centre for the valuable palm-oil trade of the Niger delta. The ardent wish of successive governments to eradicate slave-trading and the safety of the palm-oil traders had led to the presence along the West African coast of a number of British consuls who were supported by men o'war which intimidated such chiefs as attempted to impede British commerce or molest British subjects. In East Africa something of the same sort of 'unofficial' empire obtained, based upon the sway of the British consul-general in Zanzibar. The Cape had been taken from the Dutch in 1806 and held since on the grounds of its vital importance as a staging post on the sea route to India. The security of Cape Colony had necessitated the occupation of its neighbour, Natal, in 1845 and political efforts to secure a paper sovereignty over the inland Boer republics of the Transvaal and Orange Free State.

This pattern of small, economically weak coastal colonies was similar to those of the other European powers, France, Spain and Portugal, which had vestigial colonies in Africa. Before 1870 they were considered burdensome, and no efforts had been made to enlarge or invest in them. The exception had been Algeria, where the coastal regions had received a steady flow of French, Spanish and Italian immigrants in the wake of the French armies. The numbers who had been attracted to Cape Colony and Natal had been disappointing before 1870 but the recent discovery of diamonds in Kimberley was beginning to act as a spur to fortune-hunters from Britain. Yet the two South African colonies never proved as great a magnet as Australia.

There was little in the African hinterland to attract Europeans or to tempt their governments to spend treasure. Much was unknown and what information there was did little to encourage annexation. The native inhabitants were hostile, the climate was at best ennervating and at worst fatal, and tropical forests, bush, unnavigable rivers and the high interior plateau meant that movement was slow. Enthusiasts such as missionaries, concerned about millions of souls condemned to pagan ignorance and evil gods, and explorers whose reports hinted at possible but usually indistinct sources of wealth could make no headway in persuading governments to move into Africa. This aloofness was characterized by the attitude of two successive British governments. In 1868 Disraeli sanctioned a large expedition which landed on the Red Sea shore of Ethiopia, marched inland, rescued a number of hostages held by the Emperor and then retired. Six years later Gladstone approved a large demonstration of force against the Ashante after they had attacked the coastal littoral of the Gold Coast which was under British protection. The army marched to the Ashante capital, Kumasi, forced their ruler to concede terms and then retired.

Yet after 1870 the hitherto sluggish process of European penetration and colonization of Africa suddenly accelerated to a hectic pace. A series of events over which they could exercise little control forced British governments to revise their policies towards involvement in the African hinterland and finally to take often unwilling steps to secure the conquest and permanent occupation of large areas.

The first factor which determined this new course was a number of crises in Africa itself. The collapse of the stable and hitherto sympathetic regime of the Khedive Tawfiq of Egypt in 1882 imperilled the Suez Canal and with it Britain's vital lifeline to India. The eventual solution was the invasion of Egypt and the establishment of a puppet government there backed by British troops. In southern Africa the failure of the British government to foist a federation on the Boers led to a brief war in 1880–81 which marked the first stage in a struggle for domination of the area, a contest made more intense by the discovery of gold near Johannesburg in 1886. Two local crises set in motion a number of wars in which Britain asserted her control over Egypt and pushed forward her influence in southern Africa. Simultaneous with these problems in Egypt and South Africa was the unlooked-for intervention in Africa of three new colonial powers, Germany, France and Italy and, acting as a private individual rather than a monarch, King Leopold II of the Belgians. The appearance of these interlopers naturally alarmed Britain, which had hitherto been accustomed to see itself as the only imperial and world power.

What was later called 'the scramble for Africa' had begun in 1876 when King Leopold II, a rather impoverished king by European standards, placed himself at the head of a private company whose aim was the exploitation of the wealth of the Congo basin, which had been rather exaggerated by the explorer H. M. Stanley. This in turn encouraged France to put her weight behind the soldier-administrator de Brazza, who busied himself exploring the north bank of the Congo and gathering treaties from local tribal rulers who were willing to place themselves and their people under the protection of the Third Republic. A pattern had been established. In East Africa, Karl Peters, explorer and catspaw for German business interests, made similar bargains, and his backers in Germany badgered Bismarck for recognition of their rights. In 1884 he acceded, in spite of his misgivings over the future value of African real estate, and laid official German claims to Togoland and the Cameroons in West Africa, large stretches of East Africa which would become Tanganyika, Zanzibar and Angra Pequeña which would expand to become German South West Africa and, today, Namibia. In West Africa, French soldiers were pushing inland, chasing the chimaera of a sprawling French empire covering the western

Sahara and extending across the Sudan to the Red Sea. In this area Italy was looking for a toehold and occupied Eritrea and Somalia.

Britain may well have been surprised and dismayed by these developments but they were, in a sense, inevitable. The creation in 1860 of the Italian kingdom out of a number of small states and the unification of Germany eleven years later marked the successful conclusion of the two major European nationalist movements. Europe had stabilized after twenty years of intermittent wars and, thanks to Bismarck's diplomacy, an uneasy harmony was brought into being, at least for three decades. France had been the loser, and the inclusion in the German Empire of her two eastern provinces of Alsace and Lorraine made her bitter. French patriots and governments were therefore anxious to assert their country's traditional power and in so doing find compensation elsewhere. When France announced her protectorate over Tunis in 1881, Léon Gambetta boasted that she was again a great nation. Bismarck was well pleased, for he hoped that in the future Gallic energies would be channelled into imperial conquests beyond Europe. At the same time, French expansion would bring conflict with Britain, and so Germany would not have to fear a Franco-British understanding. Bismarck cared little for colonies but they were valuable pawns on the European chessboard, and as such he was willing to exploit them in moves contrived to secure Germany advantage in Europe. For Italian imperialists colonies offered land for immigration, particularly from the poor south, and a chance for the new kingdom to behave like a great European power.

In London the new, global ambitions of the Continental powers were interpreted as challenges to what had been Britain's impregnable position as a world power. They were not confined to Africa, for by the early 1890s European ambition and greed were turning towards the Far East, where the Continental powers were joined by the United States, Japan and Russia, all jockeying for political, economic and strategic advantage. Successive British governments were therefore obliged to respond aggressively, either asserting previously unquestioned power or forcibly pressing forward British interests to meet or anticipate challenge. The game was to be played, from the early 1880s until its conclusion at the beginning of the twentieth century, in Africa, the last region of the world where European penetration and influence had hitherto been limited and where there were

24

no political units which possessed the strength and resources for sustained resistance.

In one sense Britain's manœuvres in Africa were a surprised answer to the moves of other European powers, each of which was not prepared to allow Britain a monopoly of global power. They were also a response to the immediate problems of Egypt and South Africa, where Britain was determined not to let her already established influence slip away. Alongside this concern with prestige and strategy, there were also economic arguments advanced by businessmen and their political allies which urged government to acquire land in Africa. From 1870 the old pattern of world trade began to break up, to the disadvantage of Britain. The new industrial nations, Germany, France, Italy, the United States and Russia were catching Britain up, and as their manufacturing industries came of age, they were unwilling to accept the doctrines of Free Trade so dear to British businessmen. Between 1870 and 1900 France, Germany, Italy and the United States all dropped Free Trade and imposed duties on exports and imports. There tariffs were extended to their newly acquired empires. Britain's world markets were suddenly receding. This new commercial problem was summed up by the future Conservative Prime Minister, Arthur Balfour, in a speech to the Commons in 1899. 'Whenever our flag flies, Frenchmen and Germans are allowed to go on the same terms as our merchants, and if it be an advantage, as I think it is, that we should protect at all events some part of Africa from the effects of hostile tariffs, then it is in the commercial interest of the country that we should carry out this policy of annexation.'[9] Many businessmen echoed Balfour's views. In 1884 the journal of the London Chamber of Commerce called for 'the repetition in Central Africa of the action [i.e. conquest] which founded the Indian Empire'.

Hitherto British trade with tropical Africa had been small, but in the economic climate of the 1880s and 1890s even the smallest markets could not be ignored or dismissed. From 1870 onwards the British economy lurched between alternate booms and slumps, and growth was fitful. At the same time the Johnny-Come-Latelies of the industrial world, Germany and the United States, were increasing their respective shares in a growing world market, and their levels of production were surpassing Britain's. Britain, however, kept stiffly to her policy of Free Trade, which had been the basis of her earlier success and which, from the 1870s, guaranteed abundant and cheap food for her population. Still the repeated slumps and hard competition

Empire and profit: Clearing an anthill from land to be planted with tobacco, Malawi, c. 1915.

from Britain's rivals made many businessmen believe that the acquisition of lands and peoples in Africa might assist recovery in that they offered new markets and sources of raw materials. A few went overboard with zeal, such as Colonel Frank Rhodes, who, in 1893, felt certain that the natives of Uganda were clamouring for every kind of British-made artefact, including, oddly, opera-glasses.[10] His brother Cecil had a vision of southern Africa peopled by immigrants from Britain, the poor and the unemployed transplanted from the slums and rookeries of the industrial cities and living new lives as pioneer farmers and miners under the Union Jack. This did not happen. In 1920, thirty years after the first pioneer columns had entered Mashonaland, there were only 34,000 white settlers in Rhodesia. Neither did African colonies prove to be valuable markets for British goods; even South Africa with its large European population imported only slightly more British products than the Argentine.

The twenty-five years of British expansion in Africa coincided with Britain's transformation from the world's workshop to the world's banker, creditor, landlord and insurer. By 1913 £4,000 million had been invested abroad, but very little of this capital found its way to Africa, where the risks and returns compared

26

unfavourably with, say, the United States or South America. In the 1890s British investors shunned West African railway stock, and the colonial governments there had to go cap in hand to the British government for cash. In spite of the hopeful predictions of businessmen and lobbyists, Africa did not prove a 'King Solomon's Mine' for exporters and investors. Yet, in the heyday of imperial expansion, many men argued otherwise, and their voices gave backing to governments that wished to extend British territory in Africa. So visionaries, strategists, patriots and traders worked together to press for and applaud the creation of a new empire in a continent which had before been considered a void without value. For many reasons this call was taken up by politicians, and British governments contrived policies for the division and occupation of Africa; inevitably these policies meant war, for the native inhabitants were reluctant to submit to this unwelcome *force majeure*.

2. Frontiers and Wars

Southern Africa, 1870–1902

Young Hodge the Drummer never knew –
Fresh from his Wessex home –
The meaning of the broad Karoo,
The Bush, the dusty loam,
And why uprose to nightly view
Strange stars amid the gloam.

Yet portion of that unknown plain
Will Hodge for ever be;
His homely Northern breast and brain
Grow to some Southern tree,
And strange-eyed constellations reign
His stars eternally.

Thomas Hardy

Drummer Hodge had come to South Africa in 1899 to fight the Boers in a land which was already a graveyard for many British soldiers. They had died in a century of wars against Boers, Kaffirs, Zulus, Pedi, Matabele and Shona. All these wars had shared a common cause, for successive British governments had been determined that southern Africa should remain under Britain's thumb, an arrangement which was often not to the liking of its inhabitants, white and black.

This policy had its roots in the principle that undisturbed ownership of the Cape was vital for the survival and advancement of Britain's international maritime, commercial and imperial interests. Cape Town was a great port with an enormous commercial value: in 1878 manufactured goods, raw materials and foodstuffs worth £91 million passed through its harbour, a third more than was carried through the Suez Canal, which was impassable to sailing vessels. A few miles to the south of Cape Town were the British naval base and dockyards at Simon's Bay. At the southern tip of Africa, where the Atlantic and Indian Oceans met, Simon's Bay was a major link in a chain of naval bases – Ascension, Freetown, Mauritius, Trincomalee – which marked and guarded the sea lanes from Britain to India and the Far East. From Simon's Bay men o'war cruised westwards to the mouth of the River Plate, northwards to the coasts of West Africa and eastwards to the mouth of the Red Sea. Its strategic importance was great, indeed so great that in 1894 Lord Kimberley, the Liberal Colonial Secretary, asserted that possession of the Cape was 'perhaps the most vital interest of Great Britain', its value surpassing that of Gibraltar and Malta.

This had been the view of the younger Pitt's government a hundred years before, when a British expeditionary force had taken the surrender of Cape Town from the Dutch East India Company in order to deny it to the forces of Revolutionary France. In 1815 British ownership of the Cape was confirmed by the Congress of Vienna, although its significance no doubt seemed trivial to the Continental diplomats whose horizons were confined to the limits of Europe. Permanent British rule was a different matter for the Afrikaners, or Boers, of the Cape, for whom the new administration, laws and taxes represented an unwelcome disruption of a traditional way of life. The Boers were the descendants of Dutch and French Calvinist immigrants who had first arrived at the Cape in the seventeenth century and for whom it was a Canaan, a promised land where they could worship freely, farm and prosper. Just as God had invested them with the land, so he had given them lordship over its black inhabitants, who were ordained to become slaves, labourers and servants. The British government and its officials did not see things in this simple way. Under pressure from missionary and humanitarian lobbies in Britain, the colonial administration saw its duty as the maintenance of a balance between the interests of the black Africans and those of the Boers. For the Boer, new laws for the protection of the blacks were a meddling interference in the 'natural' relationship between master and man, and his resentment was fuelled by a number of incidents created by the enforcement of these laws. A further source of rancour was the land question. The Boers and the small numbers of British immigrants who arrived in the 1820s were land-hungry, and their appetites led to the pushing back of the colony's frontiers into tribal territories. The natives naturally enough resented

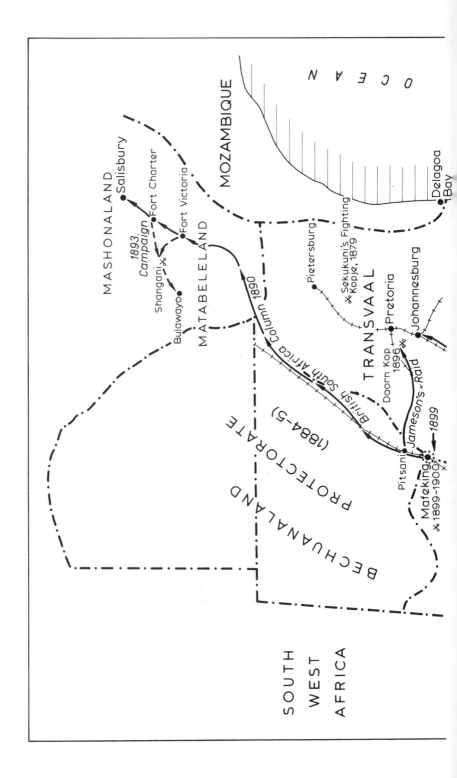

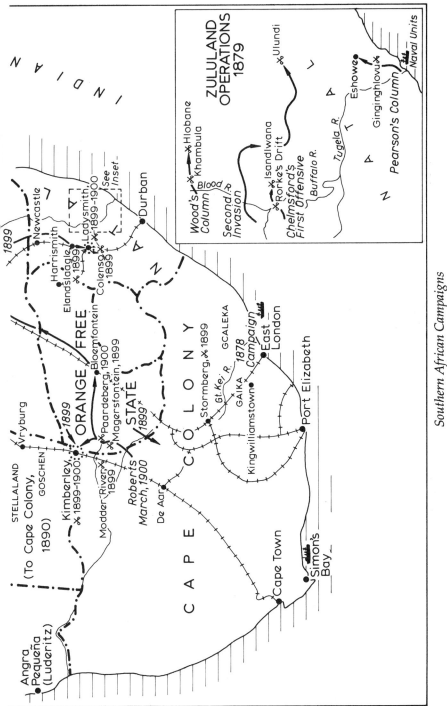

INDIAN

STELLALAND
(To Cape Colony, 1890) GOSCHEN

Vryburg

Angra
Pequeña
(Lüderitz)

Kimberley,
× 1899-1900:

Modder River,
1899

Paardeberg, 1900
Magersfontein, 1899

Roberts
March, 1900

De Aar

1899

Bloemfontein

**ORANGE FREE
STATE**
1899 ×

Newcastle

Harrismith
Elandslaagte
× 1899

Ladysmith,
1899-1900
Colenso,
1899

See
Inset

Durban

C A P E   C O L O N Y

Stormberg, × 1899

Gt. Kei R.
GAIKA
Kingwilliamstown

GCALEKA
1878
Campaign

East
London

Port Elizabeth

Cape Town

Simon's
Bay

**ZULULAND
OPERATIONS
1879**

Wood's
Column
Khambula

× Hlobane

Blood R.

Second
Invasion

× Isandlwana
Rorke's Drift

Ulundi

Chelmsford's
First Offensive

Buffalo R.

Tugela R.

Eshowe

Ginginghlovu ×

Pearson's Column

Naval Units

N

Southern African Campaigns

encroachments on their grazing lands, and for their part the settlers were incensed by continuous native rustling of their stock. Tension, generated by the advancement of the colony's boundaries, exploded into a series of nine wars between 1799 and 1878 known collectively as the Kaffir Wars from the colonists' contemptuous generic name for all local blacks. British forces, stationed in the Cape, were unavoidably drawn into these conflicts since the colonists were incapable of defending themselves. These wars were not conducive to the overall tranquillity of the region and added a considerable burden to the colonial government in terms of expense.

The upshot of the continual wrangling between the Boers and the British administration over the treatment of natives and the land question was a series of Boer migrations away from British-controlled territory. The earliest treks in the 1830s led the Boers into the coastal plain of Natal, which was annexed by Britain in 1845. This prompted a further exodus inland over the Drakensburg Mountains and Orange River to the veldt. Here the Boers founded two republics, the Orange Free State and the Transvaal, whose independence was formally acknowledged by Britain in the 1850s. Since both landlocked states depended upon the goodwill of the coastal colonies of the Cape and Natal, they did not appear to offer any serious threat to the maintenance of British paramountcy in southern Africa.

For the time being, the Boer problem appeared to be in abeyance. That of the frontier tribes was not. The British government disliked paying for the bush wars and was anxious to find some way in which they might either be avoided or else be paid for by the colonists. In 1856 the War Office turned in desperation to a scheme for the building of a chain of frontier outposts in the eastern Cape and Natal which would be manned by soldier-settlers, all former members of the German Legion which had been recruited to fight in the Crimean War.[1] According to a draft of this plan, there were to be thirty such stations, each with 250 settlers and their families and defended by fortified schools, churches and blockhouses. This ingenious if fanciful translation of an expedient of Roman frontier defence to Africa never got off the ground, and so the old headache of the volatile border remained. The only cure seemed to be a political one, obtained by the creation of a strong union of self-supporting colonies with its own elected government and the wherewithal to raise and pay for its own soldiers. Such a stable unit would serve Britain's interests for it would provide Cape Town with a secure and

A most vital interest, Cape Town: British troops disembark at the Cape in 1900 for a war to guarantee British domination of South Africa.

Refugees from British rule: A Boer farmer, his family and servants, Transvaal, 1880.

tranquil hinterland. Before 1870 this solution to the area's difficulties remained a pipedream since the Cape and Natal were sparsely populated, Cinderella colonies unable to defend themselves against their neighbours.

Boers, Pedi and Zulu

In 1869 there was an economic revolution in southern Africa which had far-reaching political repercussions, not least of which was the making of the fortune with which Cecil Rhodes stamped his own ideas on the area during the following thirty years. Diamonds were discovered in Griqualand West, which was hastily incorporated into Cape Colony, and a mere £90,000 was offered later to the Orange Free State for the land rights which it was too weak to enforce. The diamond diggings at Kimberley lured immigrants, and by 1873 the white population of the Cape was 236,000, twice what it had been twenty years before, whilst its government's income had trebled to £1.6 million by 1879. With economic self-reliance came political responsibility, and in 1872 the Cape was granted a constitution with an elected parliament.

Seen from the perspective of London, these developments opened the way for a lasting political settlement of the whole area. Disraeli's Conservative government, elected in 1874, threw itself into the promotion of a project for the creation of a southern African federation of the kind so recently and successfully applied to Canada. The new political unit was to embrace the Cape, Natal and the two Boer republics and would be floated on the revenues from the diamond mines, which would mean that it could meet the costs of its own administration and defence. This suited the interests of Britain, but would it satisfy the settlers in the colonies and republics? Afrikaners made up the majority of Europeans in southern Africa, and they needed to be convinced that the suggested federation under the British Crown would be in their best interests.

By a strange paradox, this plan which had been devised for the establishment of a stable southern Africa led directly to four years of intermittent war in which Britain was forced to send forces to fight the tribes of the eastern Cape, the Zulus, the Pedi and finally the Boers of the Transvaal. Setting on one side the question of whether the Boers would have unresistingly submitted to the suggested federation, the responsibility for the wars rested on the shoulders of the local officials of the British government. From the moral Olympus of his Midlothian election platform of 1879 and with hindsight, Gladstone blamed the wars on 'prancing pro-consuls' spoiling for a fight, and there is much to be said for this view.

The newly appointed High Commissioner for the Cape, Sir Henry Bartle Frere, was a veteran administrator from India, from where he brought his uncompromising views on the treatment of tribes which seemed to menace imperial frontiers. Frere's native commissioner, Sir Theophilus Shepstone, shared his superior's opinions that safe frontiers could be gained only by aggressive, forward thrusts of British military power followed by annexation. Shepstone was eager to solve 'the native problem', and he was scared that British paramountcy might be shaken or even irreparably damaged by a coalition of local native states, within and beyond the boundaries of British government. The most formidable of these native states was, in his eyes, the Zulu kingdom of Cetshwayo. As long as it survived as an independent state whose borders marched with the northern frontier of the weak colony of Natal, there would be no tranquillity in southern Africa. Moreover Zulu military power was a natural focus for wider African resistance to European rule. Both Frere and Shepstone were lucky that their views about local security, and in particular the alleged threat posed by the Zulu kingdom, were shared by the Honourable Frederick Thesiger (after August 1878 the second Lord Chelmsford) who took up his appointment as commander of British land forces in South Africa in March 1878. Yet before Frere and his associates could move towards an armed confrontation with the Zulus, two unexpected crises occurred which required their attention.

The defeat of Transvaal forces by Sekukuni, the king of the Pedi, placed the nearly bankrupt colony in jeopardy. As the local authorities could not handle the crisis, Frere took his cue and in April 1877 annexed the Transvaal. For the most part the Boers were frightened by their vulnerability and were not therefore unduly distressed by the sight of the Union Jack flying over Pretoria or disturbed by the subsequent arrival of British troops there. For them these events were the outward signs of what they considered a temporary measure, but for Frere, Shepstone and the Colonial Office the Transvaal's misfortunes were a happy chance which could be manipulated later so as to keep it and its people under British rule and then bring them into the planned federation.

The crisis in the Transvaal was quickly followed by another in the eastern Cape, where, in September 1877, the independent Gcaleka tribe crossed the Kei River in the first stage of an endeavour to join forces with the rebellious Gaikas. As in the earlier Kaffir wars, this challenge to British authority stemmed from the many collisions of economic interest between the colonists, who complained of native cattle-reiving, and the natives, who were unwilling to relinquish their tribal grazing lands to settler farmers. Matters were made worse at this time by a drought which was followed by famine. So desperate were conditions that Sir Evelyn Wood remembered a native mother having to sell her child to a Boer for grain. When hostilities began in September, King Kreli of the Gcalekas attacked the Fingoes, once helots for his tribe, whose territory separated him from his allies, the Gaikas. The British, under General Sir Arthur Cunyng-hame, responded by deploying forces along the Krei river in an endeavour to keep the two tribes apart. Warships from the Cape squadron played a crucial role in the first stage of these operations. HMS *Active*'s guns shelled tribesmen at Bowker's Bay, and another man o'war was used to carry a battalion of the 88th Regiment (Connaught Rangers) from East London. Landing parties from these ships, armed with war rockets and Gatling guns, were sent ashore to assist local volunteers and a scratch force of two to three thousand Fingoes, anxious to pay off old scores against their traditional oppressors. After holding back the Gcalekas, Cunynghame raided their territory, burnt down their kraals and took away thirteen thousand head of cattle. All this was very much in the spirit of the previous Kaffir Wars and similar fighting on the northern frontier of India, where imperial forces, denied a signal victory, turned to condign punishment of their adversaries through the destruction of their resources.

In March 1878, when Chelmsford replaced Cunynghame, the temper of the war changed. Assisted by his subordinates, Colonels Evelyn Wood and Redvers Buller, the new commander was determined to impose great system and cohesion on his forces and pacify the eastern Cape completely. Reinforced by the 24th (Warwickshire, later South Wales Borderers) and 90th (2nd Cameronians) and artillery, Chelmsford sent his forces into the bush to engage his enemies. Small forces, like beaters on a shoot, fanned out over the bush and flushed out their opponents in a series of small skirmishes. Buller characteristically carried a large stick with which he walloped any undergrowth which he thought might be hiding a native. The death of the Gaikas' king,

The Navy's here! HMS Active *off the African coast, c. 1870–80: her guns and her crew took part in the Ninth Kaffir War, and some of her crew fought as part of the Naval Brigade during the Zulu War.*

Sandili, in a skirmish, heavy losses and the effects of famine wore down both tribes, who submitted in May 1878. The successful outcome of this small war restored the internal security of the Cape and native resistance to the settlers there. Frere and Shepstone were now free to turn their attention to their neighbours, the Zulus.

Both men wanted war, for they had long regarded Zululand and its people as a major stumbling-block to the advancement of British interests in South Africa. Cetshwayo was accordingly presented to the Colonial Office as a savage and bloodthirsty despot who governed a kingdom which overflowed with fighting men, all anxious for war. There were then about 400,000 Zulus, and their king could summon up a force of about thirty to forty thousand warriors (a figure Shepstone often exaggerated) but they never constituted a standing army as the British repeatedly alleged. The Zulu fighting man who was fit for service joined his regiment when called to arms and then returned to his homestead and cattle when the fighting was over. This 'nation in arms' was transformed by Frere and Shepstone into a savage standing army which permanently imperilled Natal and whose

Zulu beauty: Photographs like this were collected as souvenirs by officers, but their display by a London firm of photographers in 1879 led to its unsuccessful prosecution by the Society for the Suppression of Vice.

ruler's obstinate refusal to submit to Britain was a challenge which had to be taken up for the sake of local prestige.

There were other reasons why the Zulu kingdom was a stumbling block to the advancement of Britain's interests, as Shepstone admitted when he wrote, 'Had Cetewayo's thirty thousand warriors been in time changed to labourers working for wages, Zululand would have been a prosperous country instead of what it now is, a source of perpetual danger to itself and its neighbours.'[2] At the time when Shepstone penned this revealing statement, Natal was troubled by a labour shortage, for local natives were reluctant to take the niggardly wages offered by colonist employers. Many years later, Shepstone's dream of a helot Zulu race was fulfilled, for by the 1890s many thousands of this proud people had joined the ranks of the migrant workers in the mines and on the railways and farms of the Cape and Transvaal. This is just what the champions of South African economic development had always wanted, for the enterprises necessary for colonial prosperity demanded a large, submissive native labour force. At the same time the black worker secured the cash with which to pay taxes to the colonial government.

Before he could take his place in the modern state, the native had to be shown the hopelessness of resistance to its advance. So Lord Chelmsford prepared his arrangements for the invasion of Zululand in the sanguine expectation of an unopposed trium-

phal march to Cetshwayo's royal kraal at Ulundi. Frere and
Shepstone encouraged the fancy that his advance would be
unimpeded with the prediction that many of Cetshwayo's subjects would throw in their lot with the conquerors once they saw
the impressive columns of redcoats marching through their
country. In the meantime negotiations with the Zulu king continued, but whilst Cetshwayo hoped to conclude a peaceful
settlement, he was unwilling to surrender his independence and
disarm his warriors. So the talks ended and the *impasse* was
exploited to provide a reason for the declaration of war.

On 10 January 1879 the invasion of Zululand began and with it
the Zulu War. What was at stake seemed clear, at least to Private
Owen Ellis of the 24th who informed his family in Caernarvon
that he and his fellows had been commanded 'to proceed
through and occupy the country of the Zulus, in as much as King
Cetshwayo did not submit to the terms demanded by the British
government'. Ellis, who would lose his own life within a fortnight at Isandlwana, anticipated a short war, whose outcome
was beyond doubt. 'We are about to capture all the cattle
belonging to the Zulus and also burn their kraals; and if they
dare to face us with the intention of fighting, well woe be to
them! As in Transkei [the recently ended Kaffir War] they shall
be killed as they come across us.'[3]

This prediction as to the outcome of an open battle between
the British army and the Zulu impis worried Cetshwayo. The
war was not of his making, and during the next six months he
continued to look for a settlement of his differences with the
British. His kingdom was ill placed to fight a war since the lack of
rains during the past year had dried up much of the grass upon
which the Zulu cattle fed. Zulu warriors therefore often travelled
and fought on empty bellies, for it was usual for their impis to
move across country followed by boys who carried sleeping
mats and food and drove cattle to be slaughtered and eaten by
the army. Such supplies were thin in 1879; the regiments which
attacked Rorke's Drift had not eaten for twenty-four hours, and
at Khambula in March dead Zulus were found with their mouths
stuffed with porridge gobbled from British cooking pots. The
same deficiencies which sapped Zulu fighting strength also
affected British soldiers, who had to sustain themselves by
plundering sheep, goats and cattle from kraals close to their line
of march. Cetshwayo had rightly guessed that problems of
supply would hinder his adversaries and so had deliberately
withdrawn herds of cattle from the border of his kingdom, a

stratagem which ironically also deprived his own men of rations.

This attempt to deny provender to his enemies had been part of Cetshwayo's wider strategy by which he hoped to wear down the imperial forces by hitting at their lines of communication. There were no roads in Zululand, only rough tracks over a landscape of rolling hills, ravines and rivers, and so the British invasion force depended on columns of ox-drawn wagons which moved slowly, needed large stocks of fodder and were exposed to ambush. Whilst pricking the British supply lines and so slowing down their advance, Cetshwayo hoped that he could negotiate a peace. He was mistaken both in his belief that the British would agree to terms and in the hope that his indunas (army commanders) would confine their operations to small-scale raids. The indunas wanted battle in the traditional manner in which their warriors adopted a formation which has been likened to the outline of a buffalo. There was a centre and two horns which in attack would spread out to envelop the enemy's position before the final charge and hand-to-hand combat with the short stabbing assegai and shield. This battle formation was well suited to flat country but was less effective on broken ground and suicidal in the face of troops armed with rifles, machine-guns and artillery. An engagement of these terms was sought by Chelmsford if the unexpected occurred and his march to Ulundi was challenged.

Ulundi was Chelmsford's objective, and to achieve it he had command of sixteen thousand men of whom five thousand were British infantrymen in eight battalions, many of them acclimatized veterans who had fought against Gaikas and Gcalekas the year before. There were also local forces, mounted settler volunteers and nine thousand Natal natives for whom enlistment had been offered as an alternative to paying colonial taxes. They were widely and justifiably considered to be unreliable. To accomplish the invasion, Chelmsford had divided his force into four main columns, with the 80th (2nd battalion Staffordshire) Regiment at Luneberg on the Zululand Transvaal border as a precaution against a Zulu attack in that direction. The first British column, under Colonel Pearson, was based at the Lower Drift (crossing point) of the Tugela River and was made up of a Naval Brigade, the 3rd (East Kent) and 99th (Cameronian) Regiments and over two thousand Natal natives. This force had been ordered to advance northwards towards Eshowe, thirty-seven miles away. The second column, entirely drawn from local native and settler volunteers under Colonel Durnforth RE, was based at the Middle Drift and was under instructions to probe eastwards and be ready to meet and deflect any Zulu invasion of Natal. The third column, to which Chelmsford was himself attached, had been selected to undertake the seventy-five-mile advance from Rorke's Drift on the Buffalo to Ulundi. It consisted of the two battalions of the 24th, artillery and various native units. The fourth column, also with two battalions of British regulars, was positioned to the north at Bemba's Kop on the headwaters of the Blood River, and its commander, Colonel Evelyn Wood, had been instructed to draw the Zulus away from the track to Ulundi.

Operations started on 11 January but Chelmsford's crossing of the Tugela was hampered by recent heavy rains which churned up the tracks and made the going hard for the vital trains of ox-wagons. An advanced base was set up at Isandlwana, four miles from Rorke's Drift. Here Chelmsford received hazy intelligence that a large Zulu impi had left Ulundi and was moving in his direction. According to Wood's spies this impi had the intention of attacking Chelmsford's column. For all this, Chelmsford's knowledge of his enemies' plans was sketchy, and even the addition of Durnforth's cavalry, hurriedly called up, did not provide him with a sufficient number of scouts. What appeared to be substantial sightings of a large concentration of Zulus to the south-east of Isandlwana drew Chelmsford off in that direction with over half his force just after dawn on 22 January. With no clear indication of his enemy's whereabouts, Chelmsford was gambling, but he knew that he would have to give battle soon or else face delays which would exhaust his supplies. In undertaking this quest for a decisive engagement, Chelmsford left behind him the camp at Isandlwana under the command of Colonel Pulleine of the 24th with just over six hundred men from that regiment and a further thousand colonials and native levies. The many supply wagons were not in a laager, a defensive measure which was thought unnecessary since they were all due to be returned to Rorke's Drift.

At about midday on 22 January cavalry patrols who were busy rounding up Zulu cattle about 5½ miles to the north-east of the camp stumbled on an unformed Zulu force of about twenty thousand warriors. This was the impi for which Chelmsford was vainly scouting over eleven miles to the south-east. Startled by this chance encounter, the Zulus chased the equally bewildered horsemen back towards the camp and, in defiance of Cetshwayo's orders, rushed the British position. There was no

41

effort by the indunas to muster their forces in the customary offensive formation but, in the teeth of losses of one in five men, the charge was finally pressed home against the British lines. After two hours of fighting only fifty-five of the men at Isandlwana were left alive, and they were fugitives who had escaped the encircling swing of the Undi corps which cut the path back to Rorke's Drift. The camp was plundered and burnt, and the dead and dying were mutilated before the mass of warriors turned away for Ulundi, where they would confront Cetshwayo with the news of their disobedience and victory.

Three regiments, exalted by their army's success but shamed by the smallness of their part in it, ran towards Rorke's Drift and, in contempt of Cetshwayo's order not to cross into Natal, attacked the mission station there. What followed during the afternoon, evening and night of 22–3 January became an imperial epic, the Roncesvalles of the British Empire. Just over 120 men of the 24th held the hastily fortified mission station against a series of ferocious and well-pressed attacks. The reckless Zulu regiments, which totalled nearly four thousand warriors, lost over four hundred dead and many more wounded before calling off and returning to Ulundi.

During that same night Chelmsford, recalled to Isandlwana from his wild goose chase, stepped amongst the baleful detritus of the camp and saw a distant glow in the sky from the burning roof of the mission, whose defenders he thought were lost. In the morning he found a hundred of them still alive as he drew himself and the remains of his column out of Zululand. He had lost nearly an entire battalion, two thousand irreplaceable oxen and £150,000 worth of ammunition and stores. A few weeks later, when the news of the catastrophe reached Britain, a *Punch* cartoon pictured a Zulu schoolmaster drawing the attention of his pupil, John Bull, to a text on a blackboard. It read, 'Despise not your enemy.'

The telegraphic link between London and the Cape had not been completed in 1879, and so the Cabinet heard of the disaster at Isandlwana only on 11 February. Not even the eleven Victoria Crosses awarded to the most courageous of the heroes of Rorke's Drift could remove this blemish on Britain's military prestige, which was probably the most damaging since the surrenders to the American colonists at Saratoga and Yorktown a hundred or so years before. Orders were immediately issued for reinforcements to be drafted to South Africa, and on 26 May the architects of the débâcle, Frere and Shepstone, were sacked.

Imperial heroes: The defenders of Rorke's Drift: the central bearded figure is Lieutenant Chard VC; behind him are other defenders, and around are signs of the recent struggle. Several men have picked up discarded Zulu weapons, 1879.

Imperial battlefield: Rorke's Drift, the ruined mission and the Oscarberg (in the background) from where the Zulus sniped at the defenders.

Chelmsford too was removed, and his successor, Sir Garnet Wolseley, was ordered out to South Africa to take command of the forces there the moment he landed. It was not an appointment which pleased Queen Victoria, whose misgivings had to be quietened by a Disraelian *bon mot*: 'It is quite true that Wolseley is an egotist, and a braggart; so was Nelson.'[4] Her cousin the Commander in Chief, the Duke of Cambridge, bristled with choler and blamed Wolseley and all his 'damned new-fangled methods' for undermining the fine army which he warmly remembered from his days in the Crimea.

In Natal, where an invasion was feared but did not come, the Duke's lack of faith in the British soldier was shared by many of the natives, the backbone of the supply train, who deserted in droves. For Chelmsford there was no further likelihood of a second invasion until his fresh forces had disembarked at Durban, and so the rest of his army stayed where it was. In the north, Wood's column underwent a series of adventures after Buller's mounted colonials crossed the path of a Zulu impi of four thousand, anxious for another Isandlwana. Buller's men bravely extricated themselves after a rough mauling at Hlobane on 28 March, and a day later the Zulus charged Wood's entrenched camp at Khambula Hill from where they were driven off with over eight hundred casualties. On the coast, Pearson's column, having made it to Eshowe after a short engagement at Inyezane, found itself faced with the disconcerting news that they would have to stay there until a relief force could be mustered. The fortified camp at Eshowe was relieved on 3 April, after the battle of Ginginghlovu, in which the Zulus again suffered heavily in the face of rifle and machine-gun fire. It was now clear to them that Isandlwana had been an aberration and that in normal circumstances they could not be expected to prevail by attacks in the open.

By May Chelmsford had his additional forces, including five more battalions of British troops and two cavalry regiments, the 1st Dragoon Guards and 17th Lancers. Chelmsford was now ready for a second advance to Ulundi and a decisive victory which he hoped to get before Wolseley disembarked. Once again the British moved forwards, avoiding the dismal and undisturbed field of Isandlwana, and made a laboured advance over damaged drifts, worn tracks and grassland which offered thin grazing for the transport oxen, which died in hundreds. More ill-luck dogged Chelmsford, for on 1 June Louis Bonaparte, the Prince Imperial and only son of the late Emperor of

France, Napoleon III, was killed when his small mounted patrol was bushwhacked by a large body of Zulus. In France the Bonapartists were furious and muttered about a British conspiracy, and in Zululand there was a court martial which found the patrol's commander, Captain Carey, guilty of cowardice, a verdict which was overturned on appeal. After Chelmsford's forces had burnt kraals in the vicinity of Ulundi, they were attacked on 4 July, but the feeble Zulu charges were easily beaten off. Cetshwayo's kraal was entered, looted and then burnt. Chelmsford had at last got what he wanted, even though a few days later he had to hand over his command to Wolseley. Chelmsford was never again offered an active command, but since he enjoyed considerable royal favour he secured a handful of court positions before he died in 1905, in the middle of a game of billiards in the United Service Club.

His successor, Wolseley, who was also High Commissioner for South Africa, was left with the task of ruling Zululand, where he feared that resistance would not cease until Cetshwayo was captured. On 24 August the fugitive king commanded his warriors to lay down their arms, and four days later he was taken by a British patrol. He was sent, a prisoner, to Britain and then exiled. His kingdom was partitioned and the pieces were doled out to tribal rulers on the political grounds that a divided state posed no threat to its neighbours and Britain's interests. A spate of internecine struggles in the 1880s prompted the absorption of Zululand into Natal in 1889, and in 1902 the area was opened to European settlement. Four years after, in 1906, there was a final flourish of Zulu resistance when there was an uprising against taxation. In a squalid campaign it was relentlessly crushed by local, colonial forces, which included Mahatma Gandhi, who served with an ambulance unit.

With the end of the Zulu campaign and a political settlement of the Zulu question, Wolseley was free to give his attention to the military problems of the Transvaal, which meant Sekukuni and the still defiant Pedi. Sekukuni's military headquarters was a remote and rocky 'fighting kopje', a natural fastness honeycombed with protective caves and boltholes. It was guarded by six thousand warriors, of whom two thirds were armed with rifles, many of them paid for by wages earned on the Kimberley diamond fields. This bastion was about 150 miles from Pretoria, from where Wolseley sent a request for Sekukuni asking him to submit to British terms. These included the acknowledgement of British sovereignty, the surrender for trial of cattle-raiders and a fine of 3,500 head of cattle. Wolseley, who was uneasy about undertaking a campaign in a distant region with dangerously elongated lines of communication, hoped that Sekukuni would be moved by the recent fate of his sometime ally, Cetshwayo, and give way. Sekukuni may have contemplated such a course, and at a conference of his chiefs he tested their feelings by complaints of war-weariness and called for appeasement. One of his chiefs was dismayed and shouted out for defiance. 'You are cowards,' he told his kinsmen. 'Let the white people fight for the cattle if they want them. We have no cattle to give.'[5] Sekukuni warmly applauded this spirited response and then set about buying rifles, powder, shot and even a cannon. News of the Pedis' mood left Wolseley with no alternative but to march to their stronghold and take it.

In the following campaign against Sekukuni, Wolseley commanded fourteen hundred British infantry – 21st (Royal Scots Fusiliers) and 94th (2nd battalion, Connaught Rangers, four hundred mounted colonial volunteers and ten thousand natives, most of them Swazis, old foes of the Pedi and eager to kill as many of them as they could. On 27 November 1879 the 'fighting kopje' was stormed, and after a three-hour struggle, in which the Swazis held back, it was taken. Those Pedi who had crept into caves were driven out by charges of dynamite, although, since some of them had learnt about explosives whilst working on the diamond diggings, the British engineers sometimes found that their fuses had been cut. Sekukuni was later taken and, like Cetshwayo, sent into exile. Away on the northern borders of the Cape, smaller forces under Sir Charles Warren completed 'mopping up' operations against local tribes. These were over by the end of 1879 and completed two years of sporadic but heavy fighting which had cost the British government £6 million. In return the taxpayers had gained the internal security of South Africa, where the native population would never again seriously threaten the advance of European settlement.

With the defeat of the Zulus and Pedi, the British government was able to turn again to its pet scheme for a South African federation. In the spring of 1880 Disraeli's government had lost the general election in which the Liberal leader, Gladstone, had repeatedly denounced its showy adventurism and warmongering. In his campaign call for a return to morality in government, he promised the restoration of the Transvaal's independence, but once in office he gave the matter second

He was defeated: Sekukini, King of the Pedi, 1879. 'He was an oldish man, with a grey beard and very frightened eyes, who, when taken, evidently feared the very worst – not without reason, if he imagined that the Swazis were to be let have a go at him. He was in an abject funk when his photograph was taken' – Captain Hugh McCalmont.

thoughts and came out in favour of federation. For him and his fellow Liberals, South Africa was a moral dilemma and the cause of much soul-searching. On one hand Liberal principles demanded that the Boers should be given their rights to self-determination, but on the other the harshness of their native policy was unacceptable to the humanitarians who considered British colonial government the best hope for native rights. For the time being Gladstone succumbed to pressure for the continuance of British rule in the Transvaal in spite of calls to the contrary from his radical colleagues.

Whilst the British Liberals were in a moral quandary, there were growing signs that the Transvaal Boers wanted their independence back. The conclusion of the native wars meant that the problem of the Transvaal's security no longer existed, and it was therefore with dismay that the Boers heard Wolseley's plain statement that the Vaal would flow backwards before the Union Jack was hauled down in Pretoria. Elsewhere in South Africa, Boers were indignant at British high-handedness and, as a mark of their sympathy with their blood brothers in the Transvaal, those in the Cape voted decisively against federation. With open support from the Cape and Orange Free State, the Transvaal resistance movement grew under the leadership of Piet Joubert and Paul Kruger. During 1880 there was a rash of civil disobedience in which Afrikaners refused to pay taxes, and a party of fifty rescued one of their kind who had been arrested for ill-using a native. By 16 December there were eight thousand Boers in arms, and a declaration of independence was issued.

For the first time the British army came face to face with the flexible Boer fighting unit, the commando, in which mounted riflemen and their black servants were organized into a mobile force which could hit hard. On 20 December one of these commandos intercepted a column of the 94th Regiment as it was marching from Lydenburg to Pretoria and asked its commanding officer to turn back. The colonel refused and his men instantly came under heavy and accurate rifle fire and suffered high casualties, including many officers, who were singled out by the Boer marksmen. After twenty minutes the British surrendered. The skirmish at Bronckhorst's Spruit began the first Boer War, a struggle for which the local British forces were wretchedly unprepared.

The task of bringing the Boers to heel fell to General Sir George Colley, Wolseley's successor as commander in South Africa. His position was an unenviable one, for the isolated garrisons in the Transvaal had been bottled up by the Boers, and a large commando had crossed a few miles into Natal and dug itself in at Laing's Nek, blocking the road northwards to the Transvaal. Their expulsion was Colley's first objective, and on 28 January 1881 he moved forward from his base at Fort Prospect for an assault on the Boer lines. The frontal attack by over a thousand men backed by a navy war-rocket battery came to grief under Boer rifle fire and Colley retired. A month later Colley, now reinforced, sallied out for a second attempt to dislodge the Boers. This time he aimed at taking Majuba Hill, a prominence which, in British hands, would give him the means to outflank the main Boer position. With just over five hundred men and without either war-rockets or machine-guns, Colley was able to occupy the hill, but on the following day, 28 February, it was retaken by the Boers, whose rifle fire scattered the British and sent them back down the steep slopes. Colley was amongst the dead. His successor, Colonel Wood, prudently decided to stay in Fort Prospect, where he worried about dwindling food supplies and the unlikelihood of getting any more since heavy rains had washed away the dirt tracks which connected the fort with Newcastle and the rest of Natal. On 6 March Wood negotiated a truce with Joubert, which was followed by further discussions

The Transvaal subjugated: British forces parade in Pretoria in 1881.

Boers triumphant, 1881: Colonel Evelyn Wood (centre) discusses truce terms with the Boer nationalist leaders Kruger (left) and Joubert (right). 'It is remarkable that none of us ever heard either Boer leader boast, or even speak in a tone of exultation, of their successes. This was not the case with the young men, but the leaders on every occasion ascribed the result of their struggles to the intervention of the Almighty' – Evelyn Wood

which were concluded at the Pretoria Convention the following August where full Boer independence was restored to the Transvaal.

The brief, fumbling campaign was a British humiliation and an Afrikaner triumph. The first fruit of victory was the Pretoria agreement by which British troops marched out of the Transvaal, which was again an independent republic even though the British insisted on the retention of 'suzerainty', whatever that meant. The army authorities were angry and wanted to fight on but Gladstone had given way to those in his party who adhered to the principles of self-determination. For the Boers throughout South Africa the victory peace meant the death of the federation which they have never liked and the dawning of Afrikaner nationalism, an emotion which infected not only the Boers of the republic but those under British rule in the Cape and Natal.

Mr Rhodes's Wars

The peace established at Pretoria was extremely fragile. During the next twenty years Britain became increasingly frightened of Afrikaner nationalism and its powerhouse in the Transvaal. This fear was based upon the very real possibility that British paramountcy in South Africa would be eroded and that political domination of the region would slip into Boer hands. After 1886, when the gold mines of the Witwatersrand had been opened, the Transvaal passed through an economic revolution whose momentum was sustained by the revenues from the vast gold-bearing reef. By 1898 the Rand provided over a quarter of the world's annual gold output, and the Transvaal government's yearly income had risen to just over £4 million, twenty times what it had been in the early 1880s. Much of this cash was spent on the purchase of modern weaponry from Europe, which gave the Transvaal the military strength to support her local political pretensions.

At the head of this emerging industrial nation was President Paul Kruger, a graceless but shrewd gerontocrat whose domestic political credibility rested on his impeccable nationalist background – he had been a child during the treks of the 1830s and led the independence movement in 1880 – and his ability to embody the simple, agrarian Afrikaner virtues. He wished to reduce whatever ties the Transvaal had with Britain and its colonies and was anxious to extend his nation's friendship to other European powers. One fruit of his diplomacy was the Dutch-financed Delagoa Bay railway which terminated the Transvaal's dependence upon communications which passed through the British colonies. These developments all seemed to indicate a more fundamental change within southern Africa by which economic power would shift away from Britain towards the Transvaal, which would then be able to assume the political leadership of the region.

One man was determined to reverse this change: Cecil Rhodes. Rhodes was a visionary and a politician who possessed extraordinary good luck, a more than generous share of ruthlessness and the ability to charm men into his service. He was fortunate to have been in Kimberley when the diamond diggings were in their early days and even more fortunate to exploit this advantage and the later chances which came his way. By 1890 nine out of every ten diamonds sold across the world were the product of Rhodes's De Beers Consolidated Mines, and he was investing heavily in the gold-mines of the Rand. Rhodes was a millionaire several times over, and he was always ready to use his cheque book to get what he wanted, in business and politics. What he wanted he had outlined in 1877 when he composed a confession of faith as an Oxford undergraduate. He saw it as the highest duty of an Englishman to extend his country's control over as much as the world as was possible in order to propagate Anglo-Saxon civilization. To this end, he mused on the mechanics of founding a vast secret society whose members would devote their lives to 'bringing the whole of the uncivilised world under British rule'.[6] Circumstances prevented Rhodes from taking a global stage, and so he made southern Africa his stamping ground, planting it with Union Jacks and settlers of British stock.

The political voice of Rhodes was first heard in 1880, when he was elected a member of the Cape Parliament, and four years later it sounded loudly during the fuss that had been stirred up after the creation of two new Boer republics, Stellaland and Goschen. These lay to the north of the Cape and bisected the 'missionary road' which passed towards what was then known as Zambesia. If the Boer filibusterers dug their heels in, those who followed them would be free to push westwards and encroach on Bechuanaland (Botswana) or even move north into Zambesia. If this occurred, Rhodes's vision of British expansion northwards from the Cape would be a mirage, and so he was forward in making angry demands for some sort of counter-move from the Colonial Office. In London the missionary lobbies were also speaking up for the interests of the natives of Bechuanaland who would have faced a bleak future as part of a Boer labour pool if the two infant republics grew. There was an added and, for South Africa, new dimension to this problem, the arrival on the coast of South West Africa of the Germans, whose government had, in 1884, announced its claim to Angra Pequeña. Since at the time the British government was obliged to Germany for diplomatic support in Egypt, there was no chance of demanding German withdrawal from South West Africa and wielding the naval big stick. Still there was a suspicion that, if the Germans moved inland, they could, if unchecked, eventually meet the Boers moving westwards, and the no longer land-locked Transvaal might pass under German influence.

So the British government reacted by declaring a protectorate over Bechuanaland, and at the end of 1884 an army of five

*Mr Rhode's mines: Diamond diggings and migrant workers, Kimberley,
c. 1875.*

thousand under Sir Charles Warren was ordered to the Cape. It
moved northwards, dissolved the two republics and expelled
the Boer interlopers. There was no bloodshed, for the Boers
quietly dispersed, and the whole area, including the route
north, passed into British hands.

Rhodes now had unimpeded passage to Zambesia, where his
agents joined others who were already badgering the Matabele
ruler, Lobengula, for concessions. In 1888 his men secured the
royal mark to an agreement by which Lobengula agreed to
become Rhodes's pensionary and received a large consignment
of breech-loading rifles in return for a concession to settle and
prospect for minerals in Mashonaland. It was left to Rhodes to
procure a charter from the British government for his new
company, the British South Africa Company. This was granted
by Parliament in 1889 after payments to the Irish Home Rule
party. Rhodes could now govern in the Queen's name a vaguely
defined area but was bound to follow Colonial Office guidance
in all matters of native policy. As in Nigeria and East Africa, the
government paid nothing and in return got a private enterprise colony.

In April 1890 the Company's first column set off from Mafeking on its northward trek. There were 179 settlers, British and

Boers, guarded by five hundred men – 'a corps of dare-devils' of the recently formed Company Police. This *gendarmerie* took with them a mighty arsenal of machine-guns, war-rockets and artillery and a generator-powered searchlight with which to impress the natives. Its beam of light, which seemed to drive away the darkness of the night, was remembered nearly ninety years later by an old native who had watched the column come into his land.[7]

Whilst the ox-drawn pioneer wagons were moving up country, Rhodes's ambitions were galloping ahead. He briefly contemplated a plot to kidnap Lobengula, whose kingdom he already coveted, and he planned to push as far north as Katanga, where gold and copper deposits were known to exist. Rhodes was anxious to get his hands on the sea port of Beira, and in May 1891 a detachment of his *gendarmerie* probed inside Portuguese territory, where they met, attacked and routed a small force, killing twenty. Any plans which Rhodes may have entertained for this area were soon thwarted, when the Anglo-Portuguese Boundary Agreement was signed later in the same year. By this time it had become clear that another of his dreams had evaporated, for no substantial gold deposits had been discovered in Mashonaland, and its future rested solely on the profits from farming.

Rhodes had pinned his hopes on the discovery of another Rand within his concession, whose economic development would consequently rival if not surpass that of the Transvaal. Instead, his Company found itself running a rather poor agrarian colony and was faced with troubled relations with Lobengula. It had long been the custom for Matabele impis to sweep into Mashonaland and raid its villages for slaves and livestock. This pattern of predatory warfare persisted after the arrival of the first colonists and made them and the Company nervous. It was argued that Lobengula's fifteen thousand warriors were a permanent danger to the colony's existence and prosperity, and voices were raised in favour of a showdown which would lead to the overthrow of the Matabele state, whose territory would then be open for settlement.

An opportunity for goading Lobengula into war unexpectedly offered itself in July 1893 and was swiftly exploited by the local officials of the Company. An impi of about 2,500 Matabele raided Shona villages close by Fort Victoria, which was soon filled with frightened natives and settlers. The police commandant and magistrate, Captain Lendy, a hard-dealing ex-

Stepping-stone to conquest: British South Africa Company troopers manning the earthen ramparts of Fort Charter, 1890.

Harrovian athlete of an easily recognizable type, refused to hand over the Shona refugees and, as the disappointed impi withdrew, sent a small detachment out to shoot it up. The Matabele warriors, obedient to their king's command, did not return the fire.

The Company's chief administrator, Dr Jameson, an Edinburgh physician and friend of Rhodes, blamed Lobengula for the incident and began to plan an offensive against the royal kraal at Bulawayo. At a time when the Company was facing financial hardship and had just been forced to reduce its *gendarmerie* by five hundred, it was hard to understand Jameson's belligerence, although Lendy's was typical – a year before, he had shot a local chief, his son and twenty-four tribesmen after a misunderstanding.* An offensive campaign against the Matabele did, however, have much to recommend it, for if successful it would have extended the Company's domains and removed the largest single threat to its security. Jameson certainly wanted war and went to extraordinary lengths to raise an army, for he resurrected a medieval recruiting trick by which volunteers were offered six thousand acres of yet unconquered Matabele land and a share of some of Lobengula's yet untaken cattle. Rhodes's enemies in Johannesburg noticed with amuse-

* Lendy died the following year of exertion after putting the shot at a local sports meeting.[8]

55

Conqueror and raider: Dr L. S. Jameson, administrator of the British South Africa Company during the first Matabele War and leader of the raid on the Transvaal.

ment that many of those lured by this offer were the worst riff-raff of the Rand whose progress to the battle zone was marked by heavy drinking and theft. At the same time as Lobengula's kingdom was being parcelled up to draw freebooters from the Johannesburg bars, the king was doing what he could to forestall an invasion and reach a negotiated settlement. This was the last thing that Jameson wanted, and by the first week of October two columns with over seven hundred European troopers and five new Maxim machine-guns were straining on the leash at Forts Charter and Victoria. Far away to the south, the British High Commissioner, Sir Henry Loch, was reading alarmist telegrams from Jameson in which he was told of massing Matabele impis poised for an attack on the colony but which left him with the justifiable suspicion that he and the government he represented were being bulldozed into a war.

The enthusiastic troopers did not have long to wait to begin their ride to Bulawayo. Nor did they have much to fear when they came face to face with the Matabele impis. Many of Lobengula's fighting men were suffering from smallpox, and at the battle of Shangani on 24 October an impi of between five and six thousand was beaten by rifle and machine-gun fire. A larger force of eight thousand came to grief in the same manner after another frontal attack on a column seventeen miles from Bulawayo. This defeat left the kraal open, and on 3 November it was occupied, although the two American scouts who made the first entry found only smouldering ruins, for the Matabele had blown up their supplies of powder. Only a few days earlier Lobengula had been trying to make terms – his envoys had been shot by Major Goold-Adams of the Bechuanaland Police – and when the columns converged on his capital, he took flight. He died soon after of smallpox, but some of his sons and grandsons fell into the Company's hands and were sent in captivity to Rhodes's Cape mansion where they were put to work as gardeners. Another (or at least someone who said he was a son of Lobengula) turned up in Britain and made some money by appearing in the music halls as part of a tableau which claimed to show the last stand of Major Wilson's column which had been wiped out in a skirmish on the banks of the Shangani. It was exciting stuff, for the embattled men were said to have sung patriotic songs before they died.

In July 1894 the short war yielded its harvest, and Lobengula's lands were handed over by the British government to the British South Africa Company. By this date the new lands and the rest of the Company's acreage were being called Rhodesia, and this name was accorded official recognition in 1897.

Matabele resistance did not die with Lobengula. It flared up again in the spring of 1896, when there was an uprising against the Company's administration in which nearly a hundred settlers and their families were murdered. These outrages provoked Rhodes, who urged his men to 'Kill all you can. It serves as a lesson to them when they talk things over at night.'[9] Yet for all his fire-eating Rhodes was himself willing to talk things over in July when he patched up a peace with the Matabele in a dramatic palaver in the Matopo Hills. By this time the Shona had thrown in their lot with the insurgents. Like the Matabele, they had learnt from the setbacks of three years before and chosen to wage a guerrilla war rather than offer themselves as mass sacrifices to the Company's machine-guns. The campaign was therefore a long-drawn-out struggle with a lot of hard riding in search of rebels and small bush skirmishes. It was all but over by the October of 1897 when the British officer in charge of the clearing-up operations, Colonel de Moleynes, reported to the War Office that, 'Prospectors are now out in many parts of the country and although a certain amount of mutual distrust still exists I do not think any further trouble is to be feared.'[10] In other words the Company was back in the saddle, and a Hut Tax had been introduced so that both Matabele and Shona, now well cowed, would have to find work on the settlements in order to pay it.

In terms of the wider struggle for supremacy in southern Africa, the establishment of Rhodesia was a success for Britain in that it effectively barred the way to northward expansion by the Transvaal. Rhodes had been very glad to number Boers among the settlers in Rhodesia, for they were of course going there to be subjects of the British Crown. For many years he had been anxious to foster cordial relations with the Boer voters of the Cape, where, in 1890, he had become Prime Minister. Yet even if the Cape Boers trusted him and were satisfied to remain subjects of Queen Victoria, this did not alter the unpleasant fact that it was the Transvaal and not the Cape which dominated the economic life of the region. The Transvaal, suspicious of Britain and with a spiralling prosperity, seemed fairly set on a course which might end in the extinguishing of Britain's political influence in the Cape and Natal. This prospect worried Rhodes and made him believe that only by the overthrow of Kruger's republic would Britain's future in southern Africa be assured. To remove the obstacle to Britain and bring the Transvaal into the British fold, Rhodes became the mainspring of a conspiracy which was as daring as it was shifty.

Throughout 1895 Rhodes planned surreptitiously for the subversion of the Transvaal government by a violent *coup de main*. A clandestine organization which called itself the 'Reform Committee' was founded in Johannesburg, funded by Rhodes and steered by his brother Frank. It hoped to exploit the political and economic grievances of the local mining community and stage an uprising in the city. As the miners rose in arms, a force of heavily armed men drawn from the ranks of the British South Africa Company Police and the *gendarmerie* of the Bechuanaland Protectorate would invade the Transvaal to assist the insurgents. The result would be turmoil and therefore an excuse for direct British intervention which would restore order and bring the Transvaal under British control.

Although nearly all the mining companies judiciously stood aside from the plot, the Reform Committee went ahead with its plans, and miners were drilled with arms supplied from Kimberley and paid for by Rhodes. In the meantime, Rhodes busied himself enlisting the pliant High Commissioner in the Cape, Sir

Waiting for the Matabele: Refugees from outlying pioneer farms at Bulawayo, 1896.

The Company preserved: British South Africa Company troopers with dead Matabele, 1896.

Hercules Robinson, and cajoling the Colonial Office to get possession of a strip of Bechuanaland which had been designated the springboard for the invasion. The commander of the invading army was Dr Jameson, who was enticing men from the Company and Bechuanaland police forces with offers of 7s.6d a day in wages. By Christmas Day 1895 he had recruited several hundred who were encamped at Pitsani just over the border from the Transvaal. They were in the dark as to what they were about to do, although many were convinced that they would soon join battle with a local chief, Linchwe, who was objecting strenuously to Rhodes taking his lands.

The *coup* had little hope of success. The Boers were suspicious, for there had been little secrecy about the Reform Committee's boasting or the military charades of its warlike members. When the moment for action came, the Johannesburg men thought better of it and the rebellion was cancelled. Rhodes too was having second thoughts and shied away from setting the plot in motion. His misgivings were not shared by Jameson, who was faced with a restless army, some of whose members were slipping away. On 29 December he called his troops together and gave them a speech in which for the first time he told them where they were going and whom they would fight. The Transvaal would crumble in the face of their onslaught, he said, and, in an appeal to what chivalry existed amongst them, he produced what he claimed was a written petition from the wives and children of the beleaguered miners of Johannesburg. Colonel Grey of the Bechuanaland Police then said his piece, which was more truthful and to the point: 'I cannot tell you that you are going by the Queen's orders, but you are going to fight for the supremacy of the British flag in South Africa'.[11] This was indeed so, and six hundred horsemen with eight machine-guns and artillery galloped over the border and spurred on to Johannesburg. In their haste they failed to sever all the telegraph lines, and so, when they came near the city, a Boer commando was waiting to intercept them at Doorn Kop. Pinned down by long-range but accurate rifle fire, Jameson's force was left with no choice but to surrender, having lost sixteen dead in two days. Kruger sent him and his fellow commanders back to Britain, where they received a heroes' welcome and trial for the offence of waging war against a friendly state. Jameson got six months.

For the future South African leader Jan Smuts, 'The Jameson raid was the real declaration of war in the Great Anglo-Boer conflict.' Rhodes was discredited and was forced to shuffle

Waiting for Jameson: Miners drilling in Johannesburg in 1895; in spite of this brave show, these men and their leaders thought better of the uprising and stayed put when the Raid began.

shame-facedly out of Cape politics. For the Boers the Jameson Raid was evidence that Britain would stop at nothing to get its way in and impose its will on South Africa, even if, as was true, British ministers had never been party to the cabal which had planned it. In Britain, initial dismay at the reckless illegality of the operation disapppeared when the German Kaiser sent a telegram of congratulations to Kruger which temporarily reawakened fears of the German bogey in southern Africa. The Kaiser was fishing in troubled waters, and his appearance on the riverbank made the British government even more agitated about the direction of events in South Africa. What was now at stake was the future of British power in the area, and if it was to survive, it would have to be seen to be greater than that of the Transvaal and Boer nationalism.

The Boer War, 1899–1902

From 1896 until the outbreak of war in October 1899, there was a prolonged and vinegary trial of political strength between Britain's new High Commissioner, Sir Alfred Milner, and President

They rode with Jameson: Troopers of the Bechuanaland Border Police, 1896.

Kruger. This duel had two purposes for Milner and the Colonial Secretary, Joseph Chamberlain. The first was to assert British paramountcy, and the second was to exploit an issue which would engage public sympathy in Britain. This cause was that of the Uitlanders, the Transvaal immigrants whose business was connected with the mines and who possessed no political rights. Their employers, the mining companies, endured high costs thanks to the Transvaal government's transport, dynamite and liquor monopolies, although these did not seriously impair their profits. The political grievances of the Uitlanders were pushed for all they were worth, especially the demand for the vote, a cause which, it was hoped, would find favour with the man in the street in Britain.

In its crudest form the wretchedness of the Uitlanders' position was drawn by G. A. Henty, a strong imperialist and supporter of the war, in his yarn for boys *With Buller in Natal*, which was published in 1901. For him and his readers, the Uitlanders were 'a large body of intelligent men' who had been held down in 'abject subjection by an inferior race, a race almost without even the elements of civilization, ignorant and brutal beyond any existing white community and superior only in the fact they are organized and armed'. The Uitlander community had been milked dry by taxes levied to underwrite 'a general uprising of the Boer population and establishment of Dutch supremacy throughout the whole of South Africa'. Whilst the first was not a statement in diplomatic language, the second, however far-fetched, did represent a nightmare which troubled Milner and Chamberlain.

At the same time as Henty was putting across the bluff jingo view of the war's issues, Liberal anti-imperialists were presenting the war as the consequence of a conspiracy of financiers and gold speculators who had the popular press in their pockets and the ability to bulldoze politicians into the service of their interests. One side-product of this 'capitalist conspiracy' theory was the identification of some of the plutocrat villains with Jews, the 'Randlords' of radical imagination. It was true that the mining companies with their new but expensive deep-level shafts were suffering as a result of the obstructiveness of Kruger's administration, but this did not mean that they wanted a full-scale war which might easily disrupt or damage their businesses. After the war, Milner did remove the restrictions which had vexed the mining companies, but their taxes were raised and there was a shortage of black labour. Nevertheless, the theory that the war was only the product of a conspiracy of rich men was simple and therefore had much political appeal, then and now.

For what was Britain really fighting? War had been declared by Kruger on 11 October 1899 but he had acted under pressure, knowing, as he had told Milner a few months before, 'It is my country that you want.' Certainly this was so, for the traditional policy of British paramountcy in South Africa depended on either a client Transvaal which would respond unquestioningly to British wishes or else a Transvaal under direct British rule. Neither was possible without a war, but a large-scale and costly war for an abstract political principle had to be sold to the British public in terms which would win its approval, and so, on one level, the struggle was represented as the just fight for the Uitlanders' political liberties: their oppressors had doggedly resisted reasoned arguments and therefore had to be brought to heel. And so, as elsewhere in Africa, the war was reduced to a simple, popular issue of Britain facing a backward, treacherous and obstinate foe which would have to be overcome for its own good. Thinking beyond victory, the administrator Milner believed that it would be possible to rebuild and reshape the whole of southern Africa to provide a just, well-ordered society from which Boer nationalism would have been extirpated.

The Boer War, which began in the autumn of 1899 and ended

with the signing of the Peace of Vereeniging in the spring of 1902, was the largest campaign ever fought by British forces in Africa; indeed, in terms of the numbers involved and the final cost, it surpassed all other nineteenth-century conflicts, including the struggle against Napoleon and the campaign in the Crimea. By the end of the war over 400,000 British and Dominion troops had served in South Africa, of whom 22,000 lost their lives, three quarters from wounds and disease and a quarter on the battlefield. The bill paid by the British government was over £200 million. Men and money had been mobilized to fight the two Boer republics whose total of men available for military service was 55,000, of whom never more than 35,000 were in the field at any one time. Of these, just over 7,000 were killed in action.

The military and political events of this major war have been frequently and exhaustively chronicled,* and so there is no need to examine them in detail. The conflict passed through three distinct phases, of which the Boer offensive against Natal and Cape Colony in October 1899 was the first. The Boer war plans aimed at obtaining an immediate strategic advantage through control of the rail networks of the two colonies and the occupation of Durban and Cape Town. If achieved, these objectives would have crippled British efforts to land reinforcements and disperse them, for either defence or counter-attack. The invasion of the Cape was expected to sound the tocsin for an uprising of the local Boer population for whose use the Transvaal government had already laid down stocks of arms. It was also hoped that early and devastating successes would encourage the intervention of one or more friendly European powers and so increase the pressure on Britain to sue for peace. The response from the Cape Boers, in both the early and later stages of the war, was disappointing, and whatever the result of the struggle in southern Africa, British sea power effectively deterred any outside intervention.

After not unexpected initial successes, the Boer offensives broke down by the beginning of November. The thrust into northern Natal ended with the siege of Ladysmith, in which Boer forces encircled and bombarded the important rail centre and beat off attempts to relieve it. It was much the same story in the Cape, where Kimberley was besieged, and further north

* e.g. T. Pakenham, *The Boer War* (1979) and R. Kruger, *Goodbye Dolly Grey* (1982).

64

Mafeking was blockaded. Large numbers of men were tied down to no purpose, and the British were free to disembark new troops, artillery and supplies. For Britain the three besieged towns had a magnetic attraction, and they were transformed in the public imagination to embattled outposts of empire in the tradition of Lucknow or Khartoum whose loss would have been a blow to national self-respect and honour.

That the beleaguered towns attracted so much interest and that their fate seemed inextricably bound up with patriotic sentiments was not surprising. The performance of Britain's forces in the field had been dismal. Sir Redvers Buller, from 31 October the commander in chief of forces in South Africa, had made their relief the first aim of his operations. He and his subordinate generals were also anxious to bring the Boers to battle, in the belief that a signal and overwhelming victory would presage a total Boer collapse and the restoration of imperial military prestige. So in the Cape Lieutenant-General Gatacre attempted to dislodge a strongly entrenched Boer force at Stormberg, where, after a night march of eight miles, his forces were bloodily repulsed on 10 December. Lord Methuen, stalking victory along the tracks of the Kimberley line, engaged the Boers who had entrenched on the banks of the Modder river on 28 November. The Boers, after inflicting losses on their assailants, withdrew to a more formidable position at Magersfontein, which Methuen vainly tried to storm on 11 December. His attack came to grief like the others, with losses of nearly seven hundred wounded and captured.

Buller fared little better in Natal. He was a brave general who, in spite of his flawed tactical decisions and their bloody consequences, was well liked by his soldiers. 'Sick of Africa' and keenly aware of his own incapacities, he shared his colleagues' misfortune or lack of foresight in that he always fought the Boers on ground of their own choosing. At Colenso on 15 December he sent his men forward to attack Boers who were well dug in, and they were severely cut up by shell and magazine rifle fire. His will faltered and a day later he flashed a heliograph message to the defenders of Ladysmith which told them to surrender, for he could send them no further help. Three defeats – 'Black Week' for the British public – seemed a catastrophe but none of them changed the situation in South Africa. The Boers never exploited their successes by counter-attacks which might have turned British retirements into routs, unlike the tribesmen of the North West Frontier who, as one junior officer remarked, always

65

On to Pretoria: Lord Roberts sets the pace for his staff, 1900.

harried a retreating enemy.[12] It was a small but welcome mercy. If the Boers preferred to fight by staying in their trenches, the British began to understand the futility of frontal assaults against well-directed fire from magazine rifles. The later fighting, in particular Buller's final push to Ladysmith, showed that officers and men were quick to develop a more flexible and therefore effective battlecraft.

The unhappy catalogue of defeats in December 1899 led to a change of command in South Africa by which an Indian army veteran of sixty-seven, Lord Roberts, took up the post of commander in chief, with Lord Kitchener as his chief of staff. *En route* to Cape Town the two commanders solved the strategic problem with a plan for a flank march north along the railway line to Kimberley and then a swing eastwards into the Orange Free State which would take the war to the Boer homelands. The second stage of the war had started. Roberts's manœuvres were successful, and on 27 February 1900 his forces took the surrender of four thousand Boers under Cronjé, who had been entrapped at the Paardeberg Drift. From there his forces moved to the Orange Free State's capital at Bloemfontein, which fell on 4 April, and Pretoria, which was taken on 4 June. In Natal Buller was at last making headway with his reinforcements after a major setback at Spion Kop on 24 January. Here Buller had authorized the taking of the hill whose summit was overlooked by the Boers and which proved a death-trap for over a thousand British infantry. In the next weeks Buller's troops, learning new techniques as they fought, pushed the Boers back, and on 28 February they entered Ladysmith. Within a few months his army was operating in northern Natal as the commandos fell back into Transvaal.

The fall of Pretoria seemed to mark the end of the war, and in London a sanguine War Office commissioned campaign medals which gave the terminal date of the operations as 1900. The British army had secured the capitals of its opponents, driven their armies back and left them scattered and isolated. In other words, they had won. This would have been true had they been fighting a European power, but they were not; instead they faced a new and debilitating phase of the war, a prolonged contest against Boer guerrillas. A new and younger generation of Boer commanders, Louis Botha, J. H. de la Rey, Christian de Wet and Jan Smuts, had stepped into the shoes left by the older, more cautious generals such as Joubert and Cronjé. The new men brought with them a new kind of fighting which aimed at

Beaten Boers: Prisoners-of-war preparing for embarkation at Cape Town. Some would be sent to St Helena and others to Ceylon or Bermuda; their close guard included Lancers (on the left).

wearing down their enemies, not from the safety of earthworks but by swift and wounding raids against isolated detachments, outposts and lines of communication. The British army would be beaten not by one or more decisive actions but by a series of pinpricks inflicted by mobile commandos. In the end the war-weary British would be forced to acknowledge Boer independence, or so the guerrillas hoped.

In the next two years the guerrilla generals conducted a spectacular war, or so it seemed to them, in which they repeatedly disrupted rail transport, took towns, ensnared often quite sizeable units and side-stepped the thrusts of the large columns sent out to hunt them down. Throughout this time the morale of the *bittereinders* ('bitter-enders') stayed high, and in 1902 Deneys Reitz's, one of the 'bittereinder' commandos thought that news that peace negotiations were underway meant that the British were suing for terms.[13] Yet Reitz also knew that what the guerrillas had looked on as 'important victories' were, for the British, just 'minor incidents'. This was right, for the guerrillas never weakened the British war-machine, which showed itself well able to cope with their activities, through both the deployment of sufficient troops and the taking of what turned out to be effective counter-measures.

British operations against the guerrillas began in the summer of 1900 and lasted until the making of peace in April 1902. It was a tedious war of attrition conducted by Lord Kitchener, who succeeded Roberts as commander-in-chief at the end of November 1900. Overall strategy was to wear down the guerrillas by two means. The first was the erosion of their resources, and thirty thousand farmsteads were burnt and their occupants, Boer women, children and black servants, from September 1900, taken under guard to internment camps. This drastic policy was designed to deprive the guerrillas of assistance on the veldt, which was also systematically stripped of all livestock. Previously, when farms had been razed and stock driven off, the Boer families had been left to their fate in the hope that husbands and fathers would return from the commandos to look after them, but this had not happened; indeed, it was widely believed that the Boer women had done much to encourage and stiffen their menfolk's resistance. By December 1901 the army authorities reverted to this method of handling refugees from the devastated areas although there was no direct evidence to suggest its effectiveness.

The refugee centres, which were called 'concentration camps', varied greatly, but for the most part the women, children and servants were housed in army tents and arrangements for sanitation and medical care were often flimsy. Measles, pneumonia, dysentery and typhus were endemic, and 28,000 Europeans died in the camps, 22,000 of them children, whose natural lack of resistance to illness was made worse by the poor diet offered by the army authorities. Further camps were built for the 115,000 black refugees who fled from tribal lands which were being fought over by the guerrillas and the British, but losses here, like those of blacks in the Boer camps, were never computed by the army.

Whilst the army cleared the disaffected areas of beasts and people, it waged war against the guerrillas. Vast areas were parcelled up by barbed-wire fences and watched over by small detachments in blockhouses connected by telephone lines. To these static defensive measures was added a sequence of offensives by co-ordinated columns which criss-crossed the countryside, hunting the commandos or driving them into specially contrived traps. This was a tedious and slow war in which the results seldom seemed commensurate with the effort. An eight-

*War of attrition, I: 'We went to the rebels' farms and took all their cattle
and harness, as well as pigs and chickens enough to last a month, after
which an officer, myself, and another man search the houses for firearms
and ammunition. At one place the old woman and her daughter didn't half
carry on, for the women were worse than the men, whom they put up to
all sorts of mean actions. I was taking a large bar of soap, when the girl
came behind and snatched it from me. I said, 'All right, my dear, you
need it'. She got so angry that she was going to hit me across the head with
a big piece of iron and would have done so had I not stopped her' –*
anonymous private, Essex Regiment, June 1900

War of attrition, II: Women and children at Springsfontein Camp, 1901.

War of attrition, III: Boer families and their black servants, unknown camp, 1901.

day sweep in the western Transvaal during July 1901 by Brigadier Dixon's column yielded two surrendered Boers, three hundred women and children, who were entrained for an internment camp, and three hundred head of sheep, goats and oxen.[14]
It was often observed that those Boers who fell prisoner or gave
themselves up were often older, sick or dejected men whose loss
would positively help their comrades. Kitchener found all this
stretched his patience, and he gave voice to his irritation in an
order to General Sir Leslie Rundle (whose ponderous advances
had earned him the nickname 'Sir Leisurely Trundle') which was
to be passed on to those under him: 'The operations against the
enemy not yet having resulted in teaching the Boers the useless-
ness of their struggle it is necessary to exert renewed energy and
rigour in bringing home to them the folly of continuing the war
. . . all commanders will use every means in their power to
stamp out as rapidly as possible all armed resistance in their
districts.'[15]

At the same time the conflict was becoming a civil war. Many
of the Boers who had submitted and taken the oath to Edward
VII enlisted in special corps to fight their one-time comrades.
These were the 'handsuppers' who, in the eyes of those still in
the field, were taking crumbs from the enemy, and they were
given no mercy. When a commando of two hundred passed by
Elandsfontein near Johannesburg on 22–3 July 1901, they shot a
Mr Koch, who had done 'excellent work' in persuading men to
surrender, and burnt his farm to the ground. They also retook
ten surrendered Boers, four of whom were flogged with a
sjambok (rhinoceros-hide whip); the others were thought to
have been shot.[16] Such brutality suggests that at heart many of
the commandos must have known that their cause was lost. It
did not deter other 'handsuppers', for over five thousand were
serving with British forces by the end of the war.

In spite of Smuts's spectacular and ruthless invasion of Cape
Colony towards the end of 1901, the guerrilla war was being lost
and the resisters were facing the possibility of total defeat and,
with it, a peace entirely on British terms. Kitchener for his part
wanted an end to a conflict which was increasingly unpopular at
home and was therefore willing to meet the Boer leaders and
negotiate a settlement. In March 1901 the Boers had been intran-
sigent about the surrender of independence, but at Vereeniging
just over a year later they bowed to the inevitable. The republics
gave up their independence, their people were offered £3 million for economic reconstruction, and with few exceptions a

On the track of the Guerrillas: Troopers of the Imperial Yeomanry (Border Horse) in hot pursuit of the Boers.

general amnesty was extended to all in arms. The political future would be self-government but the blacks and coloureds (of mixed blood) were excluded from the franchise, much to the satisfaction of both Boer and British South Africans. Milner settled down to reshape the future of South Africa and hoped that a flood of British immigrants would arrive to swamp the Boer majority and enforce loyalty to the Crown. He was disappointed, and his administrative work was cut short in 1906, when a Liberal government allowed the Orange Free State and Transvaal self-government. Four years later the Union of South Africa was created, a fulfilment of the dream of the federation under the British Crown, a bulwark to uphold British interests.

The Afrikaner nationalism which had been brought to its knees in 1902 and survived and in the form of the Nationalist Party became the government in 1948. Thirteen years later, under Dr Verwoerd, South Africa became a republic. What then had Britain gained? The British soldiers who had fought in southern Africa had beaten black resistance and temporarily overthrown that of the Boers. There had, in 1914, been a pro-German and anti-British uprising by diehard nationalists who thought that with German aid they might reverse the verdict of the recent war against Britain. The majority of their countrymen thought otherwise; the revolt was easily put down, and South Africa threw in its lot with Britain to reap the reward of the ex-German colony of South West Africa (Namibia) in 1919. Again in 1939 there was a recrudescence of pro-German sentiment but the South Africans chose to fight with Britain in a war which marked the end of British global power. Paramountcy in the Cape no longer mattered.

Egypt and the Sudan, 1882–1920

It dawns in Asia, tombstones show
And Shropshire names are read;
And the Nile spills his overflow
Beside the Severn's dead.
A. E. Housman

In 1869 the Suez Canal was opened, and its significance for the future of British commercial enterprise and maritime supremacy was soon understood. Within a dozen years four out of every five vessels which passed through the canal were British; to and fro went British men o'war bound for eastern waters, troopships replenishing garrisons in India and merchantmen with cargoes of raw materials and manufactured goods. The Suez Canal had become a vital artery, and its security was naturally a major concern of British governments. Before 1881 the canal's safety depended upon three factors: the powerful Mediterranean Fleet based at Malta and Gibraltar, Britain's possession of a major shareholding in the Suez Canal Company, and the willingness of Egypt's ruler, the Khedive, to dance to a tune composed by his country's European creditors and played by French and British financial advisers in Cairo. By 1881 the Khedive's Moslem subjects, most of them poor peasant farmers, had grown weary of stepping to a pace set by foreigners and unbelievers which was leaving them broken by its rigour. Popular feeling therefore backed a *coup* by a knot of nationalist army officers led by Colonel Arabi which commandeered the government and promised an end to Egypt's submission to rapacious interlopers.

Arabi's reform programme was a blow against the system of 'unofficial' empire, and it was one which the British Prime Minister, Gladstone, was ill equipped to parry, for he privately

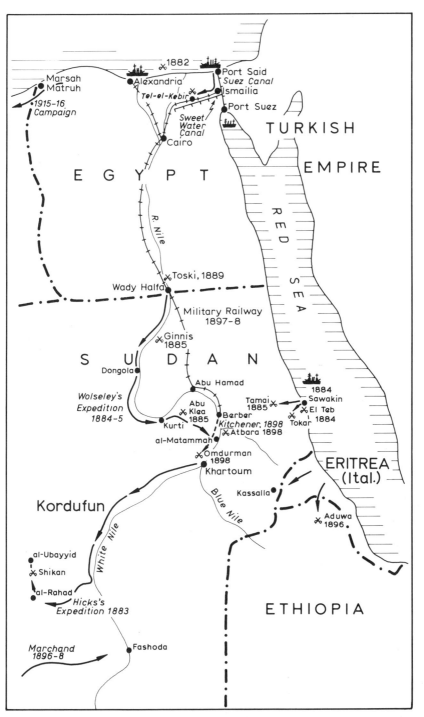

Egypt and the Sudan

sympathized with the nationalists and wished at all costs to avoid using force to assert his country's interests. Gladstone instinctively chose diplomacy as the instrument by which Egypt would be placed in hands which would work for British interests. His efforts to enlist the aid of other powers, in particular France, were not successful. At the same time he had to make a public affirmation of traditional British policy and offer protection to British subjects in Egypt. So, at the end of May 1882, he and his Cabinet fell back on the customary expedient and ordered a squadron of warships to anchor off Alexandria. Alongside these warships were others, also there as tokens of their governments' concern and as an advertisement of international displeasure with Egypt's new regime. The Egyptians were not overawed. The British and French financial commissioners were sent packing, and on 11 June rioters in Alexandria attacked Europeans and plundered their property. As a further gesture of defiance, the authorities began to mount artillery on the city's seaward defences, possibly as a deterrent against a sudden landing.

The British government was now faced with a number of uncomfortable alternatives. Its squadron could lie passively at anchor as the peril grew, it could call off and thereby inflict a wound on British pride and naval prestige, or Admiral Seymour, the commander, could insist on the dismantlement of the batteries. The first two were unthinkable, and so Seymour demanded the dismounting of the new guns on the grounds that they endangered his fleet. In accordance with Cabinet instructions, an ultimatum was delivered to the governor of Alexandria on 10 July which gave him twenty-four hours to take away his guns or else face bombardment. Foreign vessels scurried out of the harbour, and in the evening Seymour's men o'war steamed to their battle stations.

The British squadron was formidable. Seymour commanded eight battleships, including his flagship, HMS *Inflexible*, which mounted four sixteen-inch guns, and five small gunboats. The weight of his broadside far exceeded that which the Egyptian batteries could throw against him, for whilst they numbered over two hundred guns, a third were obsolete and ineffective against strongly protected ironclads. By contrast Seymour's warships were well armed with modern rifled breech-loaders, and so when his guns began their steady and deliberate fire at seven in the morning of 11 July, the outcome was never in doubt. Ten and a half hours later, the Egyptian artillerymen abandoned their pieces which they had doggedly manned to maintain a ragged answer to the naval fire. Their shot and shells had inflicted marginal damage on the ironclads and killed five sailors. The shelling had started fires within the city, where mobs were turning their rage on Europeans, their homes and businesses. Rough weather the next day prevented a landing, but on the 13th the fleet cast anchor in the harbour. At once six hundred marines and bluejackets went ashore with Gatling guns and set to work to impose order in Alexandria. Two days later they were briefly joined by some US Marines whose ship was anchored nearby and who were eager for a share in the action. Egyptian forces offered no contest to the landing parties, although once the city had been pacified there were many skirmishes in the countryside beyond. These sallies gave Captain Fisher (later Lord Fisher of Kilverstone, the First Sea Lord before and during the First World War) the chance for a few *Boys' Own Paper* stunts when he organized an armoured train, bristling with Gatling guns, which made periodic forays into the Alexandrian hinterland.

Just as the gun emplacements of Alexandria were in ruins, so was Gladstone's Egyptian policy. The naval action and occupation of Alexandria had destablized Egypt, and it was feared that Arabi would order the blocking of the Suez Canal in retaliation. This is what Arabi considered but he was deflected by the canal's builder and present administrator, Ferdinand de Lesseps, who argued that the canal was neutral. De Lesseps also convinced Arabi that the British would respect the canal's neutrality, and so there was no danger of its falling to a sudden attack. He was wrong, for the British Cabinet had decided on a *coup de main* against the canal which would be immediately followed up by a full-scale invasion of Egypt. The long-term objective was the expulsion of Arabi and his replacement by a stable and docile government which would underwrite the future security of the canal.

The first stage of the implementation of this policy was begun on 2 August, when Admiral Hewett, the commander of the East Indies station, landed men from his squadron at Port Suez in anticipation of local disorders and possible sabotage to the canal locks. Arabi was not alarmed thanks to de Lesseps's assurances and a deliberately deceptive press release which hinted strongly that the British would concentrate their forces at Alexandria. The inviolability of the canal was shattered on the night of 19–20 August when a hundred sailors from HMS *Ready* landed and took

HMS Inflexible: *Admiral Seymour's flagship at Alexandria, one of the most powerful battleships afloat.*

Egypt crumbles: Abandoned guns, Alexandria, 1882.

Ready, aye, ready: Bluejackets man Captain Fisher's armoured train, Alexandria, 1882.

over the canal's telegraph system, barges and dredgers. At dawn five hundred marines and sailors with two Gatling guns came ashore at Port Said, surrounded the Egyptian army barracks, took the surrender of its inhabitants and arrested their commander in his house. Another party took over the Suez Canal Company offices, much to the amazed fury of de Lesseps. There was no serious opposition, although one officer was beset by an Arab mob which he dispersed by striding up to its ringleader, who was told, 'Get out of this, you ugly-looking ruffian!'

Further down the canal, the battleship HMS *Orion* in company with HMS *Carysfort* had steamed to Ismailia where a landing party of five hundred was disembarked. It met with some resistance, but the Egyptian infantrymen broke off the engagement and scattered westwards towards the army base at Tel-el-Kebir, forty miles away. Some reinforcements issued out of Tel-el-Kebir, but their advance was stemmed by the action of the captain of *Orion*. He induced a heavy starboard list in his ship which was sufficient to increase the range of his twelve-inch guns to four thousand yards. One of their shells hit the railway and blew away all hopes of an Egyptian counter-attack. By speed and stealth the navy had carried out an operation in the classic Nelsonian tradition which had forestalled any attempt to block the canal and delivered into Britain's hands a lifeline vital for its continued maritime supremacy.

79

The navy had opened the way and the army followed. On 25 July the War Office had begun to gather an expeditionary force of 24,000 men drawn from forces in Britain, the Mediterranean and India. It was a mixed body of men and included Indian lancers, reservists recalled to the colours, the Guards and the Blues and Royals. Morale and excitement were high. One young officer recalled the 'immense joy' felt in the mess of the Royal Rifle Regiment when they heard that they were to leave Gibraltar and take ship for Egypt. Command of the expedition had been given to Sir Garnet Wolseley, then the rising star in the military firmament who had directed operations against the Ashante and the Zulus. Then his opponents had been ill-armed natives, but the Egyptian army, with its modern artillery and breech-loading rifles, appeared to be more formidable, even though its soldiers were conscripts drawn from the *fellahin* (peasant farmers). Wolseley was expected to bring this army to battle as quickly as possible and defeat it decisively. A swift victory was imperative so that Britain could face her Continental critics, especially France, as the unquestioned master of Egypt.

Wolseley's plan was simple and methodical. After a feint towards Alexandria to fox Arabi, his troopships entered the Suez Canal and steamed to Ismailia. It was an ideal base since it lay at the terminuses of the Sweet Water Canal and railway line which both ran straight to Tel-el-Kebir. Here Arabi was concentrating a force of thirty thousand men with sixty cannon in order to bar the way to Cairo. Wolseley's first move was therefore to gain control of the railway and canal and so secure his lines of supply and communication. After a series of probing reconnaissances in force, the British secured the canal and railroad as far as Kassassin, where they established a forward base for the attack on Tel-el-Kebir, a few miles away. Intelligence had shown Wolseley that the Egyptians had thrown up extensive earthworks behind which men and cannon had been ranged. With thirteen thousand men and fewer cannon than the Egyptians, Wolseley appreciated that the only way to attack quickly would be under cover of darkness. As the Egyptians did not bother to send out night patrols, it was possible for the British force to move forward to within two hundred yards of the fortifications. If this could be achieved, the British troops would not suffer from rifle and shell fire and could rush the defences. In Wolseley's words, 'The Highland Brigade would give a great shout and rush in; and no troops in the world would stand it'.[1] Privately he was less optimistic and feared heavy losses.

Just after midnight on 13 September, the columns of British began their advance, guided by a young naval officer who was skilled in navigating by the stars and who later lost his life in the battle. The march was slow, with frequent pauses, and there were, luckily, few hitches, although one Guards battalion fired off a few shots by mistake. In spite of this, surprise was complete and the defences were stormed under heavy fire and taken at bayonet point. It was too much for many Egyptian officers, who scampered off, but the *fellahin* conscripts fought back stubbornly for a short time. Within twenty minutes the battle was over and the Guards' bands were called up to play a medley of regimental marches, a fittingly anachronistic finale to a battle which had been won by the bayonet. Far away the cavalry cantered after the dispirited Egyptians, and the road to Cairo was open. Wolseley had gambled and won; he had beaten an army with modern weaponry and given Britain control over Egypt.

Tel-el-Kebir had given Britain unassailable control over the canal, and the Khedive Tawfiq was free from the influence of Arabi, who was later sent into exile in Ceylon. For French politicians, the crisis and the campaign had been manipulated by a devious British government to gain possession of Egypt and so bruise the interests of France. There followed a long sequence of sour wrangles in which Gladstone looked for the means to placate international criticism at the same time as setting up in Cairo an administration which was honest, solvent and amenable to Britain's interests. The solution was a regime by which British advisers directed the government of Egypt in the Khedive's name, and an international agreement was made for the settlement of Egypt's debts. Meanwhile the British government was becoming painfully aware that the problems of Cairo were now those of London as well.

The Sudan, 1883–98

One of the greatest of Egypt's difficulties in the early 1880s was the collapse of order in its huge southern province, the Sudan. During the summer of 1881 the province was suffering from a series of minor convulsions inspired by an Islamic prophet, Muhammad Ahmad, who took for himself the title '*al Mahdi*', 'the promised one'. He was a messenger of Allah, who had given him the task of purifying religion, chastising the slack and unbelieving and uniting all the truly faithful of the Sudan. Those

Masters of Egypt: Officers of the 7th Dragoon Guards relax after the battle of Tel-el-Kebir, 1882.

who accepted the Mahdi became his *ansars*, servants of Allah who fought for His prophet and lived by the highest moral and religious standards. To the British who later fought against them, they were, collectively, the Dervishes.

At the onset of his religious campaign, the Mahdi had threatened war to all who rejected his divine mission and had promised miracles to his *ansars*. In January 1883 Muhammad Ahmad and his army gave the world proof of Allah's favour when, after heavy losses, they took al-Ubayyid, slew its garrison of Egyptians and plundered six thousand Remington breech-loaders and an arsenal of ammunition. This miracle stirred the Kurdofun, and more and more tribesmen began to rally to the Mahdi. In Cairo, the Khedive had no wish to hand over the Kurdofun to the Mahdists, and he demanded the despatch of an army to retake al-Ubayyid and destroy the Mahdi. This suggestion dismayed his new British advisers, who queried the sense of a bankrupt state undertaking such a campaign. The Khedive prevailed and in March 1883 orders were given for the collection of an army of 8,600 infantry and 1,400 cavalry at Khartoum. A brave and experienced British officer, Colonel William Hicks, was given command, and his forces were equipped with the latest weaponry, including six Nordenfelt machine-guns and

Krupp breech-loaders. Hicks's opponents were thought to number nearly seventy thousand, and whilst he was willing to take the field against them, he wanted Khartoum to be put in readiness for a siege.

Hicks's army was doomed. Many of the *fellahin* soldiers had fought against the British at Tel-el-Kebir and therefore had little love for a British commander, whilst others were rescued slaves who had been drafted against their will. The native officers were 'inefficient, and as a rule apathetic', and Hicks, surrounded by backbiting and lethargy, likened himself to 'Jesus Christ in the midst of the Jews'.[2] His strategy was flawed for, rather than choosing to march to al-Ubayyid by the shortest route across open country, he took his forces south-west from Khartoum into a landscape of long grass and scattered woods. He had made up his mind after receiving offers of mounted men by a local ruler, Mak Adam of the Taqali. They never appeared and Hicks's column, infiltrated by Mahdist spies, was sniped at by their comrades hidden in the bush and trees alongside his path. As he moved forward, Hicks was unable to establish and man posts for communications and supplies for he had insufficient reserves.

The Mahdists who hovered on Hicks's flank saw an army in a state of deliquescence. On 8 November the column had dragged itself seventy-five miles in eight days, during which it had been the impotent victim of continuous hit-and-run raids. The transport camels in tight masses were easy targets for Mahdist marksmen, while others, less lucky perhaps, perished from exhaustion after having been burdened with additional baggage. After six days rest at al-Rahad, the demoralized army moved towards al-Ubayyid under the fire of sharpshooters who continued to vex its flanks. From 2 to 5 November the attacks intensified, and in the end the trap was sprung at Shikan, where the sad detritus of the force was surrounded, its cannon abandoned and its men footsore and thirsty. At the end the *ansar* spearmen charged home, crying '*Di al-Mahdi al-muzanger*' ('This is the Mahdi, the promised one'), and swept all before them, including Hicks, who died fighting. Two hundred and fifty Egyptian soldiers were captured, many of whom joined the *ansars* and with the Mahdi took rifles, machine-guns and the abandoned Krupp cannon. On the same day, 5 November, a force of Hadandawa warriors under the command of an ex-slave-dealer and Mahdist convert, Osman Diqna, routed five hundred Egyptian infantry led by the British consul in Sawakin.

Ready to tackle the Mahdi: General Hicks (seated far right) and Baker (next to him) pose before their ill-fated campaigns, Cairo, 1883.

Three days later Egyptian authority in the eastern Sudan suffered another wound when Osman destroyed another force at Tamai. Total catastrophe was averted when the guns of HMS *Dolphin*, anchored in Sawakin harbour, frightened off Osman Diqna's advance guard as they moved towards the port.

These shots were the first indication that Britain was being drawn, unwillingly, into the affairs of the Sudan. Admiral Hewett, the naval commander in the Red Sea, had already been authorized to do all within his power to maintain the stability and security of its Sudan shoreline. This coast flanked the sea route from Suez to India and was therefore important to Britain. It was also good sense to take measures which might prevent the spores of Mahdism crossing the Red Sea and infecting Arabia, then part of the Turkish Empire and, in British eyes, an essential bulwark for Middle Eastern stability. Yet the British government shrank from open commitment in the area and entrusted Sawakin's security to Cairo. In January 1884 the Egyptian general Valentine Baker (a former British cavalry officer whose promising career had ended when he was convicted of molesting a girl in a railway carriage) was ordered to Sawakin with a scratch army of three thousand, including Egyptian infantry, Egyptian ex-policemen and Turkish mercenaries, with instructions to drive Osman Diqna from the area. On 4 February 1884 Baker's army was routed by Osman's horde near El Teb (al-Taib). The Dervish horsemen cut through Baker's pickets, and the column behind was thrown into a desperate panic. 'The men turned their backs on the advancing foe, and in a paroxysm of terror fired into the square [their own], or fell on their knees praying for mercy.'[3] None was offered and 2,400 were slain, their cannon and machine-guns falling into Osman's hands. Baker, on horseback, cut his way free from the debris of his army and, like Johnny Cope, 'ran with the news of his own defeat' into Sawakin. The following day marines and sailors came ashore from the men o'war in the harbour and with their machine-guns started to set up a perimeter defence. Two days after, Hewett's initiative was endorsed in a telegram from the Cabinet.

For Gladstone and his Cabinet, busy seeking ways to rid Britain of the Egyptian incubus, the telegrams from Sawakin and Cairo were baleful reading. Three Egyptian armies had been annihilated, thousands of rifles, their ammunition, cannon, machine-guns and rocket tubes had fallen into the enemy's hands. No Egyptian army could withstand the Mahdists, and Gladstone had no wish for any more to try, since he regarded the Dervishes of the Sudan as a people struggling to be free. So on 19 February 1884 he decided that Khartoum and other inland garrisons were to be evacuated under the supervision of General Charles Gordon, who would command in the name of the Khedive. Sawakin was another matter, for here it was possible to land an army, drive back Osman Diqna and maintain a British armed presence thanks to naval support. Therefore on 12 February the Commander-in-Chief in Egypt had been instructed to organize an expeditionary force of British troops for the rescue of the beleaguered Egyptian garrisons on the eastern Sudan.

Ten days later, the Sawakin Field Force landed at Tirinkitat, north of Sawakin and a few miles from the town of Tokar (Tŭkar), then besieged by Osman's army. Its arrival owed much to the speed of telegraphic communications and the army's ability to respond quickly to a crisis. The York and Lancaster Regiment had been summoned from Aden, the Black Watch, the Gordons and the 60th Rifles from garrison duties in Egypt, and the Royal Irish Fusiliers had been diverted whilst *en route* to India. The 10th and 19th Hussars provided some valuable cavalry squadrons for scouting; there was a seven-pounder battery and naval ratings with their Gatling guns. The emergency

Dervishes: Captured Dervish warriors photographed after the battle of Atbara, 1898.

force's commander, General Graham, on landing proclaimed that, 'The English Government is not at war with the Arabs but is determined to disperse forces now in arms in the neighbourhood and near Sawakin.' Osman was not cowed, for a few days before he had warned Admiral Hewett that those without faith in the Mahdi would perish and that the British would soon be pushed into the Red Sea. Given his attitude and the prestige he had gained from his recent victories, General Graham immediately set about bringing Osman to battle, an operation which would ensure the relief of Tokar.

Graham's aim was to engage Osman at his base at El Teb, a few miles inland from Tirinkitat. Ahead of his main force were squadrons of Hussars, and behind them the main body marched as a huge column, ready to fend off a sudden attack, and encompassing the transport animals with their spare ammunition, tube wells and water-containers. To the front of the square marched the sailors with their machine-guns. After a 3½-hour advance through thick mimosa scrub, the square drew up just a thousand yards short of the Dervish position. Osman had had earthworks thrown up, and he had placed behind them Krupp cannon recently taken from Baker. These were manned by renegade Turkish gunners, and their fire on the square opened the battle. The naval gunners replied with their machine-guns and drove the Turks off. It was now safe for the square to advance, and the attack was launched. The square stepped to the right and, with the Highlanders' pipes playing, it crossed the Dervish flank and moved to assault the earthworks. The Dervishes rushed out to counter-charge with swords and spears but were thrown back by the volleys of the leading companies. First to the breastwork was Colonel Fred Burnaby, a *beau sabreur* of the Blues and the subject of Tissot's famous portrait,* in which his etiolated figure lounges with élan and insouciance. At El Teb he cut a different dash and killed thirteen Dervishes with twenty shots from a double-barrelled shotgun. His coolness reminded one onlooker of a man at the butts, but when descriptions of the incident appeared in the press, there was a wail of indignation from anti-imperialists, made more intense by the fact that Burnaby was a Tory Parliamentary candidate.

The victory at El Teb temporarily scattered Osman's forces but was too late to save Tokar, its garrison and granaries. Nevertheless, as the *Daily Telegraph* asserted, 'The supremacy of the Anglo-Saxon race over the children of the desert was amply manifested.' Thirty-four British soldiers had been killed, against eight hundred Dervishes. Nearly one third of the losses were Hussars, for, as the official account of the battle drily observed, 'The cavalry made some dashing charges; their loss was heavy.' Whilst the Dervishes recoiled from rifle fire, they did understand sword-to-sword combat, as the Hussars learnt to their cost. With only three days' supply of water for his force, Graham was unable to linger in the area of the battle, although he recovered a lost Gatling gun and some cannon. On his arrival back in Sawakin, Graham issued a call to the local sheiks who had thrown in their lots with Osman: 'You trusted in the notorious scoundrel Osman Diqna who is well to you as a bad man. . . . He has led you away with a foolish idea that the Mahdi had come to earth. We tell you that the Great God that rules over

* In the National Portrait Gallery.

the universe does not allow scoundrels such as Osman Diqna to rule over men. Your people are weak, and England always spares such people. Come in at once, or the fate of those who fell at El Teb will surely overtake you.'[4] A good price was offered for Osman's head, but those in Britain who had been distressed by Burnaby's shotgun protested that this was barbaric. It was also, like the proclamation, unfruitful, for within a few days Osman, backed by twelve thousand followers, was again in the field and menacing Sawakin.

Graham was now determined to reinforce the message of El Teb and on 13 March set out to give battle to Osman, who was known to be with his army close to the Tamai (Tamay) wells. Graham advanced by night over eight miles of desert, during which his forces came under inaccurate fire from Dervish snipers who skulked in the scrub. In the morning more appeared and taunted the British soldiers from a distance, calling them Christians, infidels and dogs. Some came closer but fell to shell and machine-gun fire. Graham had anticipated an ambush, so his force had been divided into two squares which marched in echelon, the one ready to give support to the other. When the rush of Dervishes came, the first square came under heavy pressure and fractured as the men of the York and Lancaster Regiment fell back. Still they retired firing, and their volleys were augmented by those from the second square. This weight of fire finally forced the Dervishes back, and the cavalry, with the wisdom of experience, dismounted and added carbine fire to the volleys of the infantry. The battle of Tamai was over; 109 of the British lost their lives and another 112 were wounded. Osman's dead were estimated to be two thousand.

Tamai confirmed the message of El Teb, and Sawakin was safe. Osman changed his tactics and plagued the port's garrison with night raids which were countered by landmines and surveillance of the perimeter by warship searchlights. Osman seems also to have discovered something of Gladstone's Sudan policy, for he told his followers that the British would soon pull out. Anxious to give the lie to such tales, Graham telegraphed London on 17 March for permission to undertake more offensives against Osman to teach him and his men that 'we can march anywhere we please'. But the Cabinet held Graham in check and later ordered the evacuation of Sawakin, which was left in the care of the navy and assorted Egyptian units.

Whilst Graham kicked his heels in Sawakin and regretted Gladstone's pusillanimity, the attention of the Prime Minister and the country was being drawn towards Khartoum. On 18 February 1884 Gordon had stepped ashore there with a mandate to superintend the withdrawal of Egyptian troops in the city together with anyone else who wanted to leave. He wore the uniform of the Khedive of Egypt but his orders had been drafted in London, where it had been decided that, whilst Egypt was slithering into bankruptcy, it could no longer take any effective action to assert its sovereignty over the Sudan. The province offered Britain no political advantage, although it was admitted that strategic considerations made the continued occupation of Sawakin necessary, but then this could be undertaken cheaply by the navy. The rest of the Sudan could fend for itself whilst Britain's energies were concentrated on haggling over an international agreement which would solve the problem of Egypt's indebtedness.

This was the view from London but not from Khartoum, where Gordon was able to define a picture very different from Gladstone's. He was a professional soldier who had, whilst in China, commanded irregular troops, and he had been in the late 1870s a governor of the Sudan under the Egyptian administration. Experience and local knowledge made him conclude that the Mahdi was a will o'the wisp who, like others with his pretensions, would pass away as suddenly as he had come. If it came to a fight, Gordon was convinced that he could 'smash' the Mahdi and that, for the time being, Khartoum was 'as safe as Kensington Park'. Gordon believed that, with the co-operation of loyally disposed tribes, he could eliminate Mahdism and then concoct a political solution to the Sudan's problems which would satisfy its people and the governments in Cairo and London. To show to his superiors that he was right, he sent off a cascade of cables to Cairo and London. Once he thought that he might even accommodate Muhammad Ahmad with the offer of the sultanate of the Kurdofun but this bagatelle was scorned and Gordon received, by way of reply, a patched *jibbah* accompanied by an exhortation to wear it as a mark of his conversion to Islam and submission to the Mahdi. Gordon had, in fact, mistaken the mood of his masters, who were anxious to disentangle from the Sudan, and under-estimated the Mahdi. He was, however, a brave and resourceful fighter and, in defiance of his brief, tried to enlist the help of the riverine tribes against the Mahdists and lead a few sorties against them in the vicinity of Khartoum.

These successes boosted his confidence and faith in the rightness of his policies, and in Britain they earned him widespread popularity as a Christian hero who had followed the path of duty in the service of civilization.

Gordon's early successes had come during a period when the Mahdi was giving small thought to Khartoum. After his triumph at Shikan, Muhammad Ahmad was busy fighting the troops under Rudolph von Slatin in Darfur province and bringing to obedience the Nuba tribesmen of the southern Sudan. Once he had consolidated his authority in the south, he was free to move northwards to take Khartoum and the rest of the Sudan and impose his version of Islam on its peoples. To persuade them, he required more miracles like that at Shikan, and so he had to proceed cautiously, for a setback might easily shake the tribesmen's faith. At the beginning of March local *ansars* began their blockade of the city and incidentally cut its telegraph link with Cairo and the rest of the world. In August, after the end of Ramadam and the rainy season, the Mahdi drew the bulk of his forces out of the Kurdofun towards Khartoum, and on 21 October the siege began in earnest.

Khartoum, which lies at the confluence of the Blue and White Niles, was a walled city, and to the north was the subsidiary fortress of Omdurman. There were seven thousand troops thinly spread inside Khartoum and Omdurman, but they were under a spirited and aggressive commander who was willing to make sallies against the hundred thousand men who surrounded him. Whilst the Mahdists possessed cannon and machine-guns, their turncoat crews did not appear to have been very good, for in mid-December Gordon noted in his diary that the two thousand shells fired against the city had killed only three men. Gordon was, however, anxious about the dwindling stocks of food within the city, and, after 13 January 1885, the loss of Omdurman which fell to an assault. The Mahdi too was worried and could not feel confident about the outcome of the siege. British forces had been moving down the Nile since October, and the evidence of the recent battles near Sawakin suggested that the fanaticism of his *ansars* was no match for disciplined rifle fire. Confirmation of this came in mid-January 1885, when watchers on the walls of Khartoum saw their besiegers' camp thrown into pandemonium after they had heard how the Dervish army had been trounced at Abu Klea (Abu Tlaih) and that British forces were already at al-Matammah, a hundred miles down river from Khartoum.

The Mahdi now had no choice but to storm Khartoum and take it or else face an irredeemable blow to his religious prestige. During the night of 21–2 January, his guns carefully shelled the city's walls, and his army charged and broke through. Gordon was shot dead whilst fighting in the palace, a soldier's death which would later be transformed into the familiar icon of martyrdom in which he stands, white-suited and unarmed, above his murderous assailants.[5] The Mahdi had secured another 'miracle' and in the nick of time, for three days later armed steamers approached Khartoum. The *ansars*, their zeal recharged by the recent victory, shot out their defiance, and the relieving flotilla of gunboats turned about and steamed away.

The steamers which approached the city of Khartoum on 24 January were from a force which had been created the previous August for the rescue of Gordon. As early as April 1884 General Wolseley had guessed that an army would have to be sent to extricate Gordon, and a month later his colleagues Sir Evelyn Wood and Sir Frederick Stephenson were calculating the distances and problems involved. Wood proposed a cross-desert advance to Abu Hamad, from where the force would take ship and cruise down the Nile, whilst Stephenson pressed for a dash over the largely waterless desert between Sawakin and Berber, followed by a four-hundred-mile river journey to Khartoum. Both plans embraced great risks, and Wolseley was not prepared to take gambles with stretched lines of communications and supplies – everyone knew what had happened to Hicks. He rejected both plans and chose instead one of his own which was a model of safety and sense. The Nile would be the route, for it guaranteed that the fighting men would be well victualled and watered.[6] The chance for him to give substance to his plan came in August. After several months of press and Parliamentary agitation, Gladstone had given way and agreed to send a force to save Gordon. It was much against his will, but the possible defection of three of his Cabinet, Hartington, Chamberlain and Dilke, forced the issue.

Wolseley was given command over 10,500 men who were concentrated at Wadi Halfa, from where they proceeded southwards along the Nile by means of stern-wheelers which had been seconded from Thomas Cook and Company, who had used them to ferry sightseers to the temples of Egypt. To overcome the difficulties created by the five cataracts of the Nile, Wolseley fell back on his experiences during the Red River Expedition in Canada in 1870 and recruited 377 skilled boatmen (*voyageurs*). Their task was to steer eight hundred specially built wooden whalers, each packed with soldiers and stores, over the rapids. On tranquil stretches of the Nile, the whalers would be towed by paddlesteamers, including one which had been built in sections and reassembled on the riverbank. Progress was slow. Wolseley's forces were passing sections of the river which had never been accurately mapped, and he had only fragmentary information as to what was taking place in and around Khartoum and how Gordon was faring. On 15 December he received a four-week-old message in which Gordon urged the greatest speed and predicted that Khartoum would not hold out for more than forty days. A new plan was immediately contrived and Wolseley ordered his force to split. A river column, under General Earle and supported by armed steamers, was to follow the great bend in the Nile beyond Kurti, and a desert column under General Stewart was to cross the desert in all haste and meet up with Gordon's steamers at al-Matammah. Stewart was allocated 1,100 men and 2,200 camels.

The advance guard left Kurti for the Jakdul wells on the last day of 1884. They were followed by the main force, which included sailors and a camel-mounted contingent drawn from cavalry and infantry regiments. Their path was barred by ten thousand Dervishes who had positioned themselves in front of the well at Abu Klea (Abu Tlaih) on 16 January. Stewart's force made a defensive perimeter of thorn bushes (*zaribah*) strengthened with ammunition boxes and waited for an attack. None came, and after a wait the next morning, the force advanced in square preceded by skirmishers. After an hour's ponderous advance, the square came face to face with the Dervish horde, which began a silent charge. The skirmishers turned on their heels and ran back to the shelter of the square. Some ran back to the sector manned by dismounted cavalrymen under the command of Colonel Burnaby, who ordered them to open up to let their comrades through. Before this misjudgement could be corrected, probing Dervish warriors had rushed into the gap. Surging on past a jammed Gatling, the weight of Dervishes pushed the fractured line of troops back against the mass of camels at the centre of the square. Behind them rode a bearded sheikh who coolly dismounted, staked his banner in the ground and began to read from a book of prayers, inspiring the *ansars* for a few moments before he was shot dead. Around him British soldiers who had been caught off balance fought back with volleys and bayonets, helped by the rear rank of the front of the

Death on the Nile: An artist's impression of the hand-to-hand fighting when the square gave way to Abu Klea.

square which had turned about and fired into the flank of the Dervishes. Those who had exploited the break in the square were either killed or driven off. Their main attack broken, the Dervishes fell back and confined their offensives to a continuous sniping.

As the force moved on towards al-Matammah, a chance shot mortally wounded General Stewart. Command passed to General Wilson, for Colonel Burnaby had been killed in the first rush at Abu Klea. When he at last reached al-Matammah, his position was precarious. His camels were dying from exhaustion, he was harassed by Dervish raids and his lines of communication were stretched over 170 miles of desert. For three days he did what he could to make the river steamers defensible, and then he set off up river to Khartoum. With him were a handful of men from the Royal Sussex Regiment wearing red jackets which had been specially carried with the force and which it was hoped would impress onlookers, both inside and outside Khartoum, that the British army really had arrived. Gordon had suggested this for he was convinced that the traditional red coat would truly reassure the besieged and unnerve their opponents. Two days later the steamers reached Khartoum and knew from the heavy fire that the city had fallen. They turned and steamed back to al-Matammah with the baleful news of Gordon's death.

When Wolseley heard the news at Kurti, he recalled all his columns. The desert force, now under General Redvers Buller's orders, turned back in low spirits, its retirement unhindered by the Dervishes. The river column which had, on 10 February, driven the Dervishes from their position at Kirkeban, also fell back. The news of the victories achieved by both columns did little to lessen the public outrage which had greeted the news of Gordon's death and the fall of Khartoum. Gladstone and his government shook under the storm of criticism, and much against his wishes the Prime Minister ordered Wolseley to begin offensive operations against the Mahdi. The approach of summer made these impractical, and so Wolseley and his forces concentrated at Dongola to sit out the hot season.

The centre of the Sudan campaign had now shifted back to Sawakin. It was the key to a strategy which had as its objective the complete overthrow of the Mahdi. General Graham was given command of nine thousand British forces and three thousand Indians with orders to advance inland to Berber. In their wake would follow a railway line which when finished would connect Sawakin and the sea with Berber and the Nile. This railway line was to be both the spearhead of the advance and its lifeline, carrying food, water, stores and ammunition to the fighting men. Before the specially recruited British navvies could get to work, Osman Diqna had to be brought to battle and overwhelmed once and for all. Graham proposed a sally out of Sawakin by his main force which would leave behind it a chain of *zaribahs* which would guard his lines of communication and provide defensible supply depots.

The opening move of the campaign was made on 19 March 1885, when eight thousand men moved towards Hasheen, where Osman and his main force was thought to be waiting. As the British force advanced, it was the victim of the by now customary hit-and-run sniping from the scrub. As it approached Tamai on the following day, the main Dervish army attacked with a ferociousness and foolhardiness which provoked admiration and horror. But, as before, the willpower and faith of the *ansars* were unable to prevail against volley fire, machine-guns and artillery, and the charge was stopped, leaving over a thousand Dervishes dead and many more wounded with little hope of survival. Graham believed that he had delivered a mortal blow to Osman and retired to Sawakin.

The General had left behind a detachment made up of the Berkshire Regiment, a battalion of Marines and an Indian brigade which was to advance for a short distance and construct a *zaribah*, the first of the army's supply lines. Not expecting to be attacked, the men began their tasks, protected by a thin mounted picket which was too small to warn of ambush or to delay the attackers. A sudden rush of Dervishes stole up on the soldiers and took them unawares (many were in their shirt-sleeves cutting down mimosa bushes), and the small force was all but swamped. The 17th Bengal Infantry broke, and only the disciplined coolness of the Berkshires, the Marines and the 15th Sikhs saved the day, for they were able to group in a makeshift square and hold off their attackers who had entered the *zaribah*. During this fight at Tofrek, the British forces had, in their extremity, to fire blindly into their own lines, killing camp-followers, servants and camels along with Dervishes. The ambuscade indicated that Osman was still unbeaten, and for the next two months his forces reverted to their earlier habit of night raids on the encampment at Sawakin.

By the end of March 1885 there were 29,000 British, Indian and Australian troops in the Sudan, and fifteen miles of railway track had been laid from Sawakin. The war had not been of Gladstone's making; it had been embarked on as a reaction to an upsurge of public anger after the news of Gordon's death had been announced. There was no strategic advantage to be gained from operations against the Mahdi, and Egypt could be effectively defended from the railhead at Wadi Halfa.

In the middle of preparations for this unwanted war, Gladstone had the good fortune to discover an excuse for calling it off without harming his political reputation. At the end of March, Russian forces had infringed the border of Afghanistan at Pendjeh, a move which was interpeted in Delhi and London as the prelude to an invasion of that country. The nightmare of a Russian army on the Indian frontier appeared at last to be coming true, and Gladstone prepared the country for war. A flurry of telegrams ordered troopships to be diverted from Egypt and the Sudan and forces at Dongola and Sawakin to be withdrawn for the forthcoming defence of India. There were no further sallies from the Russians, who stepped down, but Gladstone had found a reason to disentangle Britain from the Sudanese imbroglio. By the end of the year only a small Egyptian contingent remained at Sawakin, backed by Royal Navy gunboats.

In June 1885 the Mahdi died. His cause was entrusted to his lieutenant, the Khalifah (successor), Abdullah Ibn al-Sayyid Muhammad, who now held sway over the Mahdist empire. His chief concern was to keep this empire intact and to wage intermittent war against his southern neighbour, the Emperor of Abyssinia (Ethiopia). He showed very little interest in Egypt, although his advance posts sometimes clashed with those of the Egyptian army. To make sure that the Dervishes kept their distance, a force of five thousand British and Egyptian troops, supported by a gunboat, HMS *Lotus*, attacked the Mahdist base at Ginnis on 30 December 1885 and cleared the small town. After his campaigns against Abyssinia, the Khalifah ordered his general, Nujumi, to undertake an offensive probe into Egypt in 1889, but this was repelled at the battle of Toski (Tuski), with Dervish losses of fifteen hundred dead. This salutary check was delivered by an army of four thousand, nearly all of whom were British-trained Sudanese soldiers. Using rifles, they were able to confirm the invincibility of firepower against the traditional Dervish rush. Preceded by skirmishers, the Dervishes came forward and charged when just eight hundred yards from their enemies. 'A steady fire . . . mowed them down in hundreds',

96

and once they faltered and began to retire, the Sudanese attacked with the bayonet, supported by cavalry and a squadron of the 20th Hussars.[7] It was a promising performance which endorsed the opinion of many British officers that the Sudanese was a more warlike fellow than the Egyptian *fellahin*.

The victory at Toski confirmed the permanence of British military control over Egypt, which was never again menaced by a Dervish invasion. It is unlikely that the Mahdists would have found much support in Egypt, for their creed offered little to the *fellahin* save one form of alien domination in place of another. For the time being, the British government was happy to leave the Sudan alone. No other European nation showed signs of wishing to tussle with the Dervishes, and their ruler, the Khalifah, had his hands full with his efforts to impose authority on lukewarm and sometimes openly rebellious tribes within his empire, which was to Britain's advantage. For the time being, Britain's attentions were focussed further south, in Uganda, where moves were afoot to secure control over Lake Victoria and the headwaters of the Nile. At first this seemed possible, through the agency of the Imperial East Africa Company, which had been chartered in 1888 with powers to govern and trade in East Africa as the catspaw of the British government. The profits from trade were sparse and costs of administration were high, and so by 1893 the company had slid into bankruptcy. It was left to the Liberal Foreign Secretary, Lord Rosebery, to pick up the pieces and announce a formal British protectorate over Uganda. The move indicated that Britain was concerned about the Nile and with it, the Sudan.

On 12 March 1896 Lord Salisbury's Cabinet gave permission for an Egyptian expeditionary force to invade the Sudan and advance southwards as far as Dongola, three hundred miles down river from Khartoum. Salisbury's Conservative government had been elected the previous year, and it had been quickly forced to devise a policy which would guarantee British sovereignty over the Nile valley. Since the defeat at Toski, the Khalifah had wisely avoided any more adventures on the Egyptian border and remained, in Salisbury's phrase, 'keeping the bed warm for us' in the Sudan. By 1896 there were signs that others were ready to slide slyly into the bed. A French expedition had left Brazzaville in the French Congo under the command of Colonel Marchand, who intended to march eastwards across the heart of Africa and

Enter Italy: Italian Bersaglieri *find it hard going in the Sudan.*

plant the *tricoleur* on the banks of the Nile as a symbol of his nation's claim to at least some of the river. Such a gesture was dear to the hearts of France's warrior imperialists, who had conjured up fanciful schemes for a French Saharan empire reaching from the Atlantic shores of West Africa to the Red Sea and bound together by a three-thousand-mile trans-continental railway, a conduit for French political authority and commerce. To this dream was added another conceived by military engineers who, in the late 1880s, contrived plans for a Nile dam, its ends firmly embedded in French territory. French imperial daydreams such as these were Britain's nightmare. To rule over the banks of the Nile was to be able to put pressure on Egypt, whose survival depended upon the river. With the survival of Egypt went Britain's grip on the Suez Canal, and so French designs on the Nile were seen as directly hostile to Britain and her interests.

There were other indications that France was looking for advantage on the Nile. French advisers pressed the Abyssinian Emperor, Menelik II, to invade the Sudan, and his army was equipped with cannon and machine-guns imported from France. With these he defeated a large Italian force at Aduwa on 1 March 1896, a victory which not only assured his country's independence but seriously damaged European prestige in the area. The Italian advance base beyond Eritrea at Kassala in south-eastern Sudan was now vulnerable, as indeed was their coastal colony of Eritrea. Italian requests for assistance were therefore sympathetically received by Britain's government, for they provided a welcome excuse for armed intervention in the Sudan, which, if successful, would both place it in British hands and scotch French ambitions on the Nile.

For the British public the two-year campaign in the Sudan was an imperial diversion which filled the newspaper columns and generated excitement and celebration. It was widely promoted as a war of liberation which would remove from the Sudan the tyrannical and brutal rule of the Khalifah. In the words of Winston Churchill, who followed the closing stages of the campaign as a war correspondent, the Anglo-Egyptian army was 'the strong and implacable arm of civilization' which would thrash the Khalifah and his followers. The press battle-lines were clear cut. On one side, the Anglo-Egyptian forces stood for right and justice, and on the other the Khalifah's Dervishes represented a massive wrong, compounded of slavery, massacre and cruelty. There was also an element of revenge for the

Imperial warlord: Lord Kitchener, conqueror of the Sudan and victor of Omdurman at the peak of his career as Minister for War in 1915.

death of Gordon and the opportunity to expunge the shame of the subsequent British withdrawal from the Sudan.

The chosen agent of Britain's imperial will was General Kitchener, an acerbic, dyed-in-the-wool Imperialist who had been Sirdar (Commander-in-Chief) of the Egyptian army since 1892. The Sudan had mesmerized him since 1884, when he had served there, gathering intelligence during the Gordon campaign and gaining for himself a well-deserved reputation as an intrepid officer. His appointment to the command of the army in the Sudan was the fulfilment of a personal crusade, and that country would be the vehicle for his advancement as it had been a dozen years before. Yet he was carefully circumscribed by Lord Salisbury and, below him, Lord Cromer, the British Consul-General in Egypt and the prevailing influence over the Khedive's government. The Sudan campaign was the Foreign Office's show, and political direction was therefore tight; unlike Gordon, Kitchener was left in no doubt that he carried out policy, not dictated it. He did not like this much.

The conquest of the Sudan was, after the Boer War of 1899–1902, the largest operation undertaken by British forces in Africa. At the beginning it involved an eighteen-thousand-strong Egyptian army which had been collected at Wadi Halfa for the march south. There were eight battalions of Egyptian conscripts and six of Sudanese blacks, all drilled and trained by

100

British officers and NCOs, many of whom commanded in battle. This army was supported by artillery, including Maxim machine-guns, and ten gunboats. These ships were one of the keys to the eventual success of the expedition, for they provided the means to reconnoitre the Nile, probe Dervish defences along its banks and add massive firepower to the land forces during pitched battles and assaults on towns. The other key to Kitchener's victory was the railway, in particular the desert line which was started on 1 January 1897 and which eventually stretched to Atbara. Under the tireless supervision of Edouard Girouard, a French-Canadian engineer officer, the tracks were laid by the forced labour of Egyptian *fellahin* and felons from Egyptian gaols. 'You find it admirable that Egypt's ruffians are doing Egypt's work,' approved G. W. Steevens, the *Daily Mail*'s war correspondent. There was less enthusiasm for Egypt's work in Britain, where a strike in railway workshops meant that the line's six new locomotives had to be built in the United States.

Steam, whether driving the engines of trains or of gunboats, was the motor power for Kitchener's war-machine. It enabled him to overcome the size and emptiness of the region he planned to invade and gave him the ability to arm and supply his army. As Steevens observed, it also shaped his strategy: 'The Sudan machine obviates the barrenness and vastness; the bayonet action stands still until the railway action had piled the camp with supplies or the steamer action can run with a full Nile. Fighting men may chafe and go down with typhoid and cholera; they are in the iron grip of the machine, and they must wait the turn of its wheels.'[8] This the Khalifah did not appreciate, for he had never seen a train. His strategy was to withdraw and allow the Anglo-Egyptian army to come forward in the hope that its soldiers would be ground down by the heat and the distance, until, broken in body and spirit, they would be picked off as Hicks's forces had been.

Kitchener's advance was slow and methodical, its pace set by the telegrams from the Foreign Office, the dragging of gunboats over the cataracts of the Nile and the labour of Egypt's convict navvies. The start was auspicious. On 6 June 1896 ten battalions of Egyptian infantry marched through the night to the Dervish camp at Firket (Farkah), invested it and attacked. The outnumbered Dervishes fought back bravely but were finally driven off by the Egyptians, whose steadiness reassured their British officers and disabused their critics who had predicted that they would cut and run as their predecessors had when faced by

The Sudan war machine, I: Highlanders pause for a shave and some food on their journey from Abu Hamad, 1898.

The Sudan war machine, II: The gunboat Melek *conveying Sudanese troops, 1898.*

Dervishes. Rain, sandstorms and a cholera epidemic hampered the next two months' campaigning, but on 10 September Dongola was taken. In Cairo, Cromer was pleased but he favoured no further advance for at least two years. Kitchener now had the bit between his teeth and hurried to London, where he argued the case for a further push south. Lord Salisbury agreed and accepted his scheme for a cross-desert railway from Wadi Halfa to Abu Hamad – the need was for speed if the French were to be forestalled. Half a million pounds were accordingly delivered to the Egyptian government to meet the bills and reassure Cromer, who dreaded that Egypt might be unable to settle the final account.

Salisbury had also authorized a second, smaller expeditionary force along the Nile. Under the command of Major MacDonald, an officer of engineers, a contingent of Sudanese infantry was to move northwards from Uganda into the southern Sudan. The public purpose of this expedition was the exploration of Central Africa, an excuse which could have carried little weight since the explorers included several hundred askaris and were armed with a handful of machine-guns. The Sudanese were unwilling explorers, and in September 1897 they began to trouble Mac-Donald with a series of complaints about the conditions of their service. Overwork, poor pay and comparisons between their duties and the lives of their comrades, comfortably dwelling with their wives and families in garrisons, formed the gravamen of the infantrymen's grievances. None were comforted by Mac-Donald's assurances that the march north would be easy, and several companies mutinied. By early October over five hundred Sudanese were in arms and had commandeered a fort, a steam launch and a Maxim gun. All hope of the Nile expedition was lost, and the local military authorities had to spend all their energies and the next few months tracking down the miscreants. Another damp squib was a series of diversionary attacks against Osman Diqna, who was still marauding settlements near Sawakin in January 1898.

On New Year's day 1897 the first tracks of the Sudan Military Railway were laid, to begin an enterprise well suited to the ebullient mood of Queen Victoria's Diamond Jubilee year. Whilst it bypassed the Nile and snaked across the desert, columns moved towards its projected terminus, Abu Hamad, which was taken after hard fighting on 29 July. Soon after, the Khalifah ordered the abandonment of Berber, which was entered on 10 September. Kitchener was now poised for an advance on Khartoum but his lines of support were long and vulnerable to sudden Dervish raids. On 10 December he received alarming intelligence that the Khalifah had left Omdurman with the bulk of his forces to seek battle at al-Matammah. Kitchener was reluctant to fight him with only Egyptian and Sudanese forces, so he cabled for reinforcements of British regulars. On 23 December the Cabinet agreed to his request and appointed him commander of all forces in the Sudan. The panic was by now over, for the Khalifah had revised his plan and returned to Omdurman, where he busied himself organizing defences and mining the Nile. Kitchener was also looking to his defences, and his advance base at the confluence of the Nile and Atbara rivers had been fortified. Here arrived the promised reinforcements from Britain, which included the Grenadier Guards, Highlanders, English county regiments and the 21st Lancers, who had not yet obtained a battle honour for their colours.

Whilst the Anglo-Egyptian army concentrated at its camp at Atbara and the newly arrived British soldiers accustomed themselves to the heat and discomforts of the Sudan, the Amir Mahmud Ahmad advanced to meet them at the Khalifah's orders. Mahmud commanded twelve thousand men and sensibly rejected the traditional frontal charge, placing his forces behind earthworks and a *zaribah* at al-Nikhailah on the banks of the Nile. There he blocked Kitchener's advance and so had to be removed. So a night march was planned as a prelude to a dawn bombardment and assault on 8 April 1898. It was Good Friday, a day which a devout Moslem might not expect the Christians to choose for a battle, or so Kitchener reasoned. As the sun rose, the artillery shelled the Dervish defences for fifty minutes, and then the main force moved forward for the attack. The Dervish defenders fired on them and were in turn fired on by the advancing British and Egyptians, who stormed and took the position at bayonet point. After some house-to-house fighting the Dervishes retreated, leaving behind casualties thought to exceed three thousand. The Anglo-Egyptian army lost 600, of whom 120 were British. Mahmud was taken, made to act in a humiliating triumphal march led by Kitchener and then locked away in Wadi Halfa gaol. Churchill wondered why he had not been hanged then and there for his part in earlier Mahdist massacres.

Crowned with the laurels won at what became known as the battle of Atbara, the army spent the hot months from April to

Mahmud, Atbara, 8 April 1898: 'His expression was cruel but high. He looked neither to right nor to left, but he strode up to the Sirdar [Kitchener] with his head erect. "Are you the man Mahmoud?" asked the Sirdar. "Yes, I am Mahmoud, and I am the same as you." He meant commander-in-chief. "Why did you come to make war here?" "I came because I was told, the same as you"'
– G. W. Steevens

July in summer quarters, waiting for the arrival of the railway line. This reached its destination on 3 July, by which time the Nile was rising and the passage to Khartoum was open to the gunboats. A further British brigade had arrived to add further weight to the punch which was to be launched at the Khalifah and Khartoum. With the Nile flooding, the Anglo-Egyptian war-machine prepared itself for the final and decisive stage of the war and on 24 July began its southwards march along the west bank of the river. On the river steamed ten gunboats with a further five auxiliary steamers, and on the shore marched 17,600 Egyptian and Sudanese troops and 8,200 British regulars. Between them the men and ships were armed with over fifty pieces of artillery and forty machine-guns. From the midst of this formidable army, Kitchener called upon the Khalifah to send women and children from Khartoum in anticipation of the imminent bombardment. The Khalifah responded to this surprising humanity by emerging from Omdurman at the head of sixty thousand tribesmen, and shortly before noon on 1 September this horde was spotted by scouts from the Lancers. Their report was brought to Kitchener by Churchill.

That evening the army bivouacked in a tiny village called Agaiga. Behind it was the Nile, and to its front was a hastily constructed *zaribah* of mimosa scrub. Each brigade had been deployed in battle order and stood to during the night for fear of an attack in the darkness. Just before first light, the pickets of the 21st Lancers rode out to discover the whereabouts of the Khalifah's army, which they had sighted the day before. With them rode Churchill, and in the grey dawn light he descried the approaching masses, whose many hundreds of banners, each embroidered with a Koranic text, reminded him of pictures he had seen of medieval armies. As Churchill wrote later, the army of the Khalifah was indeed a host like those which once had faced the Crusaders. Its warriors chose to attack with sword and spear and were driven forward by a fiery faith and the knowledge that, whatever their collective success, heaven would be the reward for every man who died.

At 6.45 the first wave of ten thousand fighting men under Osman Azraq came over the sandy plain and hurled itself at the right and centre of the Anglo-Egyptian line. Within just over an hour, a quarter of them had fallen, none within three hundred yards of the *zaribah*. Between eight and nine, a further twenty thousand chased the Egyptian cavalry over the Kerreri Heights to the right of the main army but were thwarted of their prey by heavy fire from artillery and gunboats. A side turn brought this force into the full storm of the rifle and machine-gun fire, and its onrush was stemmed. By 8.30 the frontal attacks were over and Kitchener ordered his battalions to march off in echelon towards Omdurman. The 21st Lancers screened the advance with instructions to find the position of the twenty thousand men whom the Khalifah was thought to be holding in reserve. During this reconnaissance they charged what they thought was a thin line of Dervishes but which turned out to be a deep *nullah* (sunken stream bed), sheltering three thousand. For once in this battle, the Dervishes were able to meet their foes on equal terms with stabbing and cutting weapons, and in just two minutes, as the Lancers ripped through their line, they killed and wounded seventy-one men, nearly a third of their assailants. The gallant Lancers who had broken through rallied, dismounted and poured rifle fire into their opponents' flank. Against the weaponry of the industrial age, the medieval warriors were helpless.

The same was true elsewhere. The Khalifah's reserves made repeated rushes against the advancing columns but they were futile in the face of rifle and machine-gun fire. By 11.30 the battle was over and the cavalry harried the stragglers running back towards Omdurman. Kitchener ordered a siesta, and at two in

Omdurman, imperial victory, I: 'The Dervish advance at Omdurman, 2 September 1898. 'I never could have imagined anything so cool and brave as those men were, especially one, the last one to fall; he had been wounded in his arm and limped, yet his ambition was to get the flag, and he got it and carried it some 50 yards at a slow trot, when he was shot, and as he fell his companion took it and came on a few yards only when he fell, with the flag. I was sorry for these men; they were simply wiped out' –
Lieutenant Hodgson, Lincolnshire Regt.

Omdurman, imperial victory, II: The captured black banner of the Khalifah is carried above Kitchener and his staff as they ride towards the town of Omdurman.

Omdurman, imperial victory, III: 'Two or three newspaper correspondents, eager for loot, rode out amongst the wounded, when up jumped a Dervish with a huge spear and put them all to rout, pursuing them back to the nearest troops' – Sir Horace Smith-Dorrien

the afternoon his forces began their triumphal march into Omdurman, with the Khalifah's captured black flag fluttering over Kitchener and his staff. Eleven thousand Dervishes had died and a further sixteen thousand were prisoners. Anglo-Egyptian losses were forty-eight dead and 434 wounded, either Lancers or men who had fallen to the desultory fire of the few Dervish riflemen.

Mahdism was vanquished. The Khalifah was a fugitive; he fled westwards and was hunted down and killed near Kusti in November 1899. Gordon was avenged and the Union Jack flew over his old palace, 'tugging eagerly at his reins, dazzling gloriously in the sun, rejoicing in his strength and freedom', according to the journalese of G. W. Steevens.

Six hundred miles away to the south, at Fashoda, the *tricoleur* was also tugging in what wind there was over a camp established two months earlier by Colonel Marchand after a two-year journey. On 19 September he saw Kitchener's squadron of gunboats, crammed full of troops, artillery and machine-guns and representing the legal claims of Britain to all of what once had been the Egyptian Sudan. Kitchener was a courteous and agreeable bailiff, and his dealings with Marchand were cordial but firm. Moved to tears by Kitchener's sad news of the course of the Dreyfus scandal which was convulsing France, the colonel insisted that he would die at his post in defence of the rights of his country. He permitted the Egyptian flag to be hoisted but refused to budge until ordered to do so by his superiors in Paris.

The orders did come from Paris, much to the fury of French nationalists, who had taken time off from reviling the Dreyfusards to call for a war with Britain for the Upper Nile. Delcassé, the French Foreign Minister, who commanded Marchand to come home, knew better. He appreciated that Britain would stand firm and that, in the event of a war, the Royal Navy would sink the French, leaving the whole of the French empire unprotected. The Abyssinian Emperor, to whom France had looked for support, was hostile, and France's ally, Russia, was tepid about a conflict over a stretch of profitless riverbank. If France fought Britain for the Nile, Britain would be thrown into the arms of France's real enemy, Germany. The honourable and brave Marchand returned to France, leaving behind him his nation's claim to the Nile. He was lionized and French patriots intensified their anglophobia, which would shortly be satisfied by news of Britain's defeats in South Africa.

Marchand's departure from Fashoda marked the conclusion of an aggressive policy which had been reluctantly begun in 1882 with the invasion and conquest of Egypt. From then onwards, the overriding objective of British governments had been the need to keep the Suez Canal in British hands and thereby make safe the seaway to India. All the obstacles – Colonel Arabi, the Khalifah and Colonel Marchand – had been removed by force of arms, with the result that Britain possessed the Canal, a resentful but pliant regime in Egypt and sovereignty over the banks of the White Nile. To this end British governments had spent much blood and treasure. The overthrow of Arabi had cost £4.6 million, the unlooked-for imbroglio in the Sudan during 1884 and 1885 a further £7.2 million, and the final reconquest of the Sudan £2.4 million, of which two thirds came from the Egyptian taxpayers.[9]

Keeping the Peace, 1898–1924

Omdurman was the last large-scale battle in the conquest of Egypt and the Sudan, but it was not the end to fighting in the area. Having taken land by the sword, the British found themselves committed to holding it by the sword – in other words, waging the small campaigns of imperial 'policing' designed to isolate and chastise disaffection. The wars of the 1880s and 1890s had given Britain direct and indirect overlordship over about twelve million Moslems in Egypt and the Sudan who felt little affection for their new masters. When, in 1902, the Committee for Imperial Defence pondered over what might happen if Russia and France invaded Egypt, it was told by Lord Cromer that, 'No reliance can be placed on the friendliness of the Egyptian government, population or army.' Well into the 1920s officials in Khartoum were nervous about the possible re-crudescence of Mahdism and were anxious to have adequate armed forces, including aircraft, ready to meet it. In 1908 Abd-al-Qadir, a kinsman by marriage of the Mahdi and a veteran of the Khalifah's campaigns, proclaimed himself a prophet, gathered several hundred warriors and murdered two British officials. He was taken after a night ambush of some of the troops sent to hunt him down and hanged before crowds in his own village as an example.[10] (The public nature of his death was deleted from the published report of the incident at the insistence of the Colonial Office, no doubt apprehensive about parliamentary and press criticism.)

Internal unrest in Egypt and the Sudan had religious and political roots and was liable to encouragement from outside. In 1898 Kaiser Wilhelm II had publicly offered his friendship for the world's Moslems during a progress through Syria which marked the beginnings of Germany's courtship of the Turkish Empire. Such a declaration was welcome to the Turkish Sultan, who nursed ambitions for a Pan-Islamic revival which might rein-vigorate his fly-blown and disintegrating dominions and win them sympathy from Moslems under British and French rule. Such a possibility disturbed the British military authorities in Egypt who in 1906 felt certain that a Turkish raid across the Sinai Peninsula would trigger off a Moslem insurrection in Lower Egypt.[11] Such an emergency was beyond the capabilities of the 4,500 troops who comprised the British garrison in Egypt unless they were hurriedly reinforced from Gibraltar and Malta. Above all, 'our prestige in the East', born of victories over the past two decades, required an aggressive counter-stroke against Turkey, undertaken by the Royal Navy.[12] The first steps of the journey to Gallipoli had been taken.

The outbreak of war in 1914 gave substance to the phantoms of the Turco-German subversion when there were serious efforts to foment unrest and instability in Egypt and the Sudan. The chosen instruments of German and Turkish plans were the Sanusi of Cyrenaica, who had for several years been receiving clandestine aid, including arms and advisers, from Germany and Turkey, both anxious to hinder the Italian conquest of Libya. The Sanusi shiekh, Sidi Ahmad, was the grandson of the spiritual leader of a Moslem sect whose political power had once extended over much of the central Sahara and the Western Sudan. After the arrival of the French in 1902, Sanusi authority had withered rapidly as their subject tribes were beaten and they found themselves driven back to the Libyan plain. Here they faced new pressure from the Italians, who had invaded Tripoli and Cyrenaica in 1911 and were aiming to cut the Sanusi off from the Mediterranean coast. Sidi Ahmad was therefore willing to accept help from the Germans and Turks and agree to their plans for an invasion of western Egypt. This challenge to British power would, it was hoped, spark off an uprising by the local Bedouin and rebellions in the Nile Delta.

Sidi Ahmad launched his attack in November 1915 and, as expected, the Bedouin of western Egypt joined him. He commanded five thousand well-trained regular troops and could call on over thirty thousand irregulars under the command of a small group of Turkish and German officers. The Sanusi army also possessed artillery and machine-guns smuggled across the Mediterranean which made it a formidable force. The British authorities responded to the invasion by first calling back all Egyptian forces on the border, since their loyalty was in question, and replacing them with a hastily assembled army drawn from British, Indian and Dominion troops then stationed in Egypt. From its base on the coast at Mersa Matruh, this force fought a number of small engagements with the Sanusi, who in May 1916 came under renewed attack from the Italians. This desert war was unlike its predecessors, for aircraft were employed to search out and attack enemy units as well as a squadron of Rolls-Royce armoured cars, raised and commanded by the Duke of Westminster. There was even a bizarre moment during an engagement at Agagia where the traditional roles in colonial warfare were reversed: horsemen from the Dorset Yeomanry charged a position defended by three machine-guns which they took, but with inevitably heavy losses.[13]

Whilst the Sanusi were being defeated, Ali Dinar, Sultan of Darfur and a pensioner of the British, called out his tribesmen and raised a rebellion. He had enjoyed close links with the

Sanusi, who had been his neighbours in French Sudan, and like them he may well have been swayed by Turco-German propaganda which promised a vast Islamic state in northern and central Africa which would be created after Britain and France had been beaten in Europe.[14] A force of Sudanese troops under British officers was sent south to meet the rebels, backed by a squadron of Royal Flying Corps fighters. On 22 May 1916 Dinar's forces attacked, using the customary but suicidal frontal assault at Biringia and were beaten. As they scattered they were strafed by pursuing fighter aircraft, one of which was flown by the future Air Marshal Sir John Slessor. A new era of imperial warfare had started.

The lack of success of Ali Dinar and Sidi Ahmad did not discourage the Turks and the Germans from infiltrating the southern Sudan and Uganda with agents and propaganda designed to foment Moslem resistance to British, French and Belgian rule. Much emphasis was laid on the failure of the Gallipoli landings, Ali Dinar's revolt and the mutiny of Indian Moslem troops in Singapore in 1915; the military prestige of Britain and her allies had been shown up as a sham, and the moment was right for all Moslems to join the *jihad* proclaimed by the Turkish sultan.[15]

Turkey and Germany had hoped to feed and exploit religious antipathy in order to stir up revolts against British rule, but in Egypt political grievances were coming to the fore. British domination had been resented by the educated classes for many years, and it was intensified when, in 1914, Britain declared a formal protectorate over Egypt whose reluctant population was then called upon to lend a hand with the war effort.

The nationalist movement which hoped to sever connexions with Britain and achieve self-determination for Egypt turned to direct and violent action in March 1919. The riots, attacks on property and murder of Europeans took the local military authorities by surprise, although some officers thought that political considerations were tying their hands.[16] The local commander, General Bulfin, was, however, able to call on large numbers of British, Dominion and Indian forces still in the country, awaiting demobilization. Many of these, like some Australians brought to Bilhars, in the Nile delta, were incensed that their homecoming had been postponed and vented their anger on the local population. Elsewhere, hastily formed columns, backed by aircraft, toured the disturbed areas, rounding up agitators and suppressing riots. In Bilhars a party of mounted officers and

NCOs armed with revolvers, polo sticks, whips, riding crops and pick helves galloped to the rescue of a couple of elderly lady missionaries, who were brought back to the safety of the British cantonment.[17] Elsewhere things were less jolly, and retribution was frequently summary and bloody.

The unrest in Egypt highlighted the precariousness of the British position there, which, if it was to be maintained by a constant resort to arms, would require a large and costly garrison. Imperial authority was also being violently questioned in other areas for in 1919 British forces were deployed in Ireland, Iraq and northern India suppressing insurrections. So in 1922 an agreement was reached by which Egypt received internal self-government, and British troops drew back into the area around the Suez Canal.

The new arrangements of Egypt's domestic affairs had repercussions in the Sudan, where British predominance continued in spite of the formal arrangement of 1899 which had set up an 'Anglo-Egyptian' administration. Many Egyptians wanted the province back, and agitation spread through battalions of Egyptian and Sudanese troops, often with the encouragement of nationalist officers. Never co-ordinated, anti-British incidents multiplied until in 1924 the army commander, Sir Lee Stack, was assassinated and the 11th Sudanese battalion mutinied in Khartoum. The growth of unrest had been slow and had given time for the single battalion of the Leicester Regiment, then stationed in Khartoum, to be reinforced by a battalion of Argyle and Sutherland Highlanders. With the extra men, pockets of resistance and resentment were isolated and the men involved were disarmed. Lorries and cars enabled British troops to get quickly to the remote areas and restore order. The Khartoum mutineers holed up in buildings which were reduced to rubble after a seven-hour bombardment at point-blank range by a 4.5-inch howitzer. There were no survivors.[18] The mutinies had been stifled thanks to forewarning and the lack of cohesion amongst the disgruntled Sudanese and Egyptians but they had a salutary effect on the authorities. An airfield was levelled close to Khartoum, and aircraft were kept there permanently after 1925.

The new 'aerial policing' techniques had already been used in the Sudan in 1920, when three aircraft had been sent to bomb tribal rebels. The Governor-General was well pleased with the results and informed the Air Ministry that, 'The success that attended these aircraft was immediate and decisive and the Garjuks recognizing to what dangers they were exposed speedily commenced negotiations for submission.'[19] In 1930 tribesmen in the southern Sudan also learnt the persuasive power of bombardment from the air, when attacks were made on their remote cave hideaways.[20] Amongst the Sudanese who may have watched these planes fly from Khartoum there were, in all likelihood, old men who in their youth had seen the armies of Hicks and the death of Gordon, and many more who had witnessed Omdurman and the triumph of Kitchener.* They had seen the whole imperial process of conquest and pacification, and those who survived another twenty-five or so years would see their conquerors depart.

* There were a few men alive in the 1920s who had seen Gordon die, and it was rumoured that a few of the older 'extras' who took part in Sir Alexander Korda's reconstruction of the battle of Omdurman for the film *The Four Feathers* had taken part in the original. The last British survivor of the 1884–5 campaign died in 1974, aged 109.

West Africa, 1870–1914

I proceeded to become very 'annoyed' and told the interpreter to go into the village again and to inform the King that if he did not come out forthwith and do homage to the British flag I would set fire to his village and make war on him and his villagers.

F. P. Crozier, Lieutenant,
West Africa Field Force, 1902

In 1869 a British gunboat, HMS *Lynx*, made a perilous voyage four hundred miles up the Niger to demonstrate to the rulers and peoples of the riverine states just how far the long arm of Britain could reach. When she returned and finally cast anchor off Ascension Island, all but four of her crew had to be transferred to the fever hospital there, a salutary reminder of West Africa's traditional reputation as the White Man's Grave. But white men, many of them Englishmen, had gone to West Africa for generations, first in search of slaves and then, as part of the growing national revulsion against this traffic, as missionaries. In 1806 the British Parliament made slave-dealing illegal and in 1833 ended slavery within all British territories. These were moral gestures designed to lead others, and where such persuasion failed, force was brought to bear. A squadron of men o'war cruised off the West African coasts with orders to hunt down all slavers, liberate their cargoes and bring them back to the safety of Freetown. Here the navy had its base, one of the chain which marked the sea route to India, and here also philanthropists and missionaries worked for the reclamation of souls and the moral and intellectual improvement of the native African. All agreed that slavery was the greatest stumbling block to the advancement of West Africa and that it could be removed only by the promotion of what was called 'legitimate' trade, largely in vegetable oils, conversion and the watchful eye of British consuls and the Royal Navy.

Nigeria

This combination of missionary and commercial interests in West Africa made it necessary for the British government to maintain a political presence in the area which was given sub-

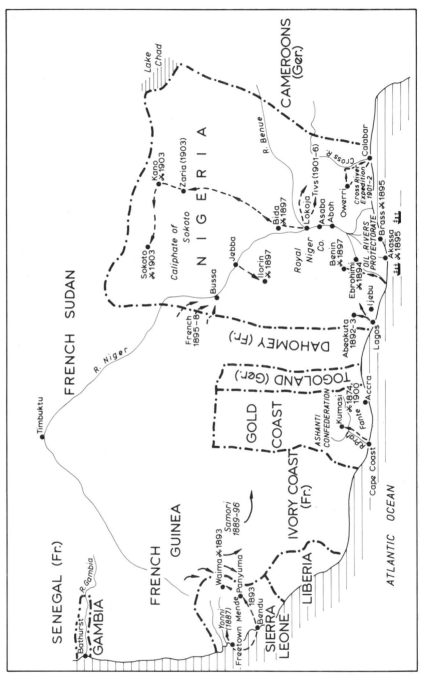

West Africa

stance by the naval squadron. Actual territorial possessions were few. Vestiges of the high days of slaving, they comprised Bathurst at the mouth of the Gambia River, Freetown, a string of castles on the Gold Coast (Ghana) and Lagos, which had been acquired after a bombardment in 1861 as a means to plug a slave-trade outlet. Military commitment was tiny; there were detachments of the West Indies regiment, recruited in the Caribbean, in each colony, local constabularies, a skeletal unit of gunners to keep the fort at Freetown, native constabularies and colonial government steamers. In each region the local colonial authorities had secured treaties and arrangements with the native states of the hinterland by which the latter accepted British protection and accepted British overlordship at least in such matters as the abandonment of slavery.

The progress of the *Lynx* up the Niger was a sign that British interests in the area were changing. Britain's new interests were commercial and stemmed from the recent expansion of the palm-oil trade. Palm-oil was the basis for soap, vegetable fats and lighting fuel, and the increased demand for these products in western Europe had attracted buyers from Britain, France and Germany to the coastal ports of Nigeria. Here they purchased the palm-oil which had been carried from the areas of production inland and which, on its journey, had been subject to various duties imposed by the rulers of the states through which it passed. Native businessmen or 'middlemen' had also taken their cut, and it was with them that the European traders dealt. With the fall in palm-oil prices in Europe in the 1870s, the coastal traders' profit margins began to wither, and many began to look for ways in which they could remove the charges of the 'middlemen' and the impositions of the native states, and so restore the palm-oil business to its former health. Conflicts of commercial interests between British traders and their Nigerian counterparts led to friction, and the British were more than willing to invoke the physical assistance of the Royal Navy if and when they found themselves threatened. In 1882, when the United Africa Company's depôt at Aboh was attacked and looted during one trade row, the local British consul was informed and men o'war were summoned. The ships hove to off the town, and when negotiations broke down and a landing party was ambushed, the naval guns opened fire. The African states of the delta got their first experience of the cutting edge of 'unofficial empire' and a pointer towards a future in which European merchants would be able to dictate terms at gunpoint.

A by-product of changes in the palm-oil market was a secondary struggle between British, French and German businessmen, all anxious to corner the trade and exclude rivals. To defend British commercial interests, Colonel George Goldie united his fellow countrymen and traders under the umbrella of the United Africa Company and started a trade war with the French. On one hand he undercut the French buyers and forced them out of business, and on the other he negotiated with the rulers of the Niger states, to place themselves under British protection. In the long term Goldie was after more than just commercial monopoly: he wanted and strove tirelessly for British political control over the entire Niger basin. In 1899, on the eve of the formal establishment of the colony of Nigeria which had been Goldie's object, a few enthusiasts suggested that his labours ought to have been rewarded by giving the territory the name 'Goldesia'.

The first fruits of Goldie's single-mindedness were bundles of treaties with native states, to which were added those secured by Captain Hewett RN from the Niger Delta. These were laid on the table at the Berlin Conference in December 1884 as legal proof of Britain's rights in the region, and they were duly upheld by the representatives of other European powers. French carping, encouraged by the Germans, was soon stilled by the threat of naval action. It was not worth France's while to stir up a fuss about exclusion from the Niger basin. 'Not even the support of Germany and her allies could protect us against the difficulties which England might create in all parts of the world if she were moved by feelings of real hostility towards us,' admitted one French diplomat. In other words, the big stick of the Royal Navy could bruise.

Claims endorsed at Berlin had to be enforced in Nigeria. To give substance to her paper rights, Britain created two new administrative authorities to impose her will on the peoples of the Lower Niger and Delta. In 1885 the coastal territories were placed under the government of the Oil Rivers Protectorate, which was answerable to the Foreign Office. Effective local authority was placed in the hands of the Consul-General, Captain Hewett, and his ability to cajole local rulers. Although 'the moral effect of Her Majesty's Ships of War' could be invoked when persuasion failed, their guns could fire only at the orders of the admiral commanding the Africa station.[1] Such prudence was not enough, and by 1893, when the Protectorate's sphere of direct influence had been officially edged inland, it possessed a

Abeokuta submits: Governor Carter waits for the town's ruler, while the court eunuchs in the left foreground look around anxiously – like the Maxim gun, the camera was mounted on a tripod.

handy force of five hundred native constables commanded by British officers, steam launches and machine-guns. Further north the lands of the middle Niger were under the government of the Royal Niger Company under the local direction of Goldie. Resurrecting the Elizabethan precedent of the East India Company, Lord Salisbury's government issued the Company with a royal charter in 1886 which empowered it to rule in Britain's name, make treaties and meet the costs of administration from its commercial profits. For the Colonial Office this was empire on the cheap and for Goldie the opportunity to keep on with his life's work, the building of a British empire in West Africa. His headquarters were at Asaba on the Niger, and within ten years he commanded an army of a thousand native troops and possessed a dozen steamers and many machine-guns.

The political and military problems which faced the Royal Niger Company, the Oil Rivers Protectorate and the older colony of Lagos were essentially the same. Each had gained and continued to gain treaties with the contiguous native states by which their rulers were bound to govern either as clients of Britain or else with an eye to British interests. Whether or not the native signatories ever fully recognized the extent of what they had put their marks to, or, as was often the case, had succumbed because of bribes or under menaces, is an academic point. What mattered in the 1890s and early 1900s was that the treaties and their interpretation created a permanent source of tension. For the British the treaties were inviolable, and infractions justified armed intervention. When native rulers relinquished their rights to impose tariffs on merchandise which crossed their lands or swore never to impede traders and missionaries, they put themselves in a vulnerable position once they broke their word or tried to reassert their diminished sovereignty. Again, when they had pledged themselves to abolish such customs as infanticide, human sacrifice, slave-trading and domestic slavery, all of which were deeply repugnant to the British, they committed themselves to the removal of well-rooted and often cherished traditions. Britain's determination to expunge every form of slavery struck at the economic foundations of many states, and this naturally encouraged resistance from those with much to lose. Friction was therefore unavoidable, and with it war. British administrators could not turn a blind eye to backsliding and breaches of faith. For their part, native rulers and their subjects were often unwilling to submit meekly to the loss of independence and the abjuration of religious and economic traditions.

Whatever the specific causes of individual clashes, the British always possessed all the trump cards. The Niger and its tributaries were easily navigable by steam launches and gunboats, and the small but highly efficient local forces with their rifles, war-rockets, machine-guns and artillery were more than a match for the armies fielded by their opponents. Nor could the native states shake off old political and dynastic rivalries to face the intruders united. In 1906 a Tiv chieftain, taken prisoner by a British punitive force, summed up the past twenty years of unequal struggle. 'Give me one piss-gun [Maxim machine-gun], and I'll beat you.'[2]

So awesome was the reputation of the Maxim gun that its appearance was often enough to coerce. In May 1892, after three years of strained and uneasy relations between the Lagos government and its northern neighbours, the Ijebu, the governor, Sir Gilbert Carter, entered their territory with a small force and some machine-guns. The Ijebu were quickly beaten with heavy losses. The news of this, and in particular the fearsome killing power of the machine-guns, shook the neighbouring tribes, and

Conquest by negotiation: Governor Carter of Lagos and his staff, backed by Lagos constabulary, some with the medal for the previous year's successful campaign against the Ijebu, with the Balé of Ogbongwo (far left). The governor was interested in the Balé's erotic carvings on the wall of his house, seen here in the background.

West African harmonies: The Gambia Police band share a platform with local musicians; such a band, playing 'God Save the Queen', preceded Governor Carter's column as it entered the towns and villages of Yorubaland in 1892.

so Carter's armed tour of Yorubaland in the following year was a bloodless excursion. Preceded by a constabulary band which played 'God Save the Queen', and escorted by Haussa constables, Carter also had his machine-gun and artillery pieces prominently displayed. The message was clearly appreciated, and the Yoruba rulers were more than amenable to signing agreements which brought themselves and their domains under Britain's sway.

This pattern of punitive column and pacification was not always so easy. In the closing days of 1896 Consul Phillips and a small armed party from the Oil Rivers Protectorate approached the city of Benin, where he intended to remonstrate with its ruler, the Oba, about his refusal to stop domestic slavery and human sacrifice. He chose a bad time, for his arrival coincided with a religious festival, and the Bini reacted to this blasphemy by ambushing his party and killing all but two. Such a brutal challenge to imperial prestige and authority provoked a swift and devastating response. Within less than a month a formidable expeditionary force of over fifteen hundred men had been collected, including the landing parties from nine men o'war which had been summoned by telegraph from the African and Mediterranean stations. The avenging columns had to move quickly, for the febriferous climate of the Niger delta would soon cut down the bluejackets and marines, and within three weeks the campaign was ended. The Bini vainly tried to halt the column's progress but their jungle ambushes were swept aside by the usual combination of rifle volleys and machine-gun fire. Much to the horror of the imperial forces, their path of advance was marked by hundreds of disembowelled corpses of men and women who had been hurriedly sacrificed to the Bini gods in the hope that they would intervene and drive off the invaders. In Benin itself there was even more ghastly evidence of desperate religious activity in the form of crucified victims and blood-caked altars. The Oba and his clergy had fled but the vile habits they encouraged died hard, and two years later, in 1899, another force had to be sent into the area to root out religious practices which were abhorrent to the authorities.

Captain Alan Boisragon, who had been a survivor of the Benin massacre and was a commander of the forces sent to avenge it, argued that it was only through such expeditions coupled with frequent surveillance by local officials that 'beastly habits' could be extirpated.[3] Yet shows of force and crushing defeats did not always achieve their ends. It was easy to overthrow a large

The Benin horrors, I: The Altar, Benin City, 1897. 'When the expedition took Benin City they found these altars covered with streams of dried blood, the stench of which was too awful, the whole grass portion of the Compounds simply reeking with it' – Captain Alan Boisragon.

The Benin horrors, II: 'Everywhere sacrificial trees on which were corpses of the latest victims. On the principal sacrificial tree facing the main gate of the king's compound were two crucified bodies' – Captain Alan Boisragon

political unit, like Benin, in battle, but the smaller ones often revealed considerable powers of self-resuscitation, which meant that they were the subjects of a sequence of expeditions. Between November 1901 and the following March over 1,750 troops were deployed in five columns over the ten thousand square miles between the Niger and Cross rivers. The aim was to bring the Ibo to heel and force them to renounce slavery, slave-raiding, the slaughter of newborn twins and the repulsive and slow killing of their mothers. At the same time the authorities at Calabar wished to destroy the influence of the infamous Long Juju and its priests. It was a hard-fought campaign, with the columns having to take one fortified village after another and face wild rushes by Ibos armed with spears, blowpipes, poisoned arrows and a few ill-aimed shotguns. By way of punishment, the beaten Ibos were forced to cut straight roads through the jungle and bush to make the task of any future pacification forces easier. At the end, the Long Juju was found – in one version it was surrounded by empty gin bottles and skulls – and blown to pieces. Yet ways of thinking of which it was a manifestation did not go away from the region, for in 1905 a government doctor was murdered and gobbets of his body were eaten in the belief that their consumption would make the eater invulnerable to the white man's guns. The government's retaliation was fast and condign, for the uprising was broken after five thousand Ibos, all assured of immunity, rushed a column well equipped with machine-guns. The murderers and their priestly accomplices were tracked down, tried and executed, and their sympathizers were conscripted for forced labour on new roads.

Further north, a similar series of expeditions was required for the suppression of the Tivs, whose resistance lasted from 1900 to 1906. The trouble began when a small force was ambushed whilst it was setting up a telegraph line, and the last campaign was prompted by the murder of Haussa merchants. When news of this last incident reached the Colonial Office, it counselled restraint and hoped that local officials would negotiate a settlement. This was not the way of the High Commissioner in Northern Nigeria, Sir Frederick Lugard, who had already set his heart on the use of force. After thirty years of dealing with such problems he knew better, and in his mind volley and machine-gun fire were a physic which both doctor and patient understood. Even before a grudging Colonial Office gave its approval, his troops were in the field.

The campaigns of the Royal Niger Company were like those

Tour of duty: the governor of the Oil Rivers Protectorate, his ADC and the ADC's dog pay a visit to the King of Addo, who has been given a bottle of champagne, c. 1896.

fought elsewhere in Nigeria, although on many occasions its hybrid commercial and political role meant that some fighting took place over trading disagreements. In November 1886 the Company's depot at Patani was attacked and looted by local tribesmen, and the new Company turned for help to the Consul General at Calabar. He procured the assistance of men o'war, which shelled local villages and sent parties to destroy huts, crops and canoes. The commander of the Africa station did not like the work, which 'saturated' his sailors with fever. He was also incensed by the cheapjack trick of the Company which overcharged the navy for coal, and he complained irritably to the Admiralty about the whole business of using warships as a cover for the extension of a private company's commercial and political influence.[4] He warned that the Royal Niger Company's business interests would lead to more trouble for him and his ships. He was right, for in August 1894 a simmering quarrel between the Company and a rival businessman, Nana, governor of the Benin river, erupted into war after two Company steamers were holed by fire from Nana's cannon. Again the Consul-General summoned up warships, which were sent into action against Nana's centre of operations at Ebrohimi, which was well guarded by cunningly concealed batteries. After some setbacks the landing parties were able to take Ebrohimi, thanks to the treachery of one of his kinsmen, who guided them through the swamps. Nana was well supplied with artillery and had, by some unknown means, got his hands on a machine-gun with three thousand rounds of ammunition.[5] Another local ruler, Koko of the Brassmen, irritated by Company regulations, attacked its factory at Akassa and killed a number of its native employees in January 1895. The navy was again called in, and the town of Brass was stormed and taken. Subsequent investigations revealed that many of the Company's employees had behaved in an arrogant and unfair manner towards their rivals and local people. Justice seems to have been incompatible with business activities which gave shareholders a steady six per cent return each year.

Goldie does not appear to have been discountenanced by such findings. His mind was set on extending his Company's unchallenged authority in the north, where the Caliph of Sokoto held a loose overlordship over a group of Moslem emirates. In 1885 Britain had claimed a nominal protectorate over this region, but this had never been seriously or effectively enforced. Relations between these states and the Company had been sour for many years, with squabbles over slave-raiding and the hindrance of trade. By the end of 1896 Goldie was prepared for a trial of strength between the Company and its nearest neighbours, the emirates of Ilorin and Bida, which would take the form of a war against them. There were many good causes for this since there had been plenty of border infractions, and Goldie could publicly announce that he was making war to abolish slave-trading and raiding. In private he admitted that his overriding consideration was to bring the armies of the emirs to battle and inflict a signal defeat of them so as to change the balance of military and political power within the region.[6] The invincibility of the Company would be demonstrated, but Goldie was aware of the risk, for a reversal might trigger off an explosion of Islamic fervour throughout the Caliphate which would fatally wound the Company and with it British prestige.

Goldie's warlike preparations were surreptitious although his scheme was leaked to the press by a voluble official in Lagos and so came to the ears of the Emir Abubarkah in Bida. What he would have heard was that a flotilla of fourteen steamers would anchor at convenient landing places along the banks of the Niger and disembark forces which would then march quickly through the bush for offensives against the fortified cities of Kabba, Bida and Ilorin. The first offensive, in January 1897, was a wild goose chase, for mistaken intelligence had informed Goldie that half the Bida forces were at Kabba. The town opened its gates, and in the market-place Goldie proclaimed the end of slavery, much to the open delight of his audience.

The battle he was seeking occurred at the end of the second march under the walls of Bida, where, on 26 January, his five hundred Haussa infantrymen found themselves face to face with between ten and fifteen thousand Nupe warriors. Many were mounted, and the whole was a feudal host with lance-armed 'knights' often in mail and their dismounted retainers clustered around banners. Overall, generalship, if it existed, was appalling, for the Nupe allowed their assailants to form squares with a machine-gun at each corner. Volley and machine-gun fire cut swathes through the charging masses, whose discomfort was made final by the arrival of the manhandled artillery pieces which fired shrapnel into the closely packed reserves. As at Omdurman, a modern army routed a medieval one.

The battle before Bida was a rehearsal for its successor, in which the eight thousand warriors of Ilorin were beaten. Their command was, however, a little more adroit, and an attempted ambush gave the Company's officers a few fearful seconds, for one knot of horsemen charged a company just as it was forming square. The square closed in the nick of time with the horsemen yards away; one officer heard an emir call to his men to seek out gaps. There were none and the brave man died with over two hundred of his riders. The Ilorin army was swept aside by concentrated fire (over eleven thousand rounds were fired by 550 men and five machine-guns), and the city fell after having been set alight by artillery bombardment.

Goldie, who was hailed in Britain as another Cortez or Clive, had got what he wanted, a straightforward show of the Company's superiority on the battlefield, and the memory of its firepower lingered on. A year later, when Captain Abadie visited Ilorin, no emir dared risk having his photograph taken for fear that the tripod-mounted camera was a machine-gun.[7] The political advantages of the campaign were, however, minimal, for Goldie's puppet emir soon stepped down from the throne of Bida, and Abubarkah was restored.

An unexpected crisis prevented Goldie from full exploitation of his successes. Since 1895 French soldier-administrators in Dahomey had set their sights on the region of Borgu and in particular possession of Bussa, the port on the navigable extremity of the upper Niger. To this end a series of fortalices were built in the area, a move which drew British forces, determined to defend the border agreement of 1890 which excluded France from this region. So, in the spring of 1898 Haussas and Yorubas of the Royal Niger Company faced Senegalese *tirailleurs* in the villages of Borgu whilst their officers played an uneasy game of facing and out-facing. Far away, in Paris and London, British and French diplomats camel-traded, and the Colonial Secretary, Chamberlain, got ready for the worst and put arrangements in hand for the recruitment of two thousand black troops (West Africa Frontier Force) who were to be commanded by Colonel Lugard. He also kept the men on the spot under his thumb, thanks to the telegraph line which had lately been extended to Jebba. The would-be protagonists took things easy and invited each other to parties. Captain Abadie found that at least one French officer was a gentleman and another was inveigled into a third-form prank by which he wrote an offensive letter in French to his superior, to the delight of his British counterparts who had just been the recipients of a similar message from this same French senior officer. In June 1898 the fun was ended by an Anglo-French accord under the terms of which Bussa stayed firmly in British hands. The French withdrew, and Lugard remarked favourably on the way they had settled the area during their brief occupation. The natives, he noticed, had 'received a sharp lesson from other white men; they had offered opposition, and had soon learnt that the game was not worth the candle'.

With the question of the frontier settled, the Colonial Office was now free to reshape the political administration of Nigeria. Lagos and the Oil Rivers Protectorate were merged as Southern Nigeria, and the territories of the Royal Niger Company were joined to what was still a paper protectorate, the caliphate of Sokoto, to make Northern Nigeria. Its High Commissioner was the colonial warrior turned pro-consul Colonel Lugard. On New Year's Day 1900 the new colony was proclaimed publicly, and the independent emirates were each sent Arabic translations of the announcements, heralds of the approaching end of their independence. The emirs were unmoved by the declaration, and Lugard realized that his first duty was to destroy their military power and transform them into compliant instruments of the new British administration. But his determination to reduce the emirs to ciphers brought him into collision with the

Colonial Office, which was chary of giving unequivocal backing to an aggressive policy whose outcome would be a war. Goldie had warned Lugard that the recent dismal setbacks in South Africa had knocked sideways the British public's enthusiasm for colonial wars, and Chamberlain also advised prudence. If Lugard went to war, Chamberlain warned, he would need a clear and politically impeccable reason which could be presented to the House of Commons 'and will satisfy the faddists [e.g. Liberal "Little Englanders" and Aborigines Protection Society] in this country'.

Faced with the realities of governing a province, Lugard was not going to be constrained by the Colonial Office, even less by the need to appease insipid lobbyists in Britain. He had, anyway, good grounds for an uncompromising policy towards the emirates, and that was their determination to maintain slavery and slave raiding. In 1898 the emir of Bida had stated that he could no more give up slave-hunting than a 'cat can be stopped from mousing'. Moreover, the northern emirs were not anxious for a compromise, and their truculence matched Lugard's. In 1902 the emir of Kano spoke for his fellow rulers when he wrote to Lugard and informed him, 'I will never agree with you. I will have nothing to do with you. Between us and you there are no dealings except war. God Almighty has enjoined us.' The continuing wrangles over slavery and the murder of a British officer whose assassins were offered sanctuary in Kano provided the excuse which Lugard had been waiting for, and operations began in January 1903.

Kano was the first target, and Sokoto the second. Both were walled cities but their defences offered no impediment to forces equipped with 75mm artillery pieces. Resistance from Kano was limited, but as the columns closed on Sokoto they were offered battle. Once again a medieval horde threw itself on squares and machine-guns.

> As we approached close to the city hordes of horsemen and footmen armed with swords, spears, old guns and bows and arrows appeared, charging the square over and over again, only to be mown down by machine-gun and carbine fire. These men faced certain death with fanatic bravery to the beating of drums and tom-toms, the sound of shrill blasts on horns, and the chanting of extracts from the Koran. The horsemen urged their horses right up to the bayonet points of the kneeling Hausa soldiers. At last, after a period which seemed like hours, as so much was crowded into it, the struggle died down, save for the

129

War against the Caliphate: A seven-pound battery of the West Africa Frontier Force deploys to counter a bush ambush, Northern Nigeria, 1904.

menacing attitude of a group of men, who bore above their heads a big flag, on which was worked an inscription in Arabic (the Hausa language is written in Arabic characters). These men would not let anyone approach them, and as they continued to direct badly-aimed fire on to the square, they were dealt with drastically, all being picked off by specially aimed rifle-fire till none remained. As each standard-bearer was killed he was replaced by another, till the flag fell on a heap of Hausa humanity.[8]

So Sokoto fell, although resistance flickered on. On one occasion forty-five mounted infantrymen of the WAFF were caught by a force of two thousand horse and one thousand foot near Kotoroshi. In what was another Rorke's Drift, the small force beat off a series of charges during two hours before their attackers fled, leaving sixty-five dead. The commander, Lieutenant Wright, received the VC.

The 1903 campaign broke the Caliphate of Sokoto as an independent entity and was the foundation of what subsequently came to be known as 'Indirect Rule', a system by which the emirs kept their thrones but governed as clients of the colonial government, guided by British residents. It was Lugard's child and was based upon what he had seen of the feudatory Indian states when he had been a soldier there. Moslem theologians found that they could accommodate a new, British-approved

Caliph on the grounds that they were now the rightful rulers who made it clear that they did not wish to interfere with religious customs. No missionaries moved into the area, and traditional society continued much as before save that there was no more slavery. Full peace was not, however, achieved for some years, for there were a number of isolated religious and political disturbances which required punitive forces to be put in the field. There were also times when the machinery of indirect rule broke down or the puppet ruler showed himself incapable of fulfilling his obligations, and force was needed to restore the equilibrium. The spread of colonial administration also needed taxation to meet its costs, and this aroused hostility. In 1915–16, when the poll-tax was increased from 2s. 6d to 4 shillings a head, a force of troops with a machine-gun were required to tour the Bussa region to ensure that the money was paid. This area was further agitated in 1916 after disorder had spread from neighbouring Dahomey, where there had been an uprising against high taxation, forced labour and conscription, all of which were part of the French colonial war effort. Once again a show of force was required to deter any defiance. 'If the troops had taken a defeat the whole of Borgawa would have been up in arms, as they were all ready to take up arms,' commented a British NCO who commanded one patrol.[9] Even after thirty years of successful campaigns, imperial authority still stood on brittle glass.

Gambia, Sierra Leone and Gold Coast

Elsewhere in West Africa, successive British governments saw little economic or strategic advantage in a forward policy and were, therefore, willing to stand aside and give the French a free rein. The result was that the existing coastal colonies were extended inland and their borders arranged by agreement with the French. In 1888 the Gambia, a fourteen-mile-wide sliver along the River Gambia, was offered for sale to the French but they found the cost too high. The Gambia, Sierra Leone and the Gold Coast (Ghana) were impoverished colonies, and the sparseness of their revenues limited both their armed forces and the scope of military action open to them. Campaigns were therefore confined to a series of police actions against isolated areas of resistance or campaigns of retaliation against tribes which refused to keep the imperial peace. Such operations were carried out by the detachments of the West Indies Regiment stationed in each colony, local police forces (such as the Sierra Leone Frontier Police founded in 1889) and, in emergencies, landing parties from Royal Navy ships. The navy was essential for the defence of all these colonies, for shallow-draught cruisers and gunboats were able to steam up rivers, carry troops and supplies and when necessary land parties of marines and blue-jackets. In 1887 there had been a proposal for the creation of a volunteer force in Sierra Leone, a militia drawn from the local, educated black population, but the value of this was doubted by the Cabinet's defence committee, which also pooh-poohed a similar scheme in the Gold Coast, where it was thought that no one could be found of sufficient calibre.[10]

Resistance to colonial rule in the Gambia was limited. In 1891, 1892 and 1894 detachments of the West Indies regiment and naval landing parties had to be sent against two local chiefs, Foda Cabbah and Foda Sillah. In each campaign the small forces were able to destroy fortified war bases but the chiefs escaped. Here and elsewhere in West Africa a persistent feature of the fighting was that the Africans were armed with muskets and chose to fight by ambushes so that every column's advance through the bush and jungle was marked by ambuscades and brief exchanges of fire. In Sierra Leone campaigns were the consequence of friction between the Freetown government and tribes in the interior which refused to be bound by their obligations to keep the peace with their neighbours or who continued

Colonial paddle steamer Gertrude: *This shallow-draught steamer conveyed troops, supplies and ammunition to field forces during several West African campaigns in the 1890s.*

African entente*: French officers with their Senegalese* tirailleurs *(background) relax with their British counterparts after strenuous work marking out the borders of Sierra Leone. A year later, in 1892, one French officer blundered into the British colony and ambushed and killed members of a British column, thinking they were Sofa tribesmen.*

to raid for slaves. After eight years of strained relations, at the end of 1887, the government decided in its frustration to 'administer a severe lesson' to the Yonni. The instructors were a force of the West Indies Regiment and a handful of sailors from HMS *Acorn* who manned a war-rocket. This proved an amazing success, terrifying the Yonni, whose chiefs submitted. No one was killed and only twenty were wounded during the bush skirmishes. A similar expedition, in 1891, up the Scarcies river, in which two fortified villages were shelled and taken, had much the same result, with three dead and eleven wounded.

A more formidable opponent for the Sierra Leone authorities was Samori Touré, whose great inland Islamic empire crumbled under repeated assaults from the French in the early 1890s.* As his first empire sagged, Samori and his Sofa followers migrated towards the Ivory Coast and eastern Gold Coast, and some of them found their way into eastern Sierra Leone. Relations with the British government were cordial – Samori secured modern guns through trading connexions with Freetown, and the pusillanimous governor, Sir Francis Fleming, and his officials were

---

* His grandson, Sekou Touré, was the late Marxist president of Guinea.

reluctant to offer any provocation to a powerful neighbour. The commander of the local armed forces, Colonel Ellis, was more robust and anxious to wage war against the Sofas, who had been preying on their neighbours and raiding for slaves. Ellis by-passed the colonial government and secured from the War Office permission to launch operations against the Sofa. Ellis's plan was to send two columns, five hundred men in all, in a pincer movement into the territory occupied by the Sofas, raze their fortalices and drive them out of Sierra Leone. In spite of ambushes and firefights during the advance, he achieved his objective. The war camps fell to shell fire, and at Tungea the Sofas lost 250 dead after an engagement with forty-eight *gendarmerie* backed by fifteen hundred native auxiliaries.

What was remarkable about this campaign was the few-minute fight at Waima on 23 December 1893. A French junior officer, Gaston Maritz, with a company of Senegalese operating from Senegal, had been deliberately misled into believing that a concentration of Sofa were encamped at Waima. He surrounded the camp in the night and then his men attacked, firing their newly issued Lebel magazine rifles. His victims were British officers and men of the West Indies Regiment, and seventeen were killed before the error was realized. Maritz died of his wounds, having discovered too late that he had engaged British forces. During the confused firing he and his men had thought that British officers in their nightshirts were Sofas. There was a great fuss in London and Paris but the matter was settled amicably when the facts were understood.

The establishment of full colonial government over Sierra Leone in 1896 brought with it a hut tax of 5 shillings annually, which became a focus for discontent amongst the Mende and their neighbours. Attempts at the beginning of 1898 to collect the tax with a detachment of troops provoked violent hostility which the single company of the West Indies Regiment could not contain. The Royal Navy was summoned and three men o'war were sent into action up the Sherbro river and along the coast. By May the uprising had spread and there were a series of massacres of Christian natives and those who had adopted European dress and customs. A further four warships arrived to take immediate preventive action whilst a larger expedition, under Colonel Woodgate, got ready for a full-scale campaign of pacification.

The pattern of this campaign was a repeat performance of the 1873–4 Ashante War. The war had arisen out of a sequence of unresolved disputes between the Asantehene Kofi Karikari and the colonial government of the Gold Coast which had blocked his inland kingdom's trade routes to the coast. In January 1873 an Ashante army, reckoned to be sixty thousand strong, crossed the Prah river and made war on those tribes which claimed British protection. The government's counter-measure, an attempt to create a Fante federation, failed wretchedly, and the Ashante advance threatened the littoral and its string of forts. Five men o'war quickly arrived and provided marines and sailors to man the castles (relics of slaving days). An attack on one, Elmina, was beaten off, and offensive operations in the form of bombardments of villages were undertaken. The new local commander, Rear-Admiral Commerell, a Crimea VC, took command and planned an armed reconnaissance up the Prah river in his flagship, HMS *Rattlesnake*. This demonstration of force went sadly wrong, for a flotilla of cutters, whalers and launches was ambushed near Chamah and forced to pull back with losses. From then on, during the autumn, there were a series of limited offensive actions by landing parties and warships which together ensured the safety of the coastal region.

The navy lacked the men to do more than fend off the Ashante invasion and, recognizing this, the government authorized a full-scale military expedition to invade Ashanteland, take its capital, Kumasi, and impose terms on the Asantehene, Kofi – or, as he was called by the British, King Coffee. This was a chance for the new, reformed army to show its paces, and command was given to the 'coming man', Major-General Wolseley, who was widely reputed a modern and 'scientific' general. The Secretary of War, Cardwell, was a trifle anxious, for, as he warned Wolseley, the local climate was 'peculiarly fatal' for Europeans, and his British troops should not be over-exposed to it. A short war was needed in which the casualties would not be high. During the autumn Wolseley and his 'ring' of acolyte officers busied themselves with highly detailed and all-encompassing preparations. On New Year's Day 1874 2,500 British troops disembarked and prepared for their advance to Kumasi, accompanied, much to Wolseley's disgust, by a bevy of war correspondents, including H. M. Stanley of the *New York Times*. Wolseley did, however, change his view after Stanley joined in the fighting and proved himself a good shot.

To meet this threat and stem the inexorable advance of the British and their native allies, the Asantehene adopted the contradictory policy of seeking a negotiated settlement and sending war bands to ambush the columns and strike at their lines of communication. Neither yielded him anything. The British, with overwhelming firepower, got the best of the fighting, and Wolseley was unwilling to talk, at least until he had taken Kumasi. This he did, after some hard-fought engagements, on 2 February, the Black Watch leading the way. Once in possession of Kumasi, whose capture was regarded as a means of bringing Kofi to his senses, terms were laid down under which he promised to become a pliable client of Britain. This achieved and a considerable amount of plunder collected, the army withdrew back to the coast for re-embarkation; the two per cent casualty rate had been gratifyingly low and a mark of the thoroughness of Wolseley's calculations and arrangements.

By defeating the Ashante in 1874, the British had, unknowingly, fractured irreparably the structure of the Ashante state. The damage to the prestige of the Asantehene left his kingdom and his successors weakened, and the area deteriorated into chaos. By the end of 1895 the kingdom was ready for annexation and direct colonial rule. There were fears that its ruler, Prempeh, might make a pact with Samori, his northern neighbour, and the expansion of the Germans in Togo and the French on the Ivory Coast opened the possibility that the region might slip from Britain's grasp. To secure British occupation, an army was mustered at Cape Coast, including a battalion of the West Yorkshire Regiment which was then being shipped home after garrison duty in Aden and India. In spite of suffering from debilitation as a consequence of this service, it was argued that these unlucky soldiers would be sufficiently hardened to overcome the local climate. As in 1874, there was careful preparation, but it proved needless, for the march to Kumasi was unopposed. King Prempeh surrendered himself to exile and his kingdom to British rule.

The first taste of British government was little to the liking of the Ashante, who found themselves pressed into road-building and the construction of a fort for the new British resident at Kumasi. Collective resentment burst into open rebellion at the beginning of 1900, when the Ashante heard the rumour that the governor, Sir Frederick Hodgson, had come to Kumasi to find the Golden Stool and then sit on it. The Golden Stool was the traditional symbol of Ashante kingship and was believed to embody the soul of the entire race. No Asantehene had ever sat on it, so the threat of its profanation by Hodgson's ample buttocks was, for the Ashante, an arrant blasphemy. In April

Hodgson was aware of growing resistance by the Ashante, who were arming themselves, and on the 25th he, his wife, their escort and local people who had thrown in their lot with the British found themselves blockaded in the fort at Kumasi. The concentration of machine-guns on the defences ruled out a frontal attack, and so the Ashante surrounded the fort with a wooden stockade and settled down to starve out its occupants. News of the revolt took the authorities on the coast by surprise, and hurried requests were sent to other colonies for additional troops for a relief force. When it was mustered, in June, there were over a thousand, including detachments from Central Africa, Nigeria and Sierra Leone and a company of Sikhs.

Two units, of 250 and 200, had reached the fort after heavy fighting in the bush and rainforest which pushed the garrison up to twenty-nine Europeans and 750 native soldiers together with refugees. This was too much for the meagre food supplies, which were so stretched that by the end of the month the defenders were down to an army-ration biscuit and bully beef each day. Under this pressure, Hodgson decided to break out with the bulk of forces on the morning of 23 June, leaving behind 115 men, more than three quarters of whom were invalids, with five machine-guns. His party, with Lady Hodgson in a hammock carried by porters, broke through the defences and in two days made it to the lands of a friendly chief. Those left behind had all but given up hope by 12 July, when the two British officers prepared poison to take when they were overwhelmed. The barking of Colonel Carter's fox-terrier put such considerations out of their mind, for it heralded the arrival of his badly mauled column and the relief of Kumasi. Soon after, at Aboasu, the main force engaged the Ashante, who with a gesture of hopelessness abandoned ambushes, rushed their adversaries and were shot down in large numbers. This, the third Ashante war, was the most costly in terms of lives of all West African campaigns. The governor's ill-judged whim cost the lives of just under seven hundred soldiers and porters, and a further seven hundred odd were wounded.

By contrast with operations in southern Africa, Egypt and the Sudan, the campaigns in West Africa were minor affairs, seldom involving armies of more than five hundred in unequal contests against natives with inadequate firearms or grievously mistaken tactics. Nevertheless, they were often hard-fought struggles in the most unsparing of all African climates in which both conquerors and conquered showed skill and bravery.

East and Central Africa, 1880–1920

> I will see no traders with their guns and gin. My people shall fight
> with the spear, and drink water, like their forefathers before
> them. I will have no praying-men to put a fear of death into men's
> hearts, to stir them against the law of the king, and make a path
> for the white folk who follow to run on.
>
> Ignosi from R. Haggard, *King Solomon's Mines*

There are several striking features about the subjugation and
pacification of Britain's colonies in East and Central Africa. The
first is that such a large area was conquered by such small forces,
most of them locally recruited, and in such short campaigns.
Two considerations made this possible, the first being the overwhelming firepower possessed by the British, which of course
was common to all wars in Africa. The second was the lack of any
concerted resistance by the local political units, of which the
most substantial, the sultanate of Zanzibar, had been under
Britain's thumb for several generations and was in no position to
oppose partition when it began in the 1880s. Elsewhere, Arab
slaving chiefs and tribes, most of which had never seen a white
man until the 1890s and early 1900s, and the degenerate and
craven Mwanga, kabaka of Buganda, could offer little more than
desultory and unco-ordinated resistance. The exception to this
collapse was Somaliland, where Muhammad bin Abdullah-
Hassan (the 'Mad Mullah') not only defied and outmanœuvred
imperial armies but set up a cohesive state in the hinterland
which was held together, like his followers, by a common
Islamic faith. Only in 1920 was he finally defeated. During this
period there was also a remarkable degree of co-operation
between the colonial powers, who were more than willing to
help each other in an emergency. Royal Navy warships avenged
the murder of German businessmen at Witu in 1890, German
gun-boats lent a hand in the war against slavers on Lake Nyasa,
and the Italians assisted in the campaigns against the Mullah,
whose activities affected their own colony in Somalia. Yet
whilst, at a distance, the occupation of East and Central Africa
might appear a walk-over for the British, there was armed
defiance and much hard fighting. Success rested with the unflin-
ching application of the standard principle of colonial warfare
which involved a fast response to unrest and the unrelenting
application of force to its centre. In Kenya in the early 1900s this

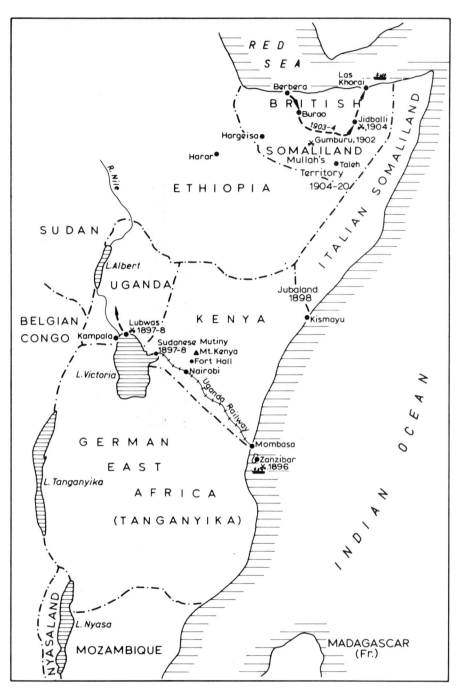

East and Central Africa

was known as 'hammering' the natives, the delivery of a military shock which would both pacify and deter.

The acquisition of colonies in East and Central Africa was a piecemeal affair which relied for much of its impetus on the efforts of private enterprise. When these proved unequal to the task, it was left to the British government to pick up the pieces and add Nyasaland (Malawi), Kenya and Uganda to its colonial responsibilities. Such action would have been unthinkable before the early 1880s, for the whole area had been loosely under the sway of Britain, whose consul-general at Zanzibar pulled the strings at the Sultan's court, a manipulation which ensured the promotion and protection of British interests on the mainland where the Sultan claimed a vague sovereignty over the small states which stretched as far as the great lakes. Behind the consul were the men o'war of the Royal Navy, which were ready not only to intimidate the Sultan – whose palace was conveniently close to the shore – but to patrol the coastal waters in pursuit of slaving dhows. Gunboats and cruisers steamed up and down the coast to support the shallow-draught steam pinnaces and whalers which cut out and boarded the slavers. It was a prolonged and uphill contest, but in spite of many Captain Marryat exploits of naval derring-do during the 1860s and 1870s, the results were disappointing. Out of the forty thousand black slaves annually shipped from the coast, only 2,500 or so were rescued by the navy. In 1873 the consul-general insisted on the closure of the Zanzibar slave market – an Anglican cathedral was built on the site – and three years later the Sultan was made to put his hand to a declaration which outlawed the trade, not that much notice was taken of this by his distant but nominal subjects.

In 1885 this system of informal empire broke down. Germany proclaimed its protectorate over much of the coast and interior and Zanzibar itself. The explorer Karl Peters and his businessmen backers in Germany hoped that these gains would become the nucleus of a prosperous German East African empire which might, in time, rival India as a source of wealth and glory. Much diplomatic give and take followed, and by 1890 Zanzibar returned to British patronage (in exchange for Heligoland), Germany took what became Tanganyika, and Britain secured Kenya, Uganda and Nyasaland. This was applauded by those in Britain who had raised their voices for and given cash in support of the struggle against slavery, and by others who anticipated rich profits from the commercial exploitation of the area. East

African slavery and its miseries were well known in Britain through the writings of David Livingstone. He had repeatedly exhorted his fellow countrymen to encourage what he considered 'legitimate' commerce. His arguments had prompted his fellow Scotsmen to create a partnership of missionary zeal, provided by the Church of Scotland, with business enterprise, provided by Scots investors, which was known as the African Lakes Company.

The Lakes Company's area of evangelizing and trading was the hinterland of Lake Nyasa, where it quickly collided with other business interests, those of Arab slavers who had recently penetrated to this well-populated area. This collision led to a series of wars between 1887 and 1895. The first shots were fired by the brutal and brutish Mlozi, for whom the Company was a stumbling-block in the way of his creation of a 'sultanate' on the northern shores of Nyasa. He opened his attack with an attempt to seize the Company's base at Karonga, and in the following year, 1888, the Company struck back with an attack on his bases nearby. The Company's rag, tag and bobtail army of local tribesmen, natives from Natal and white officials was armed with muskets, rifles and hand-grenades improvised from tin cans. Its commander was an imperial adventurer, Captain Frederick Lugard, who was badly wounded in the abortive siege. What, for the missionaries had been an anti-slavery 'crusade', came to a sticky end.

In 1891 the military balance changed decisively. The government declared a protectorate over Nyasaland after scaring off the Portuguese and agreeing boundaries with the Germans. To impose order, extirpate the slave-traders and garrison the colony, two hundred Sikh troops were imported, together with a miniature navy. Control of the lake was essential, and taking a leaf from the missionaries' book, the navy ordered three gunboats which could be built in sections, shipped up the Zambesi and its tributary the Shire and man-hauled on wagons to bypass rapids. In October 1892 the parts were delivered to the mouth of the Zambesi. They reached their destination the following summer after assistance from the Germans and were assembled by naval artificers helped by two from the builders, Yarrow of Poplar. The *Dove*, of twenty tons, was launched on the upper Shire river, and the *Adventure* and *Pioneer*, each of thirty-five tons, steamed on Lake Nyasa. They possessed cannon and Nordenfeldt machine-guns and were able to sweep the lake clear of slaving dhows – their commander, Commander Robertson,

East African watchdogs: HMS Thrush *(above) a gunboat which saw action in the West African riverine campaigns of the 1890s as well as taking part in the bombardment of Zanzibar in 1896.* HMS Racoon *(below) a second-class cruiser which took part in expeditions against the East African slaver Rashid Mubarraq in 1895 and the bombardment of Zanzibar.*

The Sultan preserved: In 1896 a coup placed Sayyid Khalid on the throne of Zanzibar, but he was ordered to stand down by the British consul. When he failed to obey, a naval flotilla shelled his palace, and after thirty-seven minutes he submitted. There were over five hundred casualties from the close-range fire, only one of which was British.

A grateful ally: Sayyid Hamud, Sultan of Zanzibar, restored to his throne by British warships, Admiral Rawson, his fellow captains and the vizier pose together after the bombardment of Zanzibar.

Scourge of the slavers: HMS Boadicea *in the 1880s.*

imitated Admiral van Tromp and set a broom on his mast to advertise his purpose. In November 1893 the coastal slaving bases were shelled, and the obdurate slaver Makanjira and his mother, a partner in his business, surrendered. Mlozi was run to earth by the consul, Harry Johnston, with a force of four hundred backed by artillery and machine-guns, and his headquarters were taken. He fell prisoner and was hanged the next day for the murder of forty-five Africans whom he had killed before and during the previous day's battle. His local power and that of his client tribes was broken by the government and served as an example to others. The missionaries were well pleased; they had not only offered prayers for the success of the campaign against the slavers, they had, on occasions, lent a hand, placing their steamboats at the disposal of the armed forces. There had also been some aid from the Germans on the Tanganyika shore of the lake. They had cut off slave routes overland to the coast, and their gunboats had joined in the shelling of slavers' forts.

The missions in Nyasaland produced, by the turn of the century, a class of educated Africans in whom the first seeds of nationalism were apparent. There was some contact between this class and Negro movements in the United States where one pastor, John Chilembwe, had studied. He ran his own church and spoke out against the recruitment of black troops to fight in Somaliland and, after 1914, against the Germans in Tanganyika. In January 1915 he raised a revolt, taking advantage of the withdrawals of troops to fight in East Africa and hoping for

Rescued: East African slaves rescued by Royal Navy warships, Zanzibar and (below) underground barracoon for keeping slaves before shipment, East Africa, c. 1880.

East Africa divided: A German officer and his British counterpart walk side by side to mark out the borders of Nyasaland (Malawi) and Tanganyika, c. 1898.

support from the tobacco plantation workers. The rising began in a Grand Guignol manner with the horrific murder of four Europeans and then degenerated into farce when Chilembwe's followers tried to break into the armoury at Blantyre. There they mistook the noise of revelry from a European club as war cries and the starting of a motor-bike for a machine-gun. Their nerve broke and for the next few days they were hunted down by panic-stricken Europeans. Several were hanged and Chilembwe was shot dead in a skirmish. The incident stirred up much alarm, especially in military circles. Captain J. E. Phillips, the army's intelligence officer for East and Central Africa, feared that extensive missionary activity was upsetting traditional African society in the region. He was troubled too by the growth of African churches, particularly those which looked to Ethiopia, still independent, as a source of religious and nationalist aspiration. In a memo of July 1917 he predicted that the Chilembwe revolt was a foretaste of what might happen if American influence was unchecked. To meet such future subversion, he urged the spread of secular education, the encouragement of divisive tribal loyalties and the possible creation, on the German pattern, of an 'elite' of soldiers which could counter-balance that of the educated Africans.[1]

Just as the first moves in the occupation of Nyasaland had been undertaken under the umbrella of a private company, so the colonization of Kenya and Uganda was placed in the hands of another, the British Imperial East Africa Company, which had been founded in 1888. As in Nigeria, Lord Salisbury was anxious for imperial government at no cost to Britain, and so the company was chartered to govern with the profits made from trade. In strategic terms its agents were also expected to extend their own and Britain's influence over Uganda and with it Lake Victoria, the source of the Nile. This necessitated an inland trek from the coast to Mengo, the capital of Buganda and the seat of its ruler, Kabaka Mwanga. The small column was led by Lugard, who, as he moved across country with his Sudanese askaris and Maxim gun, signed treaties with native chiefs by becoming their blood brother. (Blood from cuts in the arm would be mingled, and the brothers would then eat a gobbet of meat which had been soaked in their blood before signing the written agreement.[2]) There could be no blood brotherhood with Mwanga, a mendacious and cruel pederast whose features suggested to Lugard 'irresolution, a weak character and a good deal of sensuality'. Mwanga had ruled since 1884 over a kingdom which was falling apart and he rightly feared that it would pass into European hands. He stood, feebly, in the midst of a three-cornered civil war between his Moslem, Catholic and Protestant subjects. He was in no position to resist Lugard's demands, even though they were backed by a small force, and in 1890 he submitted to British tutelage which left him in the position of an Indian prince, the disarmament of his unruly subjects and the presence of Company garrisons. In the next two years, by a mixture of diplomacy and force, Lugard quietened the warring factions.

These exertions and commitments elsewhere were too much for the East Africa Company, which was facing bankruptcy by 1893. Its collapse would prelude a recrudescence of anarchy in Uganda with the attendant massacres of converts, and the possibility that another European power might seize the opportunity and Uganda as well. In 1894 the Company's responsibilities were taken over by the government, and plans were set in motion for the building of a railway which would connect its new administrative capital, Kampala, with the port of Mombasa. There were good commercial reasons for this railroad, which would become a conduit for trade and development, but it also served a military purpose in that, when complete, it would ease the task of pacification and strengthen Britain's grasp on the Nile.

Pacification was in the hands of Sudanese askaris, many of

them veterans from Egyptian service who had been driven southwards to Equatoria during the Mahdist wars. There were also Sikh regulars, imported from India, and in coastal areas the Royal Navy's landing parties. The pattern of warfare in the 1890s and 1900s was one of sending columns to break centres of revolt, usually against that unwelcome imperial innovation taxation, or tribal disorder which invariably meant either attacks on isolated Europeans or cattle-raiding. Where, as in the 1896 Nandi campaign, the natives wisely avoided a head-on collision with the columns, their cattle would be confiscated, villages burnt and crops destroyed. It was small-scale warfare but hard and brutal.

The evidence of one action may stand for many others. In August 1902 a native constable had been murdered in the vicinity of Fort Hall, north of Nairobi, and his assassins had been joined by neighbouring tribes for 'an orgy round the dead policeman's body'. Lieutenant Meinertzhagen, the commander of a small detachment of King's African Rifles, was convinced that, if such a crime was unpunished, the natives would suspect weakness and be tempted to further outrages.[3] It was therefore agreed that the village was to be attacked.

> The village had bonfires burning and the Wakikuyu were dancing round them in all their war-paint. It was really rather a weird sight. The alarm was given by a native who tried to break through our rather thin cordon. He refused to stop when challenged and was shot down. There was then a rush from the village into the surrounding bush, and we killed about 17 niggers. Two policemen and one of my men were killed. I narrowly escaped a spear which whizzed past my head. Then the fun began. We at once burned the village and captured the sheep and goats. After that we systematically cleared the valley in which the village was situated, burned all the huts, and killed a few more niggers, who finally gave up the fight and cleared off, but not till 3 more of our men had been killed.[4]

Reeling under these blows, the tribe submitted and handed the murderers over for trial. Amazingly, they received six months' hard labour.

The ability to carry out these operations in Kenya and Uganda

(Opposite) The Lake Nyasa navy: Following the creation of a small flotilla of prefabricated gunboats in 1892, the British produced another to fight the Germans in the 1914–18 war. Like the first, the boats were carried in sections across country and then reassembled, although by now transport difficulties were eased through the use of a steam tractor for part of the journey.

149

depended upon the loyalty of the Sudanese askaris who made up the bulk of the colonial forces. They were good troops. 'Just, honourable, dealing fair by all; slow to anger, but swift to strike, and that right heavily, when the occasion demands' was the judgement of one of their commanders, Major Macdonald.[5] In the autumn of 1897 he had been given orders to move northwards into Uganda and then proceed down the Nile in a clandestine expedition which had been intended to head off the French and, eventually, make contact with Kitchener's larger army, then marching southwards towards Khartoum. The plan misfired as a consequence of a mutiny by the Sudanese which led to the most bloody fighting experienced in East Africa. The grievances of the Sudanese were concerned with the conditions of their service, large arrears of pay and trepidation about the imminent march to the Nile. As the mutiny developed, there were indications that the mutineers were considering the expulsion of the British from Uganda and the establishment of a Moslem state there, a political objective which may have had something to do with the intervention of Mwanga, the ex-kabaka, who had many axes to grind against the British. Some blame for what happened rested with the British officers who had been seconded to the expedition and who, a colleague admitted, were driven by an 'insatiable desire . . . to get brevets, DSOs and medals' and were therefore disinclined to care much for the feelings of the men under them.

The mutiny infected three columns between 24 and 26 September, and the mutineers, six hundred in all, with many of their wives and children, withdrew to Lubwas on the shores of Lake Victoria. Here, on 16 October, they began to put their military knowledge to use and built fortifications which included underground, shellproof bunkers on a peninsula. They also acquired a small steamer and a machine-gun, equipment which they knew how to use. At this stage they no doubt anticipated that their fellows at Kampala would follow their example, and they had been joined by over two hundred Waganda Moslems. There is also some evidence that they did not expect retribution and were uncertain as to Britain's ability to send further troops to the area. Still, an officer had warned them before he was shot that 'Many of my countrymen will come up, and that if you do this thing, you will have reason to regret it.'

This major's countrymen's immediate concern was to contain the mutiny. Major Macdonald was quick to move to Kampala, where he disarmed restive askaris, and then to Buddu, where

Mwanga had thrown in his lot with mutineers. This sector of the uprising was quietened after Mwanga's forces were decisively beaten at Kisaliva on 14 January 1898. Meanwhile, at Lubwas the main body of mutineers were blockaded by a scratch force of Swahili infantry, Sikhs (including 150 rushed from Mombasa) and over fifteen hundred Waganda tribesmen. The commander, Captain Woodward, was keen to have a go at the mutineers and during November and December alternated skirmishes with headlong assaults. Thanks to a mutineer sergeant who could use the machine-gun, these attacks were beaten off with heavy losses, especially amongst the Waganda tribal levies. On 9 January 1898 the mutineers abandoned Lubwas, escaping by means of the dhow, which Woodward unsuccessfully tried to sink with Maxim gun fire. For the next five months the mutineers attempted to move towards the Nile and were pursued by British columns. There were a number of skirmishes, but by the end of April what was left of the mutineers' force had been scattered. Eight, including two sergeants, one of whom had manned the machine-gun, were shot at Kampala, and many others received sentences of between ten and fifteen years hard labour. In the course of the mutiny and the fighting which followed, seven British officers were killed and 853 other British forces.[6]

The Sudanese Mutiny of 1897–8 was one of the might-have-beens of African history. It created alarm throughout Uganda and took the authorities unawares – reinforcements from India were able to reach Mombasa only in March 1898, a month before the mutiny collapsed. It had been a purely military movement, created by the sufferings endured by the soldiers, and it aroused little resistance elsewhere, apart from that of Mwanga and the mutineers' co-religionists. What is perhaps most interesting is the willingness of local tribes to join forces with the British columns, even if this did mean that they became machine-gun fodder. For their part, the mutineers did little to enlist help from the local population, and their progress was invariably marked by a trail of wrecked and plundered villages.

The Mullah's Wars

It was in Somaliland that the British military authorities faced their sternest test in East Africa. The protectorate had been acquired in 1884 on the grounds of its strategic position, which

151

lay directly across the Red Sea from Aden. It was a poor colony and one which, until 1899, presented few serious policing problems, and these were overcome by small expeditions to show the flag to the interior tribes. In that year Colonel Hayes Sadler, the consul in Berbera, had written to Lord Salisbury with a nervous request for two machine-guns for an expedition inland which would demonstrate local British power. This had been jeopardized by Muhammad bin Abdullah Hassan, 'a man in the prime of life . . . dark-coloured, tall and thin, with a small goat's beard'.[7] Muhammad bin Abdullah had been to Mecca, where he had studied, and had returned to his native country as a preacher, teacher and healer of disputes. He called upon his listeners to reject religious and moral slackness and embrace a stringent Islamic faith. Innovations such as taxes, which had come with 'infidel' rule, were to be abhorred, and all Somalis were to unite around their faith and live their lives according to the will of Allah and His revelation, the Koran. There was much here to alarm the British, who understood the appeal of Mahdism, even though Muhammad bin Abdullah never claimed to be a Mahdi, and feared the way in which Moslem zealotry could unite the Somalis against their new rulers. Such fears were quickly realized. In 1900 Muhammad bin Abdullah (or, as his enemies called him, 'the Mad Mullah') had waged war against the Ethiopian infidels in the Ogaden with considerable success, and two years later his tribal following was estimated at over thirty thousand, with the likelihood that a further forty thousand would join him if he entered their lands.

The successes of the Mullah directly challenged British authority. Tribes followed him, others were coerced, and he was able to raid and move as he wished across the hinterland. The response was a series of expeditions against him in 1903 and 1904 which involved over sixteen thousand British, African and Indian troops. The plan was for columns to march to and fro in the hope that the Mullah would engage or else that his forces would be trapped and brought to battle. British officers hoped for another Omdurman, but on three occasions their forces suffered miniature Isandlwanas. At Erigo in 1901, Gumburu in 1902 and Gadbali in 1903, small units were cut off and suffered reverses in which two machine-guns fell into the Mullah's hands. When faced with larger forces, the Mullah preferred tip-and-run skirmishes to full-scale battles which were frustrating and wearing for his opponents.

On the track of the Mullah: Detachments of the local Camel Corps and their transport set off for another day's fruitless advance in 1903.

The Officer in Charge, Eildab, reports by wire that at 6.45 a.m. this morning a party of about 20 of the enemies' horsemen attempted to raid the ponies of the Tribal Horse when grazing – shots were exchanged but no casualties – Captain Molloy and 100 Tribal Horse started in pursuit, supported by Major Bridges with 200 Tribal Horse and 50 mounted Hants [Hampshire Regiment] under Captain Deane. Captain Molloy pursued enemy 3 miles beyond Badwein and exchanged shots – but enemy who had a long start got clean away, and Captain Molloy's horses were all done, so leaving 25 men to track them up, the whole force returned to Eildab.[8]

Six weeks later, on 10 January 1904, the keeper of the Headquarters Diary had more encouraging news. A mile from Jidballi a column had been engaged by a large force and there was a brief pitched battle. In spite of the admirable skirmishing skill of the Somalis, egged on by the ullulations of their women folk, none had got within four hundred yards of the square. Five imperial troops had been killed and nine wounded, and Somali losses were calculated at over four hundred. The Mullah learnt his lesson and avoided such precipitate battles in the future. He escaped the columns, which withdrew, and at the end of the year Brigadier-General Swayne regretfully informed the Foreign Office that the prestige of the Mullah was as high as ever it was and that he continued to follow 'in the footsteps of the prophet'.

Such fruitless expeditions displeased the Foreign Office, for they wasted money, and after further skirmishes it was decided in 1912 that the hinterland of the protectorate was to be abandoned, much to the fury of local military men. The Mullah had emerged as a defiant and successful head of state, ruling by Islamic law over many of the interior tribes. He had even begun a policy of building border strongholds which marked the edges of his authority. One, at Shimber Berris, was demolished after a bombardment in 1914 as a demonstration to local, friendly tribes that the Mullah could not have everything his own way. The local military authorities were well pleased with this and were seeking to obtain hand-grenades for future attacks but the demands of the World War took priority. The 1914–18 War gave the Mullah a respite which he used to cultivate an accord with his western neighbour, the Abyssinian Emperor Lij Yasu, and through him to court German and Turkish interest. He also continued to accumulate modern weapons, although one of the prizes in his armoury, a machine-gun taken from the British, was offered as a gift to Lij Yasu in 1916.[9] This was all very

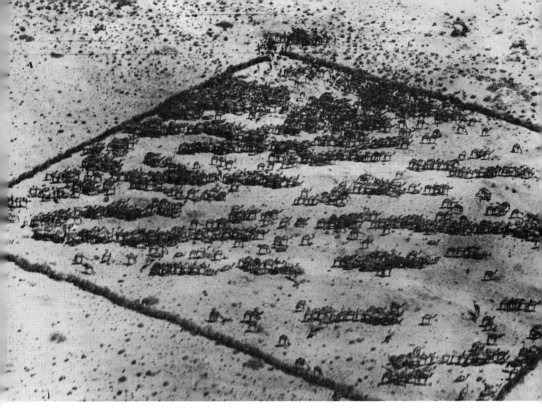

The Mullah's stockade: An aerial photograph of Medishe, taken in 1920, showing some of Muhammad bin Abdullah's stock of camels. In the past they had given him and his followers the mobility to avoid British columns.

troubling for the British, especially as the Emperor was anxious for the Mullah's friendship and there had been rumours of 'Africa for the Africans' sentiment in Addis Ababa. 'The continued immunity of the Mullah, who now stands alone as an unsubdued native potentate in Africa is a source of anxiety,' commented the Commissioner in Berbera in October 1918, but there was little he could do about him. Somaliland's annual revenue of £85,000 was insufficient for a prolonged war in the bush.[10] There were also signs that, in spite of pleas to the contrary, Muhammad bin Abdullah was still hostile to the British and was anxious to erode their authority. In May 1916 his followers had seized and ransacked Las Khorai and massacred many of the Warsangeli, a tribe which had renounced its allegiance to the Mullah four years before. Order and 'a satisfactory moral effect' were quickly achieved after a shelling from the guns of HMS *Northbrook*, and the Mullah's adherents fled inland.

155

The problem of the Mullah's continued defiance was part of a wider restlessness in East Africa during the First World War. The events in Europe were known about in Africa, and many Africans had been recruited to fight there. When they returned, they brought stories which fomented discontent: 'Round the camp fires there has been much talk – in the lingua franca which never fails the African – starting from stomach and wife, and the distance which they themselves have been brought from home to hardship, and touching on the killing of white by black as illustrated before their eyes.'[11] Those who had done that killing in the white man's war returned with new skills, and in March 1918 the commissioner in the Zeila district of western Somaliland reported that ex-soldiers from the French army had used their skirmishing drill in tribal battles. Ex-British askaris from Somaliland had shown their section drill to Lij Yasu, and other ex-servicemen were plying a trade as cattle-guards.[12] Against this background it is understandable that, once the war had ended in 1918, measures were put in hand for the overthrow of the Mullah. The *coup* involved the use of aircraft to strafe and bomb the Mullah's inland forts. Although one officer, Colonel French, thought that it would be a 'nice little show for the Post Bellum army of occupation in Egypt', the operations in February 1920 were intended both to remove an obstacle to British government and to display the force of which Britain was capable. The final fall of the Mullah is described in the next chapter, where it represents the last phase of imperial warfare.

II

BATTLE

1. The Savage Foes

There's a breathless hush in the close tonight
Ten to make and the match to win –
A bumping pitch and a blinding light,
An hour to play and the last man in.
And it's not for the sake of a ribboned coat
Or the selfish hope of a season's fame,
But his captain's hand on his shoulder smote.
'Play up! Play up! And play the game!

The sand of the desert is sodden red –
Red with the wreck of the square that broke;
The Gatling's jammed and the colonel dead,
And the regiment blind with dust and smoke.
The river of death has brimmed its banks,
And England's far and Honour a name,
But the voice of a schoolboy rallies the ranks,
'Play up! Play up! And play the game!

Sir Henry Newbolt

Sir Henry Newbolt's verses are perhaps the most well-known reaction to an imperial battle in Africa, although they have been derided by subsequent generations which recognized few if any signs of sportsmanship in the mass slaughter of total war and found the comparison distasteful. Yet by making the battlefield the complement of the cricket pitch, Newbolt gave permanence to some of the deepest sentiments cherished by late-Victorian and Edwardian officers. War and sport shared a common ground, for they called for the same moral and physical qualities. Gallantry, nerve, self-control, fitness and cheerfulness in the face of setbacks were the highest attainments of the imperial warrior, and they were also the virtues which marked him out at the crease or in the steeplechase field. Above all there was the moral discipline which insisted that, whether in sport or war, the game was played fairly, cleanly and according to the rules. It was an age when the batsman left the crease before the umpire had given him out, and adherence to this and the other principles of sportsmanship was the true touchstone of an officer and a gentleman.

'The height of soldiership is to be a sportsman,' recalled General Fuller, looking back to his days as a subaltern on the eve of the Boer War. Many of his brothers-in-arms, their heads still full of what they had lately heard in the chapels and on the playing fields of their public schools, were convinced that winning mattered less than having played well. Lieutenant 'Bobo' Jelfs, an old Etonian, asked his mother whether people in Britain looked on him and his fellow defenders of Ladysmith in the light of 'rotters' or 'heroes'. His own view was simple: 'I think we have "played the game" in keeping all those Boers busy here.' The siege was being conducted with a spirit which Newbolt would have applauded; it was a house-match final where a slogging partnership of tail-enders was struggling to prevent the follow-on.[1]

Not only did the spirit of the playing field hang over the battlegrounds of Africa but the fighting itself was often rendered in the terms of a sporting contest. A small 'scrap' with the Boers in 1901 was warmly recollected by General Younghusband as 'a thoroughly sporting fight'. This was as it should be, for he and many others like him considered the Boer War as 'the last of the gentleman's wars', a conclusion which might have been contested by other participants but was understandable in the light of the soldier's experience of the First World War. The great mounted infantry sweeps across the South African veldt were likened to beating the converts, and when such operations had ended, column commanders reported with enthusiasm on the size of their 'bags' – in other words, Boer prisoners.

The experience of the sporting shoot merged with that of the battlefield in one account of a skirmish in Matabeleland in 1893: 'It was amusing to hear the shouts of joy when a Matabele was hit, every man who had fired in that direction claiming to have shot him. Perhaps this may account for the enormous totals of "killed" which we recorded: for if every man's "bag" were counted in, it would make a formidable score, far exceeding the bodies found on the field.' Even the enemy appeared to rise to the sporting occasion. One Matabele warrior won the admiration of his opponents by the way in which he ran and dodged the combined fire of four machine-guns for a few seconds before his death. One onlooker was anxious to 'snap' the corpse of 'so plucky a fellow' but his camera failed. The photographer was Captain Donovan of the Army Service Corps, who sub-titled his record of the first Matabele campaign, 'Sport and War in Zambesia'. Fellow big-game hunter and officer Sir Claude Champion de Crespigny also managed to merge sport and war during his trip to Kenya in 1905, where he, 'had the luck to arrive just in time to join the Sotik punitive expedition, so that I was able to combine a certain amount of fighting with some excellent sport'.[2]

The skills of the game-hunter were of great value on the battlefield. During the 1885 Sawakin campaign, a civilian, A. B. Wylde, was deeply impressed by the shooting of those officers who had hunted game in India: 'It was a pretty sight seeing a good shot at work, and what awe the Arabs stand in of a first-class rifle shot. The sportsman has had more to do in winning our battles for us than anyone else, and what would have become of India unless our officers, military and civilian, had been inured to field sports and ready at any moment to take the opportunity when it offered of going out to kill a man-eating tiger, a rogue elephant, or any other dangerous beast.'[3] One such officer, the Honourable Guy Dawnay, was singled out for praise as 'one of the coolest big game shots' in the entire army, whose fast and accurate shooting 'saved the lives of several of our men and officers who were being attacked by two or more Arabs'. All this made Wylde consider that Britain could gain much if it put together an army of crack sporting shots and sent them into Africa.

The British officer always enjoyed his sport and did not allow himself to be deprived of it by war. Packs of hounds were imported into Portugal and were hunted by the young bloods of Wellington's army, and during the Crimean War officers potted partridges on the hills around Balaklava. What was different in the 1880s and 1890s was that the moral and physical qualities of sportsmanship, and in particular those needed for team games, had been elevated and enshrined in a code of conduct by the public schools. When the schoolboys became officers, they took that code with them so that it came to pervade and dominate the regimental mess or wardroom. Both institutions welcomed young men who brought with them a willingness to keep to the rules, serve the team and show physical stamina. These were the outward stamp of an officer's mettle, and it was his duty to pass on his values to the men under his command. 'Lancers do not do that' were the everyday words of reproof given by junior officers to miscreant troopers in the 16th Lancers during the 1890s. They might easily have slipped from the mouth of the team captain when he admonished a novice player who had shamed his side with a foul stroke or a lapse of sporting manners. This was understandable, given the intensity of regimental loyalties and the need for a regiment to become a team in which every member knew his duty and performed it selflessly. The bonds of mutual confidence between officers and men and a sense of corporate identity, shared by all, were the strengths of a good school team and of a fighting regiment.

In retrospect this wish to invest the waging of war with the jauntiness and spirit of a sporting contest was strangely unreal, almost escapist. Since 1850 war had rapidly shed any remaining trappings of the tournament, thanks to the industrial revolution. Railways now meant that mass armies could be moved easily and quickly and fed in the front line, whilst industrial technology was arming soldiers with repeating rifles which were accurate at ranges of over a mile. By 1890 the magazine rifle meant that the fighting man could load and fire whilst hidden from his enemies, and his firepower of up to eight or nine rounds a minute was augmented by that of machine-guns like the Maxim which fired six hundred every minute. Artillery had likewise developed, and by 1900 field guns were lighter, could be fired rapidly and possessed ranges of several miles. This new weaponry was the midwife to new concepts of warfare. Concealed and entrenched soldiers, backed by artillery, could create a horrendous and seemingly impassable 'killing zone'. This gave a formidable advantage to forces in defensive positions and made offensive operations hazardous. No longer could masses of men charge forward, and advances became perilous dashes by small groups of scattered men who had to make the best possible use of cover.

The British army was well aware of these developments but it was cushioned from their consequences until the outbreak of the Boer War in 1899. For the past forty years its main battle experience had been gained in India and Africa, where native forces possessed few if any of the advantages of the new military technology. What had been learnt in these campaigns inevitably coloured the thinking of many senior officers, such as Field-

Marshal Sir Evelyn Wood who, as commander at Aldershot during the 1890s, cherished 'sporting' officers and, in the eyes of one subaltern, was wedded to tactical ideas which he had picked up in combat with Afghan and Zulu tribesmen a dozen years before. In this school of war there remained plenty of scope for the manly, sporting qualities expected of the British officer, even though the lessons learnt had little in common with the curriculum of the modern, European battlefield. This much was appreciated by Sir Horace Smith-Dorrien when he chose to leave the Egyptian army and take a place at the Staff College at Camberley. His brother officers chafed him and were at a loss to understand why he had thrown away the chance of swift promotion. He countered them with the claim that, 'One could never become an up-to-date soldier in the prehistoric warfare to be met with against the Dervishes.'[4]

Yet when British forces engaged 'prehistoric' foes, they did so with all the paraphernalia of contemporary technological war. They employed steamships and railways where they could, were armed with repeating rifles, machine-guns and shell-firing artillery and, when they became available, made use of motor vehicles and aircraft. Their opponents were not so well off. The armies of the native states of Africa often possessed firearms, but for the greater part these were single-shot, muzzle-loading pieces of the kind which had become obsolete in Europe by 1860. In pitched battles, native warriors still relied on such traditional, close-combat weapons as thrusting spears, swords, clubs and bows, arms which had rarely been seen on European battlefields since the end of the Middle Ages. Fighting with these weapons, the native had either to wait in ambush for his adversary so as to take him unawares or else rely on his own courage or religious faith and charge him in the open. His success depended upon his physical strength, fitness and skill at arms and on his being in a countryside he knew better than his enemies.

The fearlessness and ferocity of many tribesmen impressed their British opponents. In the aftermath of the battle of El Teb in 1884, Sergeant Danby of the 10th Hussars overheard his commander, General Graham, remark that he had never before witnessed such a hard-fought struggle. The sergeant agreed and wrote home that, 'Without a doubt these Arabs are the most fierce, brave, daring and unmerciful race of men in the world; they fear nothing, give and expect no mercy and they are indeed skilled with their knives, swords and clubs.'[5] There were similar expressions of awed admiration for the Dervish after Omdurman, where warriors had rushed headlong into massed rifle and machine-gun fire, heedless of massive losses. As in India, the warmest praise was for the simple, brave warrior races with whom soldiers could easily identify. For one young officer, the Zulus were 'a very noble race' whose martial pride was in danger of being sapped by too frequent contact with Europeans. The Zulus too reciprocated this respect. Several veterans of Isandlwana told Colonel Tulloch of their admiration for the courage of the embattled remnants of the 24th in the closing moments of the fight. The Colonel noted, with regret, that the influx of missionaries into Zululand had spread moral debility amongst its people.

The Zulus had been dreaded for their fighting fury, and in 1879 newly arrived young soldiers were made nervous by their officers' tales of the cunning and courage of their foes. Scared soldiers at Fort Newdigate panicked after a false alarm of a night attack, grabbed their rifles and fired wildly into the darkness. There was no assault but three British casualties, victims of confused shooting, and the fort earned itself the contemptuous nickname 'Fort Funk'. The feral skill and savagery of the native warrior could be admired but they were not expected to discountenance the British soldier.[6]

The reactions of these soldiers was understandable. The very recent defeat of British forces at Isandlwana gave substance to stories of Zulu fortitude and aptitude in making the best possible use of local terrain. After the battle, in which just under a thousand imperial troops had been killed, much blame was placed on the failure of British officers to laager their transport wagons and so turn their camp into a small fort which might have absorbed the shock of the Zulu charge. As it was, the surprised troops of the 24th Regiment were able to deploy in lines and pour a murderous volley fire into the advancing impis. Volley fire at the command of officers was the usual tactic of British formations and, since it created a 'killing zone' in which native forces were either halted or broken, it was usually successful. This much had been understood by the Zulu king, Cetshwayo, who had ordered his indunas not to seek such a battle in which he rightly concluded his impis would be destroyed. His instruction was ignored and the Zulus attacked the camp in the customary way, seeking to encircle their opponents. They suffered heavy losses but the British infantry eventually found themselves running short of ammunition and were forced to fall back, a move which gave the Zulus a chance to come to grips and turn a withdrawal into a rout. This is what happened, although small parties of British infantrymen fought back with great courage.

> The Zulus who took part in that fight spoke enthusiastically about the grand way in which the last small squares on the slope of the hill met death. With their ammunition all expended, and nothing but the bayonet left, the Zulus say the British made fun of them, chaffing and calling them to 'come on'. In the final *mêlée* the Zulus said our men fought so desperately that each soldier killed at least ten Zulus. Of one man who had taken refuge in a deep crevice in the rock they spoke with unbounded admiration. This man, all alone, kept up the fight, firing steadily, killing with every shot, until his last cartridge was gone, when he coolly fixed his bayonet and dashed out amongst them, stabbing right and left till overpowered by assegai-thrusts.[7]

What cost the British the battle was the remarkable willingness of the Zulus to endure fire and suffer losses which, together with the four hundred killed the following day at Rorke's Drift, caused a dismayed Cetshwayo to claim that an assegai had been thrust into the belly of his people. Zulu doggedness in standing their ground in the face of volley fire rather than the mulish intractability of regimental quartermasters and the immovability of their ammunition-box lids had been responsible for the British defeat.

Isandlwana may have taught the British to respect their enemies but it also confirmed Cetshwayo's fears about frontal attacks on British troops. He recognized that his only chance of victory lay in hit-and-run raids against the often ill-guarded and ponderous wagon trains which trundled along the British lines of communication. Undeterred by the losses at Isandlwana, his indunas turned down this sound scheme and looked instead for fresh traditional battles. The consequences were disastrous. For four hours impis attacked a British entrenched position at Khambula but were beaten back by rifle fire, leaving just over eight hundred dead. At Ulundi in July 1879 the Zulu fighting spirit, already chastened by losses, flagged and their charges petered out after about half an hour. Sir Evelyn Wood was surprised: 'When the attack slackened and our men began to cheer, led by men who had not been at Khambula, I angrily ordered them to be silent, saying, "The fun has scarcely begun"; but their instinct was more accurate than mine, who, having seen the Zulus come on grandly for over four hours in March, could not believe they would make so half-hearted an attack.'[8] At Khambula each infantryman had fired thirty-three rounds, at Ulundi between six and seven. As long as ammunition supplies held and a steady rate of volley fire could be sustained, imperial forces were safe from being overwhelmed by the weight of their enemies' numbers.

This was certainly the experience of the British forces at Ginginhlovu (renamed 'Gin, gin, I love you' by the other ranks) when parties of Zulus, making the best use of the long grass, began darting forwards toward the defended laager.

> They would then suddenly sink into the long grass, and nothing but puffs of curling smoke would show their whereabouts. Then they advanced again, and their bullets soon began to whistle merrily over our heads or strike the little parapet in front. We had been ordered to reserve our fire, and then fire by volleys at 400 yards' distance. The Gatling had begun, however, and it was with difficulty that I could make the order to fire heard by my company. Not ten minutes had elapsed from the time that the first moving mass of the enemy was seen among the trees on the Inyenzane to the moment we began to return their fire; so rapid had been this perfect advance on the part of our savage enemy.
>
> After the first volley, which could hardly be expected to have done much execution, since there were but a number of darting figures at irregular intervals and distances to aim at, I ordered my men to go on firing very steadily. A few men showed signs of firing wildly, but a smart rap with my stick soon helped a man to recover his self-possession.[9]

It was soon over, for 'the enemy, unable to make headway against our fire, gradually withdrew, slinking off through the long grass like whipped hounds'. It is not an inappropriate simile, since the author, Captain Edward Hutton of the 60th Rifles, wrote later to his father that he was enjoying every moment of the campaign in Zululand: 'It is to me like a shooting expedition, with just a spice of danger thrown in to make it really interesting.' For one man the spice proved too sharp, for on 6 April 1879, four days after the battle, a court martial reduced a colour sergeant of the 60th to the ranks for running off from his post.[10]

Apart from pitched battles, like Ginginhlovu, there were smaller frays when British soldiers found themselves in hand-to-hand combat and fought native warriors on more or less equal terms. Here the fighting was brutal and confused, as Lieutenant Carrington of the 24th informed a fellow officer after a skirmish against the Gaikas in Natal in February 1878. He was in command of a small section of mounted infantry which was attempting to clear a ravine of some Gaikas who possessed muskets.

> We were soon hotly engaged. The Kaffirs were in long grass and thorn trees and would hardly budge. I got within twenty yards frequently and got outflanked by them but by charging round on them and leading a lot of Fingoes [native auxiliaries] we ousted them and were then hotly engaged with a lot of devils hidden by stones and small breastworks. We led our horses and fired on them up to within twenty yards and had a right hot corner. I rode my horse and four scoundrels kept potting at me and at last hit my horse in the jaw and he spun round like a top. He was only ten yards off so I potted him with my revolver. Another of my men had his horse shot dead under him. Another knocked out of line with a bullet in the hock. Another (a man of mine) shot thro' the thigh, another dragged off his horse by a Kaffir, which Kaffir he killed, but his horse has not been seen since. Sergeant Leslie was assegaied in the hand, but knocked the fellow over with the butt end of his gun and then shot him.[11]

Carrington's men were infantrymen who had been hurriedly transformed into cavalry, of which there was a shortage in South Africa. Until reinforcements came from Britain, the army in Natal and Zululand had to make do with local volunteers from the settler communities or else create mounted infantry detachments from the line regiments. The duties of the mounted men were reconnaissance and the pursuit of broken Zulu forces, a task performed with ferocious zeal by Captain Cecil D'Arcy of the Frontier Light Horse after the fight at Hlobane. His horsemen galloped after the fleeing Zulus, 'butchering the brutes all over the place. I told the men "no quarter, boys, and remember yesterday."' The day before had witnessed a setback by the British forces with heavy losses, and D'Arcy, presumably a settler in Natal, would have added reason to hate a race which seemed to have threatened his own and his colony's existence.

There was another, more spectacular charge by the 17th Lancers, who were ordered to pursue the running Zulus after Ulundi. It was the first time that the regiment had charged since Balaklava, when it had been part of the Light Brigade. It was a thrilling moment, so much so that one officer, his jaw broken by a lead slug from a Zulu musket, bandaged it up and cantered off, sabre in hand. The same spirit infected an NCO, who wrote exultantly to his brother in Devon: 'We had a glorious go in, old boy, pig-sticking was a fool to it.' His enthusiasm seemed to know no bounds: 'You should have seen us. With tremendous shouts of "Death, Death!" we were on them. They tried lying down to escape, but it was no use, we had them anyhow, no mercy or quarter from the "Old Tots". We only stopped when we could go no further and the horses were completely done up, then we stopped a little while, after which we went to Ulundi, which we burnt.'[12]

The Zulu was traditionally unnerved by cavalry; the Dervish in the Sudan was not. In the campaigns there in 1884–5 and 1896–8 cavalrymen's duties were confined to scouting or, in the dash to save Gordon, as mounted infantry riding camels. There were, however, a few charges, but the results were discouraging since the Dervishes were well able to cope with enemies armed like themselves with sword and lance. Kitchener was displeased with the famous charge of the 21st Lancers at Omdurman, for afterwards they were in no position to carry out the task which he had allocated them, the pursuit and capture of the Khalifah. An infantry officer who had watched the charge noted that the Dervishes were 'used to cold steel, but did not flinch and though the Lancers went through them and cleared the nullah, they suffered more loss than they inflicted'.[13] It was a carping observation and one which would have induced apoplexy in a cavalry mess and won little sympathy among the public in Britain for whom the bravado of the cavalry charge still possessed, like Lady Butler's paintings, the quintessence of war's glory.

Both Zulu and Sudan campaigns were fought largely by infantrymen, regular British soldiers assisted by often quite large detachments of sailors and marines. All shared common objectives which comprised the destruction in battle of the forces of native rulers whose activities either imperilled or frustrated the furtherance of local, British interests. The best way to achieve this end was for the British forces to take the offensive and deliberately seek battles in which victory was usually assured, thanks to superior firepower and the suicidal attachment of native generals to the traditional mass attack. An offensive strategy was also essential, for it was interpreted politically as the only way to uphold and embellish imperial prestige. Wolseley, who had had plenty of experience of such operations, summed up the whole business in a brutal sentence: 'When you get niggers on the run, keep them on the run.' Yet whilst the strategic philosophy of African warfare was one of continuous offensive, battlefield tactics were defensive. Chelmsford, after the shock of Isandlwana, cautioned his subordinates 'to adhere strictly to solid formations such as square and echelon movements; the enemy was be treated as cavalry'. This doctrine was thereafter followed religiously when British forces found themselves in the field against native armies which outnumbered them and moved swiftly to attack in mass. On many campaigns the doctrine was extended and commanders built their own defences. In the Sudan *zaribahs* of mimosa scrub were thrown up when time permitted, either to defend camps or to guard formations which were threatened by Dervish attack. As the fighting columns criss-crossed the countryside of Matabeleland in 1896, they set up small earthen forts which were garrisoned, nails driven into the bush to remind its people of the permanence of the British South Africa Company's power and to deter insurrection against it.

In seeking to bring their enemies to battle in Zululand or in the Sudan, British generals had to proceed with care, for in little-known country their forces were in danger of ambush. In the Sudan, columns of British soldiers and sailors marched in a loose square formation which enclosed the supply animals and were preceded by cavalry screens which scoured the scrub for a sight of the enemy masses. When attack was imminent, the units would close up and form the classic square. This was the formation which Chelmsford adopted to meet the Zulu charge at Ulundi, and his example was repeated in the Sudan in 1884 and 1885. Here was the brave face of imperial battle beloved by artists and magazine illustrators, who pictured the unshakeable British square, each man firm-jawed and resolute, beset by fiendish and sinewy Dervishes, their eyes alight with fanaticism. This was the scenario chosen by Newbolt for his paean on the sporting warrior, and like the painters he was not completely out of touch with reality. For the soldier marching, manœuvring and fighting were the occasions when years of parade-ground drill and training counted, for an automatic response to the words of command and steadiness became matters of life and death. In these battles every soldier had to have unquestioning faith in his officers and a willingness to obey their orders swiftly. After that great epic of the imperial battlefield, Rorke's Drift, a subaltern of the 24th concluded, 'The men have the pluck, but without a good officer they are like sheep.'

The struggles between the infantry squares and the Dervishes followed a pattern in which the tribesmen rushed through the hurricane of rifle and machine-gun fire and tried to come to grips with sword and spear. They seldom did so, but at Abu Klea there were moments when they did and the square fractured. From his section, Lieutenant Count Gleichen did not see the inrush and was suddenly embroiled in a scrimmage.

I found myself lifted off my legs amongst a surging mass of Heavies and Sussex [Regiment], who had been carried back against the camels by the impetuous rush of the enemy. Telling the men to stand fast, I forced my way through the jam to see what had happened. Heavies, Sussex, and camels of all sorts were pressing with terrific force on our thin double rank, and it seemed every moment as if it must give; but it didn't.

On getting through to the other side of the press, a gruesome sight was seen. Immediately in front were swarms of Arabs, in desperate hand-to-hand fight with our men, hacking, hewing, hamstringing and yelling like a crowd of black devils on a ground literally piled up with dead and dying. On the right the Mounted Infantry were pouring in their fire with deadly effect, the niggers falling in hundreds. At my side Dr Briggs, minus his helmet, his patients all killed or scattered, had drawn his sword, and was frantically endeavouring to rally the men near him. I shouted myself hoarse trying to get the men to aim carefully, but my voice was lost in the din. A rain of bullets whizzed dangerously close past my head from the rifles behind into the fighting mass in front. Numbers of Arabs went down in that hail, and I fear several Englishmen too. Everything depended on the right and front faces standing fast.[14]

Discipline had saved the day; unengaged rear ranks turned about and poured their fire into the centre and shattered the Arabs as well as killing a few of their own men.

For newspapermen and their readers at least, the British soldier's deadly cool in handling the bayonet was a token not only of military but of national superiority. More usually the struggle was one of .45 Martini bullets against religious frenzy. This was certainly the case at Tamai in 1884, as it was seen by a civilian:

We stood and watched the battle; the right of the Arabs was just coming into action, and their formation, which was like a half-moon, overlapped the front and right face of the 1st Brigade right up to the zareba. Buller had his men well in hand, just as if they were at a review. He commenced firing volleys at them. The Arabs who were in irregular formation, and from three to ten deep, came along at a run, and it was just like a big black wave running up to a beach. It began to break on the crest, the white foam being represented by the men that fell simultaneously with every volley, and the way began to grow less the more it neared the square. Within 250 yards it nearly ceased, and not one man could get near enough to use his spear. It was an awful sight, and as an exhibition of pluck, or rather fanaticism, it could not be equalled. Poor deluded Arabs! thinking that they could do anything with their spears and swords out in the open against disciplined British troops armed with rifles.[15]

Yet for the soldier standing in the square, waiting for his orders, the sight of the Dervish charge was terrifying, and the terror must have been more intense with the knowledge that the enemy would never take prisoners. For one soldier of the York and Lancaster Regiment it was too much, and he threw down his rifle and scurried to the centre of the square. A week later at Sawakin a court martial found him guilty of cowardice, and he was sentenced to two years hard labour, an unhappy exception to a rule of remarkable courage.[16]

Unlike journalists, the fighting soldier saw little of a battle. He faced his front, listened to his orders, loaded, fired and ejected the cartridge case. The Martini had a mean kick, and shoulders soon became bruised, whilst fingers were seared by the barrel which heated up quickly or by cartridge cases which jammed in the breach. What he could see was immediately to his front and was soon wreathed in black powder smoke. That at the battle of Bida in Nigeria in 1897 it was so thick that an officer manning a Maxim gun could not see his target, although the porters who had carried the gun were able to run forward to watch the effect of its fire, a sight which made them dance for joy.

After battle, most soldiers who wrote home offered few details of the fighting they had just experienced. The day after El Teb, Sergeant Danby of the 10th Hussars apologized to his cousin Adie: 'I would here like to describe all the awful deeds of yesterday, but time does not allow.'[17] What he did write contained nothing of the hand-to-hand fighting in which his unit had engaged but he did remind her to buy the *Graphic*, whose war artist had included him in a sketch of the march to Tokar. Likewise a survivor of Rorke's Drift who wrote to his brother referred him to the newspapers for a description of the events he had just been part of. It was left to newspapermen and officers writing memoirs to provide vivid word-pictures of the fighting. When he kept a diary or wrote home, the private soldier was more concerned with the problems of daily survival than with what he did on the battlefield or what he saw others do, and so his prose centres on discomforts and diet.

What people at home did read of eyewitness accounts of

imperial pitched battles did not always please them. Press reports of El Teb and Tamai in 1884 provoked some Liberal anti-Imperialist MPs to ask why so few Dervish prisoners had been taken and to draw from the Secretary for War some statement about the alleged killing of wounded men on the battlefield. To fend off these questioners, the Secretary telegraphed General Graham and within a day received an answer which graphically described the aftermaths of the two recent battles.

> At El Teb no wounded man injured unless he attacked our men. 15 prisoners were made by Gen. Davis. 2 others feigning death attempted to murder a Sergeant of Black Watch. My Aide de Camp Lt. Scott rescued five men from a heap of wounded at El Teb, of whom one made an attempt to attack with his knife but was disarmed. Of these I sent one with a letter to the Garrison of Tokar; the rest were afterwards released at El Teb. At Tamaii the wounded continued to fight to the last. General Stewart was nearly stabbed while giving water to a wounded man – Colonel Moffat R.E. & a mounted infantryman were stabbed and injured by men feigning to be dead. Many other cases occurred. Generally speaking the enemy neither gave, nor accepted quarter, & our men were obliged to kill them in self defence. It is however no question of colour or nationality – Our men like these blacks who fight so well, & are friendly with them when they will allow them. If wounded European soldiers were to continue fighting they would be killed by their enemy in self defence.[18]

Others present bore out Graham's testimony, although a few of the British soldiers surprised and attacked by seemingly dead Dervishes were in fact scouring the battlefield for souvenirs. A few may have hoped to have found something of value. The Abyssinian irregular horsemen did, however, wander about and kill wounded men, an activity which was not checked, on the grounds that they were taking revenge for the deaths of colleagues slain in earlier battles. Similar scenes followed the Sudan battles of the 1896–8 campaign, when some wounded Dervishes either attempted to stab British and Egyptian soldiers or else cried out to them for the *coup de grace*. British officers were at pains to point out that death at the hands of a Christian would secure an immediate place in paradise for the Dervish.

Whilst officers and men often expressed admiration for their foes, there were often undercurrents of fear and contempt which could explode after the tension of battle had passed. After the defence of Rorke's Drift, shaken and wearied soldiers took a

Zulu, who had fallen their prisoner, and hanged him from a 'gallows' which had originally been put up to stretch and dry ox-hides.[19] It was an action which could be understood, if not pardoned, by men who had fought for many hours in fear of death, who had seen their comrades die and who knew that the rest of their battalion had been wiped out and that Zulus had tortured captured drummer boys.

The same purblind, harsh anger infected the troops who fought against the Mashona and Matabele in 1896. The native rebels had 'gone beyond their own etiquette of war, and have killed our women and children', and this, in turn, had generated a spirit of revenge which had not been felt by British troops since the suppression of the Indian Mutiny nearly forty years before. What F. C. Selous identified as 'the latent ferocity of the civilised race' ran riot on and off the battlefield. A professional soldier who came across the bodies of murdered settlers felt this wild spirit: 'I left the laager that day holding staunchly the opinions of Mr Labouchere and his supporters, condemnatory of the slaughter of the blackman; but a quarter of an hour among such sights as these sufficed to convert me into a zealous advocate for their prompt extermination.'

At Westminster Labouchere and his anti-Imperialist allies pressed Joseph Chamberlain, the Colonial Secretary, for his comments on press tales of no quarter being given to natives and of running men being ridden down by horsemen, a feature of the battlefield which somehow distressed them. Chamberlain side-stepped the question of needless brutality and asserted that, 'I will make it my care to see that considerations of humanity are not lost sight of as far as is consistent with the suppression of rebellion, the punishment of murderers, and the prevention of the recurrence of the present troubles.' What armies did on distant battlefields was anyway 'beyond the power of any administration to prevent'. Reports of these cross-bench wrangles galled the fighting men in Rhodesia, one of whom damned 'armchair philosophers in England, who can see no good in a colonist, nor any harm in a savage'.[20] For their part it was natural that the political enemies of Empire were quick to condemn it on the grounds of what occurred on its battlefields.

In fighting battles against Zulus or Dervishes, British generals became host to a strange phantom, a belief that they knew the type of gesture which would make an impression on the native mind. In offering cash for the head of Osman Diqna in 1884, General Graham thought that he was following a readily understood local practice, although news of the incident provoked disquiet in Britain. Likewise in 1898 Kitchener had the captured Mahmud dragged in chains through the streets of Berber, and after Omdurman had the Mahdi's bones exhumed. For a short time he considered having the skull sent to a museum in London, no doubt as *quid pro quo* for the Mahdi's use of Gordon's skull as an inkpot, but then, in the face of criticism at home, he had it thrown in the Nile. His justification was to prevent the bones becoming religious relics.

In Zululand in 1879 Wolseley sanctioned the use of torture by forces seeking to find the whereabouts of Cetshwayo and lamented that he could not, for political reasons, chastise the Zulus with a strategy which was downright barbaric:

> Up to the present beyond shooting & wounding some 10,000 men, we have not really punished the people as a nation, and our leniency in now allowing all the people to return to their Kraals, retaining all their cattle, may possibly be taken for fear. I should therefore like to let loose the Swazies upon these northern tribes at once, but I have to think of the howling Societies at home who have sympathy with all black men whilst they care nothing for the miseries & cruelties inflicted on their own kith and kin who have the misfortune to be located near these interesting niggers.[21]

Later the Swazis had their chance at Wolseley's bidding when large numbers joined his column which had been sent to overthrow the Pedi and their king, Sekukuni, at the end of 1879. After British troops had stormed and taken Sekukuni's stronghold, the Swazis moved in to kill men, women and children, a sight which sickened Wolseley's *aide*, Lieutenant MacCalmont.[22]

Such a scene, far from journalist and war artist, was mercifully rare on the imperial battlefield, although it was as much part of the story of the British conquest of Africa as Newbolt's broken but resolute square. The campaign against Sekukuni belonged to another kind of imperial warfare, the 'small' wars of punitive columns and small-scale expeditions against local rulers with limited forces but a will to defy British authority. For the most part these wars were fought in West, East and Central Africa, and like the larger campaigns they were undertaken as offensives whose common objective was to display the invincibility of British arms and the folly of resistance. Unlike their larger counterparts, these actions were fought by native troops under

British officers, although in coastal regions men o'war and their crews were brought in as reinforcements.

Battles, when they occurred, were small-scale affairs, for few of the native rulers in East or West Africa could muster forces as large as those commanded by the rulers of Zululand or the Sudan. In practice, this kind of warfare became the speciality of a handful of British regimental officers who had sought employment and advancement in colonial or Chartered Company forces. They brought with them the habits and training of the British army which they attempted, usually with much success, to instil into native infantrymen and constables. At the end of the day, it was hoped that the native recruit would respond to orders and fight like a British regular, for it was only by immediate, unquestioning response to commands that he could march, change formation and fire volleys in such a way as to overcome his enemies in jungle and bush. After the 1897 Bida-Ilorin campaign, Major Arnold, commander of the Royal Niger Company's forces, felt well pleased with the fruits of years of drill and training. He invested his native constables with the highest possible accolade when he reported on the campaign to the War Office. 'It was', he observed, 'difficult for officers to realise that they were not commanding European troops.' A subordinate British officer echoed this judgement, applauding the coolness and steadiness of even the reputedly unwarlike Yoruba as they came to 'feel and know the power firearms and discipline gave them'. 'Implicit obedience to orders saved the day' when units were in tight spots or under attack from opponents who outnumbered them.[23]

In essence the doctrine of the small war was the same as for the larger. Once challenged or disobeyed, the local British authorities had to respond immediately and take the offensive against the source of resistance. Where possible this meant that native forces had to be brought to battle and beaten decisively. A signal victory demonstrated the foolhardiness of flouting the government's will. The message was bluntly delivered by Colonel Winton to the Yonni chiefs of Sierra Leone in 1887 after their defeat at his hands: 'The Queen has shown you her power by sending her force and taking the country which now belongs to me and the governor. When people make war, those who have been conquered have to suffer for their misdeeds.'[24] The chiefs were then given a warning demonstration of Maxim fire and 'were much impressed.'

The instrument of such chastisement was the fighting

Column warfare: Before battle – native constables from the Niger Coast Protectorate pause during their march to Benin, 1897.

column, a force of police or infantry, well armed and often with a high proportion of machine-guns, which was capable of engaging many times its own numbers. In East and West Africa the number of troops available was limited, and so commanders were often unable to establish bases along the line of march. It was therefore necessary for the column to be self-sufficient, carrying its own ammunition, medical supplies, food and, in Somaliland, water. These were carried by native porters in East and West Africa, camels in Somaliland and wagons and pack animals in Rhodesia. This requirement created many difficulties, not least the need to give adequate protection to the cumbersome lines of porters or camels which formed either the body or the tail of the column and were vulnerable to ambush. A further problem was that of terrain, for thick bush or jungle forced columns into single file and what paths existed were narrow or little known. One answer was a local guide, but these were often unreliable or reluctant. 'A most timorous individual' who was showing the way through the Gambian bush for the columns hunting Foda Sillah in 1894 lost his way many times through either ignorance or terror.

That this fellow may have been terrified was not surprising. In West Africa the native response to the column was ambush, and nearly all the fighting in this area was confined to sharp skirmishes with hidden or semi-hidden foes. In 1887 the Yonni of Sierra Leone crept through the forest and the bush so that it was

176

'impossible to see them'. On one day a column was ambushed six times within two miles, and its commander never saw more than fifty of his opponents during several weeks of marching and fighting. This experience was shared by the forces which had been sent out to take Foda Sillah and destroy his war bases in the Gambia. The operation had started badly after a naval landing party, waiting on a beach for their boats, had been fired on from the thick forest a few yards away and suffered several casualties. In the operations which followed, the columns of soldiers from the West Indies Regiment found themselves fired on by unseen sharpshooters on either side of their path through the bush and jungle. On one occasion this fire was directed by a native perched high in a tree overlooking their route.

To meet these emergencies, the officers in command relied on the drill and training of their men. As it moved through the bush, the column was in three sections, each of a hundred men. The first was the advance guard which was followed by 1½ companies (150 men) with a Maxim gun and seven-pounder, both dismantled and carried in pieces on the heads of porters. The rearguard comprised fifty men, who protected the remaining porters with their loads of ammunition, food and medical supplies. When the trackway was narrow, the whole column processed in single file and was at its most vulnerable. To meet ambush in these conditions, a special drill had been devised by which the front rank halted, turned right and fired volleys into the bush at the commands of an officer, and the second rank turned leftwards and did likewise. Where the bush was less dense, it was possible to send out flanking parties which fanned out ahead to draw fire or give warning of an ambush. After 1900 and the stern lessons of the Ashante campaign, it became common practice for the men in the flanking parties to work in pairs: one would cut through the foliage with his machete whilst his companion kept watchful guard with his rifle. Contact between the flank men and the rest of the column was maintained either by shouting or by blows on a whistle. Sometimes, when an ambush was anticipated, a soldier was ordered to shin up a tree and scan the surrounding countryside.

Battle in this countryside and in these conditions was often sudden and sharp. When one of the columns chasing Foda Sillah came across one of his stockades, it halted, assembled its seven-pounder and rocket tubes and began a bombardment which soon broke the defenders' nerve, so they fled. After what had seemed a cheap success, the column advanced and entered the

177

stockade, and the soldiers settled down to cook their meals. Within a few moments sentries came running back with the news that a concentration of Foda Sillah's warriors was advancing to retake the stockade. The subsequent engagement was recorded in the diary of a British officer:

> We manned the stockade and replied to their fire with volleys, keeping the men down under cover. The enemy still kept creeping up closer, the more advanced posting themselves behind clumps of thick cotton trees, about 50 yds from the stockade, from which they boldly stepped out to deliver their fire, and then jumped back under cover to re-load. Major Madden ordered Capt. Westmorland's Co. to deploy outside so as to bring a cross fire on these trees. A number of the enemy were using Martinis which they had captured from the Navy; the majority used long guns, either flint or percussion, which they loaded up with 4 or 5 hammered iron bullets, & it was these that did all the damage.
>
> Endeavoured with varying success to get the men behind the trees when they exposed themselves. The gun, maxim and rockets were brought into action, and the fire directed upon the bush from which the heaviest firing came. The rockets were very useful, the first one particularly so, it went very low and set fire to all the long grass in its flight, and bursting caused a great yell from the bush. Matters went on like this for over ½ an hour, we had 1 Sergt. & 8 men down, Major Madden then ordered Captain Westmorland's Company to charge with the bayonet, which they did spiritedly, I accompanied them, & shot the man behind the nearest tree with my revolver. The enemy could not stand the bayonet, and all fled into the bush appearing utterly demoralised. We advanced to the edge of the thick bush and fired a few volleys after them.[25]

The natives' precipitate flight was, in all likelihood, the consequence of their lack of bladed weapons with which to fend off the bayonets. They were soon back, and the column had to endure several more days of sniping. Foda Sillah's war camp was razed, his stocks of guns and powder destroyed, and he scurried off to the safety of neighbouring French Senegal. The column's worst experience was exposure to the fire from two gunboats, anchored off-shore, whose shells fell short during the bombardment of one war camp. This was all the more vexing since the soldiers found that those naval shells which had dropped on the target had failed to explode.

Battle against any African fighting force, like Foda Sillah's, which possessed firearms and knew how to use them effectively, made the progress of a column risky. The columns sent to relieve Kumasi in the Gold Coast (Ghana) suffered grievously from repeated ambushes by Ashante warriors, many of them marksmen. Major Aplin's column of 250 lost five dead and 139 wounded after a series of ambushes, including one in which their assailants had felled a large tree across their track. From behind this bulwark Ashante sharpshooters poured a deadly fire which threw back a party which charged them with bayonets. A similar experience occurred to Major Trenchard in Southern Nigeria in 1905 when his column was halted by a mighty trench and suddenly beset by hundreds of Ibo warriors. His men were unable to form line and fire volleys, but Trenchard rose to the occasion by firing flares whose explosions, high above their heads, terrified the Ibo and sent them running off. The more usual response was to pour volley and machine-gun fire into the bush in the hope that some of the men concealed there might be hit. This had been the pattern during the week's march through the jungle to Benin in 1897, and although the expedition was successful, it was thought to have wasted much ammunition and inflicted few casualties. The answer proved to be a more careful reconnaissance of the line of march which was embodied in the drill of the West Africa Frontier Force in the 1900s with much success.

Whatever the countryside and whoever the opponent, vigilance was always necessary in such warfare. During operations in Jubaland in 1898, a well-armed company of forty Bombay infantrymen under the command of a native officer was suddenly rushed and engulfed by Somalis, who had lain in wait for it, hidden in thick bush on either side of a narrow track.[26] The officer had taken no precautions, and so his men had not fixed their bayonets, which placed them at a disadvantage against their sword-, spear- and shield-armed adversaries. In the hand-to-hand combat which followed, twenty-seven sepoys were killed, including their officer, before the rest coalesced into a tight knot from which they were able to drive off their attackers with volley fire.

The night attack was the form of sudden ambush which was most feared, with good reason, and commanders of columns were well advised to see that their camps were well protected by night. As they marched to Ilorin, the forces of the Royal Niger Company set up camps which were guarded by tripwires which ignited lamps which would alert sentries. The lack of such precautions could invite disaster, as the forces involved in the Blue Nile expedition of 1908 discovered. Sent to arrest Abdul al

Qadir, the column's commander had neglected to post adequate sentries, laid out his perimeter in the form of an extended semi-circle rather than the traditional square and did not protect it with a thorn *zaribah*.[27] Qadir, anxious to get his hands on the rifles of the Sudanese company, rushed the camp at 2.30 in the morning with five columns of Dervishes. Crying "Allah", the warriors broke through the thin cordon attacking the Sudanese infantrymen, who fought back in small knots, using their bayonets. Their dazed officers ran from their tents and brought their men into an oblong formation around the wounded. By morning the Dervishes had been driven off, leaving thirty-five dead. The British force had lost seventeen killed and thirty-nine wounded out of just over a hundred. Experiences like those taught British officers in command of columns to be wary and never to under-estimate the determination and ingenuity of their opponents.

Qadir's night attack was a part of a much wider effort by African rulers to discover ways in which they could counter-balance the enormous advantages of the heavily armed columns which entered their countries and forced them to bow to the imperial will of Britain. In Matabeleland in 1893 the small columns of the British South Africa Company had inflicted a series of heavy defeats on the Matabele, who, in the rueful admission of one warrior, found that they could not 'stand against the Maxim'. Three years later, when they were ready to try to regain their independence, the Matabele had evolved new methods of warfare. No longer would the massed impis, armed with shield and assegai, charge in the open and offer themselves as targets for machine-guns. Instead the warriors turned to guns, a shift of weaponry in part made possible by Rhodes's delivery of a thousand Martini rifles to Lobengula in 1889 as part of the deal by which he gained permission to settle and look for gold in the Matabele kingdom. With these weapons, the Matabele fought a guerrilla campaign with tactics based upon skirmishing and shooting from cover.

The response of the Rhodesian authorities was to criss-cross the disaffected areas with columns of mounted men, for there were no mosquitoes or tsetse flies in this country which could infect and kill horses and pack-animals. The self-contained columns, usually possessing one or more Maxim gun, spent long periods in the saddle riding over a terrain which was well watered and grew sufficient fodder for the horses. Still, as in the

Column warfare: Waggons of the British South Africa Company police in defensive laager, Mashonaland, 1890.

Boer War a few years after, many horses were worn to death by the pace. The mounted columns' purpose was to hunt down their enemies and engage them. Sometimes they caught up with and took their foes by surprise, and sometimes they were themselves ambushed. Then wagons, circled into a laager, served as both a camp and a strongpoint against a heavy attack. This was its value when a party of roughriders from Giffard's Horse was caught on the hop by a large party of rifle-armed Matabele close to Salisbury: 'Giffard then sent out a galloper to call the troops into the laager, not a moment too soon. Captain Fynn's troops was fairly rushed by the enemy who poured a fire into them at close range. Here Trooper M'Kenzie was shot through the head and dropped dead from his horse. Trooper Fielding was wounded in the leg and his horse shot under him. Captain Fynn, however, brought his men into the laager in good order, returning the enemy's fire.'[28] Out of this scramble of horses and bullets, the troop could dismount and fire from under the wagons. Such sharp and confused engagements were rare; for the greater part, the campaign comprised long rides in which columns combed the country for signs of their enemies. This was the 'scouting' war which Baden-Powell fought and relished, developing his theories and techniques of tracking and fieldcraft.

To win, British forces and their native allies turned to bush-craft and stealth, tracking the guerrillas' spoor and stealing up

181

on their camps. The excitement was pure champagne for Baden-Powell, who recalled with Hentyesque enthusiasm the storming of a Matabele stronghold in the Matopo Hills:

> We could see the enemy close to us in large numbers, taking up their position in a similar stronghold. Now and again two or three of them would come out of a cave on a flat rock and dance a war-dance at our troops, which they could see in the distance, being quite unsuspicious of our near presence. They were evidently rehearsing what they would do when they caught the white man among the rocks, and they were shouting all sorts of insults to the troops, more with a spirit of bravado than with any idea of their reaching their ears at that distance. Interesting as the performance was, we did not sit it out for long, but put an abrupt end to it by suddenly loosing a volley at them at short range and from this unexpected quarter.[29]

Baden-Powell's party then scrambled off, and the machine-guns were brought up for the main assault. They were manhandled by Cape Boys across streams, through bogs and up the slopes of the kopje. The fighting which followed resolved itself into a series of small struggles on the hillside and amongst the rocks.

> For the systematic attack on the stronghold a portion of it is assigned to each company, and it is a pleasing sight to see the calm and ready way in which they set to work. They crowd into narrow, bushy paths between the koppies, and then swarm out over the rocks from whence the firing comes, and very soon the row begins. A scattered shot here and there, and then a rattling volley; the boom of the elephant gun roaring dully from inside a cave is answered by the sharp crack of a Martini Henry; the firing gradually wakes up on every side of us, the weird whisk of a bullet overhead is varied by the hum of a leaden-coated stone or the shriek of a pot-leg fired from a Matabele big-bore gun; and when these noises threaten to become monotonous, they are suddenly enlivened by the hurried energetic "tap, tap, tap" of the Maxim or the deafening "pong" of the Hotchkiss. As you approach the koppies, excitement seems to be in the air; they stand so still and harmless-looking, and yet you know that from several at least of these holes and crannies the enemy are watching you, with finger on trigger, waiting for a fair chance. But it is from the least expected quarter that a roar comes forth and a cloud of smoke and dust flies up at your feet.
>
> It's laughable to watch a Cape Boy prying into a cave with his long bayonet held out before him, as if to pick some human form of winkle from the shell. Suddenly he fires into the smoke which spurts from the cave before him. Too late; he falls and then tries to

rise – his leg is shattered. A moment later, three of his comrades are round him; they dash past him and disappear into the hole, two dull, thud-like shots within, and presently they come out again, jabbering and gesticulating to each other; then they pick up the injured man by his arms and drag him out into the open, and, leaving him there for the doctor's party to find, they are quickly back again for further sport.

For Baden-Powell it was truly a sportsman's war, and like many true sportsmen, many of the fighting men were amateurs who were just as happy to take shots at a lion which strolled too close to a column as they were to kill Matabele. Stripped of its sporting language, this was an arduous and brutal struggle in which the columns ranged the countryside, burnt kraals, machine-gunned and stormed stockades and cornered and overwhelmed resisters in remote caves. It was a warfare of improvisation in which fighting techniques were learnt on the march and in battle and there was little room for the manœuvres of the drill book.

Whilst the Matabele turned to guerrilla warfare, other African peoples and their leaders looked for other ways in which to defeat fighting columns. The simplest and most effective was to avoid battle altogether and so deprive the enemy of his objective. This was the strategy of an Arab warlord and slaver, Raschid bin Mubaraq, whose brutality along the Kenya coast provoked an expedition against him in 1895.[30] Warships were summoned and landing parties put ashore but Mubaraq skipped off, hid up-country and finally fled to German East Africa, where he sought sanctuary. All that the sailors and marines could do was to destroy his strongholds and villages near the coast, exchange fire with some of his adherents and then return to their ships. It was very frustrating, and one senior officer complaining to the Admiralty suggested a prolonged campaign of pacification. Since 'the enemy escapes into the bush and cannot be got at', the naval columns were performing a futile task and losing men to no purpose. The answer was to garrison Indian troops in the towns and then deploy a regiment of Sudanese in the countryside to come to grips with the elusive foe. This cost money, and the colonial government had little.

Where it was not possible for the column to gain a decisive victory, commanders fell back on an expedient which had become customary during the sporadic campaigns on the North West Frontier of India, the destruction of the enemy's resources. This occurred in 1886 when men o'war steamed up the Niger

Column warfare: Indian troops with camel transport crossing the Somaliland interior, 1903.

after the sacking of the Royal Niger Company's depot near Patani. There was no resistance, save for some harmless shots from cannon mounted on the river bank, and so naval detachments went ashore and fired canoes, coconut palms and huts at each village. Crops and livestock were destroyed during the Somaliland campaign of 1902–4 which led to a famine in which many thousands, including women and children, died.[31] Since Abdullah Muhammad Hassan had not given his pursuers the opportunity of fighting a decisive pitched battle, their only choice was to ravage his potential resources and return to the coast. The political effect was negligible, for the Mullah remained as strong as ever he was. This type of warfare distressed many of those taking part. Among these was Captain Austin, a young officer serving in one of the columns which was pursuing fleeing Sudanese mutineers in Uganda in 1898. After one skirmish he discovered that amongst the casualties were some of the wives and children of the mutineers. 'Unfortunately there must be from 10 to 15 of these wretched women and children wounded, which emphasises the hateful type of warfare we are indulging in.' The author later published an account of his experiences but omitted this type of detail, which his superiors might well have considered unsuitable reading for the public.[32]

A more robust and commonplace military view of dealing with Africans on campaign was expressed by Baden-Powell. He was convinced that they must 'be ruled with a hand of iron in a

184

velvet glove: and if they writhe under it, and don't understand the force of it, it is no use to add more padding – you must take off the glove for a moment and show them the hand. They will understand and obey.' This was a view which was well appreciated by other commanders, especially those who found themselves in charge of small forces in remote areas peopled by hostile natives. This precariousness was understood by Colonel Meinertzhagen, then a junior officer, in Kenya: 'Here we are, three white men in the heart of Africa, with 20 nigger soldiers and 50 nigger police, 68 miles from doctors and reinforcements, administering and policing a district inhabited by half a million well-armed savages who have only recently come into touch with the white man.'[33]

Faced with recalcitrance or uprising, a junior officer in such a position could easily show the iron fist in the form of swift and overwhelming retaliation designed to deter by terror. In 1902 Meinertzhagen discovered that a European settler had been murdered by natives in a peculiarly vile manner and decided to make a signal example of the culprits' village:

> I gave orders that every living thing except the children should be killed without mercy. I hated the work and was anxious to get through with it. So soon as we could see to shoot we closed in. Several of the men tried to break out but were immediately shot. I then assaulted the place before any defence could be prepared. Every soul was either shot or bayoneted, and I am happy to say that no children were in the village. They, with the younger women had already been removed by the villagers to the forest. We burned all the huts and razed the banana plantations to the ground.
>
> In the open space in the centre of the village was a sight which horrified me – a naked white man pegged out on his back, mutilated and disembowelled, his body used as a latrine by all and sundry who passed by.

This retribution was undertaken at Meinertzhagen's command and was his own responsibility, since his political officer had retreated into a nerveless, legal neutrality. There were no repercussions for either man.

This was an atrocity which was contrary to the accepted conventions of war in Europe, which forbade violence against those who were unable to defend themselves. Did such conventions extend to Africa? For some commanders they did. Colonel Warren, who commanded columns in northern Cape Colony in 1879, forbade the shelling of encampments which were known to contain women and children. Elsewhere, and on occasions where small numbers of Europeans found themselves isolated and faced with a hostile population, it was easy for the conventions of humanity to be abandoned by frightened and desperate soldiers. If their fellow-countrymen had been murdered or ill-used, as in Rhodesia in 1896, deeper passions were aroused. During the 1919 uprising in Egypt, when rioters had slain British officers, the authorities hit out blindly in the conviction that terror would induce a cowed docility. Lieutenant Mackie, a young officer like many others awaiting demobilization, remembered how local forces from the Bilhars garrison rode out in small units to bring back 'agitators' who were known to be stirring up nearby villages.[34] When these 'paid' agents were taken, they were brought back to the camp for questioning, a task performed by a sergeant major. He 'carried a rhinoceros hide sjambok or whip, and yells sometimes heard from his quarters' were a testimony of his methods. Everyone was nervy and there was something close to panic in the isolated camp for a Ghurka infantryman turned a machine-gun on a mass of Turkish POWs whose protest was interpreted as the start of a break-out. Many were killed before an officer pulled the soldier away, but this and much else took place away from the eyes of higher authority and newspapermen.

However reprehensible, such incidents were the unavoidable product of the small wars of Africa where the prevailing doctrines of the period called for a fast and overwhelming offensive against resistance of all kinds. Yet British Military Intelligence was able to remark on the severity with which the German authorities in Tanganyika put down the 1905–6 revolt there. Six chiefs were hanged in Dar es Salaam, and it was rumoured that out of thirty boys, each the son of a chief, fifteen were shot whilst the rest were sent back to their villages to spread the news of what had happened.[34] On the other side of the continent, the Hereros of Namibia found that the cost of resistance to the Master Race was shipment by rail into the desert, there to be left to die. Here, as in Tanganyika, Rhodesia and, for that matter, the Great Plains of the United States, a vicious edge had been given to colonial warfare by the presence of European settlers who were hungry for land which had either been cleared of its inhabitants or peopled by cowed natives who would serve as a workforce. This pattern would repeat itself in Algeria and Palestine.

By 1914 the British had all but finished their conquest of Africa, although the colonial authorities were still troubled by occasional but small-scale outbreaks of lawlessness and disobedience which necessitated the despatch of fighting columns into disaffected areas. Yet at this time many military minds were considering a replacement for the cumbersome and often expensive columns. When examining the problems posed by Abdullah Muhammad Hassan in Somaliland in 1915, Colonel Cubitt decided that the only answer was the use of aircraft. Aircraft were fast, and their range meant that they could easily detect forces in the bush which might otherwise have remained hidden from forces on the ground. They could fly great distances into the remotest districts and were not hindered by such physical obstacles as rivers or waterless deserts. Aircraft were well armed with machine-guns and could carry small bombs tucked under their wings which enabled them to strike hard against enemies who lacked any means to fight back. The aeroplane was therefore an ideal alternative to the column, and the Colonel urged its use against the Mullah, who was still defiant in his inaccessible desert strongholds. 'In a country of great distances and no roads, we should not be able to surprise him really effectively except by air,' argued the Colonel.

In 1919, with the war in Europe and the Middle East over, the Colonel's suggestion was acted upon. The aircraft carrier HMS *Ark Royal* delivered six crated DH9 fighters to Berbera, and Somali labourers prepared a landing strip at Eil Dur Elan which had been designated as the RAF base for the operation.[35] The aircraft were armed with machine-guns and bombs, twenty pounds of high explosive and twelve-pound incendiaries, which were to be dropped on the Mullah's forts at Medishe, Jidali and Taleh. Special targets were the vast herds of camels which had been, in the previous campaigns, the means by which he and his meynie had slipped past the punitive columns. On the ground, detachments of the local camel corps were ordered to intercept any of the Mullah's forces in the field which had been previously detected by the aircraft.

Before the first raid, at the end of January 1920, a single aircraft flew to the Mullah's headquarters and showered it with leaflets in Arabic which were designed to spread alarm amongst his supporters. The tone of the message owed much to Rider-Haggard but offered little hint of the terror which would follow:

This letter is sent by the British *Wali* [governor] of the Somalis to the Dervishes of the Mullah, Mohammed bin Abdullah Hassan. It is carried by British officers, who, like birds of the air, fly far and fast. Their journey from me to you will occupy but one hour. Now listen to my words. The day of destruction of the Mullah and his power is at hand. He is a tyrant who has destroyed the country; and this will be. The arm of the British government is long. BUT I tell you this one thing. My quarrel is with the Mullah and his leaders and not with his *meahs* [followers]. And in the past I have spared the lives of Dervishes who have willingly left the Mullah. Some, indeed, have been given government work. None have been killed or harmed, although the Mullah has lied to you about this and deceived you. Now today also, when you are in my hands I will give you the *amman* [peace] of the British government if you will surrender. And to your leaders I give no *amman* at all. These men have deserved the punishment they will get and I offer a reward for their capture.

Their names:

Muhammed bin Abdullah Hassan, Ogaden Bagheis . . . 5,000 rupees [£150].

And so on through his kinsfolk and leading followers.[36]

A day after this had fallen and had, presumably, been read by the Mullah, the raids began. Jidali and stock grazing close by were bombed on 21 January, and the same day Medishe was hit. Here one bomb killed the Mullah's uncle and singed his own robes. For the next fourteen days further sorties were flown against the forts and fleeing columns of Somalis. At the same time local land forces chased what was left of the Mullah's army, in co-operation with the RAF. Two naval landing parties, armed with Lewis light machine-guns and hand-grenades, stormed the Mullah's coastal castle at Galibaribur and took it. Many Somalis were killed, including seventeen members of the Mullah's family, although he got away, to die a natural death within the year. The warfare of the Western Front had been imported into Africa to excise the last resister to British rule.

There was much argument after the 1920 operations in Somaliland between the traditionalists who advanced the claim of the camel corps as the major cause of the Mullah's overthrow and the modernists who championed the RAF and its fighter bombers. The first alleged that the bombing caused few deaths (forty at Medishe), that the desired element of surprise was minimal since many Somali migrant workers would have seen aircraft in Egypt and that the Mullah's spies would have given him word of their coming despite official claims that their crates contained

The new arm of imperial retribution: DH9 Fighter shaded from the sun at Eil Dur Elan, Somaliland, 1920.

The Mullah falls: Bombs falling on the Mullah's forts at Taleh, Somali-land, 1920.

equipment for oil drilling. The governor of Somaliland was emphatic in favour of the RAF: 'The credit is primarily due to the Royal Air Force who were the main instrument of attack and the decisive factor. They exercised an immediate and tremendous moral effect over the Dervishes, who in the ordinary course are good fighting men, demoralising them in the first few days.'[37]

This was heartening news to the Commanding Officer of the newly created Royal Air Force, Lord Trenchard, himself a veteran of column warfare in Nigeria in the early 1900s. He had seen his aircraft as the natural replacements of the fighting column in every part of the empire. Since 1918 they had taken part in the small wars on the Indian frontier, Iraq, Aden and Egypt, and Trenchard was expansive in his advocacy of the aircraft as the new, efficient and only way to police and protect the empire. His zeal was necessary, for the RAF had to fight to justify its existence and secure government cash in the face of opposition from the older services. During the 1920s Trenchard called for a network of airfields, linked by wireless, which would bind every territory in British Africa together and obviate any further need for land forces there. In Rhodesia the warplanes would be flown by white settlers (sons of the men who had volunteered in 1893 and 1896), and on the arid and distant borderlands of Kenya and Abyssinia cattle raiders would be spotted and chastised by bombers.[38]

Not everyone was convinced. Was this new kind of colonial warfare not inhumane? Trenchard responded to army criticism, made all that more sharp by the fear that its traditional imperial role might be usurped, with the comment that in the past soldiers had never abandoned their rifles for blowpipes when fighting primitively armed foes.[39] This was a side swipe at some old war-horses who had grumbled that fighting with aircraft was 'unsporting'. In Iraq and Aden leaflets had been dropped on potential targets which urged women and children to leave – and husbands and fathers too, it must be supposed. Anyway on the North West Frontier Trenchard saw little need for such niceties since in his eyes, which had seen something of this sort of thing in Nigeria, there was no difference between 'the Afridi tribesman and his womenkind who murder the wounded and mutilate the dead'. Yet, however persuasive, Trenchard's case had no real application in British Africa after the fall of the Mullah. The fighting columns and the 'sportsman's' wars were over.

2. The White Man's War

He [Milner] said in a questioning sort of way, 'Surely these mere farmers cannot stand for a moment against regular troops?'

I replied that this depended on locality and other conditions. In the open they were no use against cavalry and artillery, on their own Boer ground they were the most formidable foe in the world. He did not like this.

General Sir Ian Hamilton

Those who resisted Britain in Africa were not all tribesmen with obsolete arms and an unwise attachment to self-destructive frontal charges. The Boers of South Africa were more formidable opponents, and like the British soldier they fought with the weapons of industrial technology, repeating rifles, machine-guns and artillery. Here the difference ended, for the Boer soldier was not a professional: he was a citizen in arms who as often as not understood bushcraft, was skilled in concealment, knew the country well and could shoot accurately. His fighting unit was the commando, which, in 1899 at least, travelled to the battle zone by train. In the field the commando was a mobile body of mounted infantry supported by supplies carried on packhorses or in ox-wagons and assisted by black servants who tended animals and did the chores of the camp. When the Boer went to war, he also carried his Bible, for it contained much to encourage him, with stories of another chosen people meeting and overcoming their enemies in defence of a land given to them by God.

On the battlefield the Boer's tactics were defensive. His commanders always chose positions which made the best use of natural, defendable landforms, usually high ground but so placed as to allow his forces an easy means of retreat. Natural

191

fastnesses were made more unassailable by the digging of trenches (there were over a thousand yards of these at Magersfontein) throwing up breastworks of earth and stone and building dry-stone sangars, small walled enclosures for riflemen. Having selected positions of natural impregnability from which to deploy the fire of their riflemen to its best effect, Boer generals were often unwittingly assisted by their British counterparts. In 1880–81 and 1899–1900, British generals showed a fatal willingness to engage the Boers on ground of their own choosing, with disastrous results, for their men were exposed to the full force of their enemies' fire with little chance to reply effectively. Further welcome assistance was sometimes rendered by divisional commanders, such as Major-General Fitzroy Hart, who led his Irish Brigade into a loop of the Tugela river where it was haplessly exposed to fire from three sides. Elsewhere on the battlefield, at Colenso, the artillery commander Colonel C. J. Long brought his guns to within less than eight hundred yards of the hidden Boer riflemen and within a few minutes lost nearly all his transport horses and many of his men. 'The only way to smash the beggars is to rush in at them,' he remarked before the engagement, which suggests that like many others he had little idea of the killing power of magazine rifles at close range.[1] Precipitance of this kind was a battlefield bonus for the Boers, earning British generals, such as the luckless Buller, a reputation for purblind stupidity and Boer riflemen the accolade of marksmen which was not entirely deserved for it was usually the weight of fire rather than its accuracy which pushed up the British casualty figures.

Thus high casualty figures were the immediate result of Boer tactics and the frequently ill-judged British response. At Talana and Elandslaagte in October 1899 British casualties were twelve and eight per cent respectively, and both were seen as victories. Methuen's attempt to cross the Modder river in December led to losses of twenty per cent, which was close to the levels reached during the pitched battles of the Franco-Prussian War, the most recent 'modern' European war. Such figures were a shock to the British public, who, in the opinion of one veteran general, had been lulled into the false view of war thanks to the cheap successes of so many colonial campaigns 'against ill-armed though brave adversaries, when the enemy lost thousands and we counted our casualties by tens, or at most hundreds'.[2] Another veteran of such battles, General Lyttleton, thought that the recent victory at Omdurman was 'not a real trial of our

nerves', a view which may have owed something to his experience of intense Boer fire during the battle of Spion Kop.[3] Whilst
these comments contain a considerable amount of truth, it is
surprising that the writers and many like them gave no indication that they were aware of what had happened in the few
months of the first Boer War during the winter of 1880–81. In
many ways what took place then offered a forewarning of what
occurred eighteen years later.

When hostilities started in December 1880, British forces
found themselves under heavy and well-aimed rifle fire of the
kind which they had so recently used against the Zulus. At
Bronkhorst's Spruit, the 94th was intercepted and fired on by a
Boer commando. What happened was related to a Court of
Enquiry by Provost-Sergeant Newton:

> On the 20th December 1880, at about 2 p.m. we were on the line of
> march between Middleberg and Pretoria, the signal was given
> that the Boers were on our left; they showed themselves over a
> ridge about 200 yards off; the column halted and fronted at once.
> The Colonel proceeded out to meet one of the Boers, who was
> advancing with a flag of truce; he remained there about three or
> four minutes, and then returned towards the column on the road.
> Just before he reached the column one shot was fired from the
> right of the Boers; then the Boers fired a volley which killed or
> wounded all our officers and about thirty men. We returned the
> fire for about 15 or 20 minutes, till the Colonel, who was wound-
> ed, ordered the cease fire to sound. . . . There were 63 or 64 of us
> killed, and about 90 wounded; the remainder were taken
> prisoners.[4]

Men who survived the subsequent actions at Laing's Nek and
Majuba Hill related similar experiences. At Majuba the Boers
had, by stealth, occupied the summit and scattered its defenders, and were able to fire on the reserves below who were
enfiladed. Losses from fire were high, and nearly half the
attached naval forces were casualties. Whilst General Colley's
dispositions were not of the best, it was the 'hot' fire of the Boers
which unnerved his forces and made the survivors from the 58th
(2nd Battalion, Northamptonshire Regiment) determined to
improve the quality of their shooting when they returned to
Britain. Yet what had occurred in this short campaign was
largely ignored by British generals, who, with a few exceptions,
under-estimated the fighting abilities of the Boers. On the eve of
his departure for South Africa in 1899, Buller was sanguine
about the forthcoming campaign, and he assured the Secretary

He learned from his mistakes: Sir Redvers Buller, the popular and courageous commander of British forces in Natal who, after his mis-judgements, learned how to fight the Boers and relieve Ladysmith. He displays a VC won fighting the Zulus and campaign medals for that war and others against Ashanti and Dervishes.

for War, Lord Lansdowne, that operations against the Transvaal and Orange Free State would be concluded within a few months.[5] He was soon disabused, along with many fellow officers who shared his optimism.

The unexpected shock of the defeats of 1899–1900 naturally led to a spate of recriminations within and beyond the army establishment. The peacetime training of the army was blamed, and it was argued that Magersfontein and Colenso had been lost on the exercise grounds of Aldershot. General Sir Edward May, a gunner, thought otherwise and claimed that the British army's faults were the consequence of what had been learnt on colonial battlefields: 'Officers . . . who had gained high positions for gallantry and resources displayed when fighting against opponents ill-trained and equipped, met for the first time in South Africa an enemy as well armed as they were, and capable of developing the resources modern science had placed at their disposal.'[6]

If the soldier who fought Dervishes was ill-prepared to fight Boers, his brother-in-arms who had spent his time on peace-time manœuvres in and around Aldershot was even less ready for modern war. In 1893 one side in the mock combat wore full dress and the other field dress, and a highlight of the exercise was a charge of the Royal Scots Greys against artillery, which appears to have been judged successful. Four years before, another force of cavalry was considered to have ridden down over four thousand infantry after a charge over undulating ground. A participant remembered that, like other cavalrymen, he performed to a drill book based on the practices of the eighteenth-century Prussian commander von Zeithen.[7] It must have been a very handsome sight, but recollecting this dashing pageant of scarlet and blue, even General May had his misgivings. Both actors and audience, he wrote, would shortly fight on battle-grounds 'where it was impossible to spot the enemy at all, when there was no smoke . . . and when destructive losses were incurred from positions altogether beyond the reach of shock action'.[8] For this there was no preparation, although the cavalry did get one opportunity to show their mettle with sabre and lance when they successfully cut down the remnants of a retreating Boer commando at Elaandslaagte.

If many generals were unready for a prolonged war against the Boers, how prepared were their troops, for whom exposure to intensive fire from an unseen enemy was also a novelty? A simple, vivid reaction was that of an unknown private in the Royal Field Artillery who looked back over six months of fighting in Natal in a letter to his brother and sister, written in March 1900:

> Just A few lines to tell you I ham in the best of health so far, hoping you hare hall the same. Dear Brother, we was in the Battle of Colenso and lost about 1147 men killed and wounded, my regement was vevy lucky, them onley lost 3. We have onley lost about 6 men since we been out hear. It is A hard countray for us soldres. They gett up the hills hand we halft to gett them out the best way we can, that how we lost such a lot of officers and men; has soon has thay see A officer about twenty men fire at him. I dont now how soldires fac the bor fire, it is murder for the Braves soloders in the world. Wen you recived this letter you hear of ladysmith being taken by hower men; we har drawing the Bor fire at the front with Gen. Buller has gon rounde the flanke, they will gett in A nice trap be for long. Thay are fighting for all they ar worth.[9]

For those who came directly under the Boer fire, the image of the rainstorm came readiest to mind and pen, with expressions such as 'bullets like rain' and 'a perpetual rain of bullets'. Sometimes, at extreme ranges, men were momentarily unaware that they had come under fire – like Walter Stackwood, a volunteer in the New Zealand contingent: 'I was scouting and I heard the shooting but never thought it was at us until I noticed little puffs of dust every now and then. I thought the birds were having a dust bath.'[10]

Under such a fire, often from thousands of magazine rifles, the courage of the British soldiers was often impressive, as Lieutenant Jourdain of the 1st battalion of the Connaught Rangers witnessed during the battle of Colenso. His battalion was part of the Irish Brigade, which had been ordered to ford the Tugela river beyond which several thousand Boers were entrenched, supported by artillery. Ignorant of the precise whereabouts of the crossing place and misled by an African guide, the brigade commander, Major-General Hart, led his men into a tight bend of the river and heavy fire from three sides. Part of what followed was remembered by Jourdain in a letter home: 'I walked with one man shot through the leg, who talked quite cheerfully with me. I saw one man walk into camp with bullet wounds through both legs. There was a man who had part of his hand shot off, who was carrying a rifle, and went along quite gaily . . . one man who was shot through both legs, sat down and blazed off all his 150 rounds at an invisible enemy.'[11]

Even if some of these courageous men were too numbed by shock to feel the full pain of their wounds, their fortitude was impressive. Such breeziness and grit were not, however, limitless, and the nerve of men helplessly pinned down by intense fire could break. This happened after General Woodgate's Lancashire Brigade occupied the summit of Spion Kop on 24 January 1900. When the flat hilltop had been reached, there were shouts of 'Majuba', a *crie de joie* which soon rebounded on the utterers, for their goal was woefully exposed to Boer fire from surrounding heights, and they were unable to dig trenches in the shallow, stony earth. Private Rutland of the 2nd Middlesex, which had been called up to support the stranded battalions, recaptured his own and comrades' helplessness:

> After reaching the firing line, we were in for a rough time, they started to use their pom poms, or (Buck up) as Tommy has christened them and they done a lot of damage, the Boers knew the exact distance and consequently the shells fell all around us. I was lying on the ground firing with the remainder on the extreme right of the firing line when Captain Muriel told us to go about 60 yards to our right front and about 30 of us went. 2 or 3 was hit getting there and directly we got in position, Colour Sergeant Morris was talking and telling us where to fire, he was hit through the nose, he was my right hand man and directly after this a young fellow was shot on my left.[12]

A new kind of war: Khaki-clad British infantrymen take cover in shallow trenches and behind tussocks of grass in front of a Boer position, 1900.

One in six of this small detachment had been a casualty in a few moments. All about 'the groaning was sickening', and Rutland was warned by some of the wounded that he and his comrades were entering a 'slaughterhouse'. Some men had already tried to surrender but had been forestalled by Colonel Thorneycroft, and after the battle, buzzes flew about the camps which hinted at cowardice or, in the *argot* of the period, 'funking'. These were heard by Lieutenant Jourdain:

> On the other side of the position the York and Lancaster Regiment were the objects of ridicule by the 2nd Royal Dublin Fusiliers, who threw stones at them when they retired, on account of the unsteadiness of the men. There were also stories about the South Lancashires, when stationed behind 'Gun Hill', who when a shell happened to pitch over the guns, behind which they were, would run and throw themselves on the ground in a most absurd fashion. There were instances of General officers hitting, kicking, praying men to go on, and in some instances threatening them with death, but to no avail.[13]

Similar tales filtered through to the disappointed defenders of Ladysmith, where reports that a 'funking regiment' had bolted made Lieutenant Jelfs hope that its colonel had been shot.

Whatever their behaviour under fire at Spion Kop, no one was shot, let alone court-martialled. There had, in fact, been very few charges brought against men for cowardice in the first months of the war. A corporal of the Coldstream Guards received two years hard labour for 'misbehaving' before the enemy during the battle of the Modder river where his regiment had been forced to lie prone for several hours by Boer fire in temperatures of up to 90°F. It was hard for a man to run off under such fire, for, as others observed, merely to raise a head invited a usually fatal fusillade. Two private soldiers of the West Yorkshire regiment each received twenty-one days field punishment (which involved two hours daily exposure to ridicule strapped to the wheels of a wagon) for leaving the ranks whilst in action during the advance to Ladysmith in January 1900. As the war progressed, the numbers of men charged with similar offences increased and the punishments awarded became more severe.[14]

The pitched battles of the early months of the war had led to many quick changes in the way in which British soldiers fought. Since the 1880s training had been directed towards a loose, open order of advance so that, contrary to what has sometimes been written, British troops did not approach Boer positions in solid masses. On the South African battlefield this mode of movement was quickly adapted so that advances were made by small groups, strung out, with each man making use of whatever cover he could find, even ant-hills. The object was, of course, to offer the most elusive target possible for riflemen. With the same end in mind, officers abandoned the trappings of rank (General Woodgate clambered up Spion Kop grasping a rifle), bright surfaces were painted khaki, and the Highlanders abandoned their sporrans, which had proved to be all too conspicuous targets for the sighting of Boer rifles. All this was common sense and was understood by generals and privates alike. Buller had censured his men after Spion Kop for needlessly risking themselves under fire, and Roberts, on his arrival in South Africa, advised his men to adopt flexible tactics when moving forward under fire. In sum, all this meant that combat units had to become smaller if they were to survive within the Boer fire zone. This battlefield necessity did, however, create problems of morale and discipline. How would small sections, adrift on the battlefield, behave?

Deprived of the assurance of the mass and often out of contact with their battalion, small units might easily succumb to the temptation of retreat or surrender when under fire. This had occurred during the fight at Nicholson's Nek on 30 October 1899. A column of a thousand men from the Royal Irish Fusiliers and the Gloucestershire Regiment with a battery of light guns carried by two hundred mules had been commanded by General Sir George White to occupy the Nek and hold it against the Boer advance as part of his plan to avert the siege of Ladysmith. White's counter-stroke miscarried, and his main force came to grief at Lombard's Nek and was thrown back into Ladysmith. The smaller detachment at Nicholson's Nek soon found itself in trouble after its mules had bolted in the night, leaving it without artillery and ammunition reserves. It then faced intense Boer rifle fire and another Majuba:

> Both sides were maintaining a vigorous short-range rifle contest, in which the [British] soldiers were being badly worsted, for they were up against real old-fashioned Free State Boers for whom they were not a match in sharpshooting of this kind. Time after time I saw soldiers looking over their defences to fire, and time after time I heard the thud of a bullet finding its mark, and could see the unfortunate man fall back out of sight, killed or wounded. We joined in the fight, and for the next hour we slowly but surely pressed the English to the far edge of the hill.
>
> As we gained ground we began to come on their dead and wounded, and realized what heavy losses we were inflicting, for behind almost every rock lay a dead or wounded man, and we knew that we should have possession of the hill before long.[15]

This was indeed the case. Among the victims of the Boer fire was a small group of eleven men, including three officers, all of whom were wounded. Only two were able to return fire, and the senior officer, Captain Duncan of the Gloucesters, contemplated raising the white flag: 'I was very angry at having been as I imagined deserted, and I considered that the position of our small and isolated party hopeless. I remembered a picture I had seen of the surrender of Dr Jameson's force and I thought that if they were justified in surrendering when they were not in such a hot corner as my small body was that it was a justifiable thing for me to do. The recollection of that picture put the idea of surrender into my head.'[16] Once the captain had hoisted the white flag, a chain reaction began, and other nearby units did likewise, believing, if not hoping, that it was the signal for a general surrender. The incident aroused apoplectic fury amongst some senior officers, one of whom believed that it set a low standard which was lamentably followed throughout the rest of the war but happily not repeated during the First World War.[17] The blame, he thought, lay with the British public, whose revulsion against high losses had, by some unexplained process, transmit-

Opening fire: A 'Pom-Pom' (Maxim firing one-pound shells) fires at a retiring Boer commando (the blur, right middle ground) at a range of over a mile.

Shelling the Boer: Heavy bombardment was quickly found to be an antidote to entrenched riflemen.

*Chasing the Boer: Small detachments water their horses during a sweep
across the Veldt, 1901.*

ted itself to junior officers in the field. This was ridiculous, for
the fault lay with generals who had been oblivious to what had
happened to Jameson's force under continuous long-range fire
from magazine rifles. It was, however, axiomatic that general
officers refrained from too blunt public criticism of their colleagues during this period.

The lessons which could have been learnt from what had
happened to Jameson's amateur army were, however, finally
understood by the beginning of 1900. By a combination of
superior numbers, which allowed outflanking of entrenched
Boer positions, and the use of artillery in such a way as to prise
them from those positions, the major Boer field armies were
either driven back or beaten. That part of the war dominated by
pitched battles had ended but there emerged in its aftermath the
tedious campaign against the guerrilla commandos. Again, the
British army had to adapt to a new kind of warfare in which one
part of its forces garrisoned towns and strongpoints and the
other hunted for the commandos.

In this new kind of warfare there were few large-scale battles.
It was a campaign marked by skirmishes which were the outcome of ambushes or raids by guerrillas or encounters between
them and the imperial forces hunting them. For the large num-

bers of soldiers detailed to guard towns, depots and lines of communication, daily life was a stale routine of fatigues and sentry and picket duties, and it was consequently easy for detachments to drop their guard. When combat occurred, it was often unexpected and therefore confused and bewildering, since soldiers were often unready.

In mid-December 1900 the garrison of Helvetia in the eastern Transvaal had been alerted by Military Intelligence that they might be the target of an attack by Botha's commander before Christmas. They were misinformed, and the non-appearance of Botha or any other hostile Boers may well have encouraged complacency and laxity. When the town was raided in the early hours of 29 December, seven men were drunk, including a telegraphist, and many of the men on picket duty outside the camp may well have been asleep (a common enough offence at the time) since when the action started they were without boots or rifles. Their commanding officer, Major Cotton of the Liverpool Regiment, excused this slatternliness with the claim that he had too few officers to do the rounds of the outlying pickets. He had command of three hundred men from his own regiment and a further 250 from the 19th Hussars, and he had placed pickets (small units of six men, usually with an NCO) on the hills around the town who were ordered to stand to at dawn. This they did not do, no doubt taking advantage of the lack of inspecting officers, but their routine had been noted by the Boers, who attacked an hour before dawn. The pickets were obviously dazed when fire was opened, but they fell back to the sangars from where they were determined to offer a stiff resistance, or so Colour Sergeant Johnson told the subsequent Court of Enquiry:

> The enemy were firing on us at this time, we fired in the direction of the flashes, Major Cotton, Lieutenant Jones and Lieutenant Van der West, 19th Hussars, all came into the closed sangar, also several of our men, and afterwards, the men of the 19th Hussars; I think there must have been between 40 and 50 men there before the end. I shot two of the enemy at about 30 yards from the entrance; Major Cotton was wounded in the head, he sat down on the ground and did not move again; the men kept up fire on the enemy till about 6.30 a.m. I head Lieutenant Jones tell Lieutenant Van de West that Major Cotton wanted them to surrender, but they both said they wouldn't: about 6.30 a.m. Major Cotton thought it was best to surrender to save life; at that time there had been one man killed and 6–7 wounded; there was plenty of ammunition remaining; Lieutenant Jones was working very hard

all the time; Major Cotton asked Lieutenant Jones to hoist the white flag, which he did, but we kept on firing as many of the men did not want to surrender.[18]

The offensive spirit was strong elsewhere in spite of the disorder on the hillside. Small groups returned fire and gunners were determined not to lose their gun: 'Infantry came rushing back to the gunpit, they were in a state of utter confusion, some without rifles and some had no boots on. I saw Sergeant Seaton, he was shouting at his men and trying to rally them but it was too late; the enemy came all round the gun pit and overpowered us. I heard the enemy call on Captain Kirke to put his hands up, he had snatched a rifle from an infantryman and shot one of the enemy dead, he was then shot and wounded himself and was taken prisoner.'

Cotton was unfortunate. He was an experienced soldier who had served in the Afghan and Burma campaigns, and his scalp wound had unbalanced his judgement, a circumstance which did not exculpate him in the eyes of his court martial judges for he was later dismissed.[19] Kitchener was angered by the affair and, although Lieutenant Jones was found not guilty, the Commander in Chief still insisted on his resignation. To make his feelings known, Kitchener issued an order in April 1901 which forbade officers to seek the advice of their subordinates if and when there was a possibility of surrender, for such discussions were 'subversive to discipline'. Other officers found guilty of giving their posts in too easy a way were also dismissed, and heavy sentences were passed on NCOs and other ranks for unjustifiable surrenders or cowardice. At Rhenoster in September 1900 a NCO was sentenced to death (commuted to ten years by Lord Roberts) and sixteen other men were given between three and ten years. In the same town in May 1901 another thirteen men were given sentences which ranged from five to fifteen years, in every case NCOs getting the heavier term.[20] These men were exceptional to a general rule of steadfastness under fire, as evidenced by the accounts of the fighting at Helvetia, where the chance that a soldier was one of a very small detachment does not appear to have undermined his morale – rather the contrary.

At the gun pit at Helvetia there was an opportunity for close hand-to-hand fighting, which was uncommon during the war, for the Boers possessed no bayonets and preferred to run off rather than face a bayonet charge. To many Boers cold steel, whether lance, sabre or bayonet, were the weapons of Africans, not white men, and they were rightly terrified of them. When the cavalry charged at Elandslaagte, abject burghers cried out to be shot rather than stabbed or hacked but to no avail. Many were spiked as they lay on the ground, and the grim business was summed by one sporting officer as 'Most excellent pig-sticking . . . the bag being about sixty'.[21] In later engagements the Boers reserved a special vindictiveness for Lancer regiments. There were occasional tussles with the bayonet, one described by a private in a letter to his parents: 'We crawled back a bit and stuck every one in the sangar with our bayonets and it was full of blood.' This may well have been bravado, like that of a colonel of the Worcesters, who offered £10 to the man who got his bayonet in a Boer as the regiment moved forward to the attack.[22] His promise was ill-worded for he had intended the money only for the first man who killed a Boer, but, luckily for his purse, the Boers abandoned their position.

For the columns seeking the guerrilla bands, action was usually at long range, surprise shots from distant and unseen enemies, and engagements were often over in a few minutes: 'F. and I with 4 men went on to a farm where we had been told a Boer lived. When we got within about 800 yards of the farm we were fired on from a Kopje to our left front. One bullet came unpleasantly close to me, striking the ground – we only had three rifles as one man's horse was shot under him before getting to the farm so he remained there where he was and another fell into the water and didn't recover his rifle.'[23] Once the Boers began to work round the rear of this rather ill-fated patrol, its commander, Captain Eastwood of the King's Dragoon Guards, took his chance and galloped off with his men, chased by the Boers. They reached the farmhouse, and their pursuers rode away. Such brushes were common throughout the last eighteen months of the war and perhaps did much to foster the sporting image which this kind of campaigning won for itself, at least with certain officers. Riding across country, it was not hard to think in such terms, as did the volunteer Imperial Yeomanry-men from the Northumberland Hussars, who galloped after the Boers with cries of 'Tally Ho' during an engagement at Windsor-ton in 1900. For some enthusiasts it was like a day's hunting over the Cheviots, with all the 'splendid exhilaration of the charge or the chase with "Brother Boer" as quarry'.[24]

But like the North Country foxes, 'Brother Boer' knew a few tricks, as another yeomanry detachment, the 5th Victoria

Mounted Rifles, found to their embarrassment.[25] On 5 July 1901 over three hundred troopers of this Australian unit were bushwhacked just after they had made camp after a day's hard and fruitless patrolling near Wilmansrust in the Transvaal. Many weary men finished their camp fatigues and rolled themselves in their blankets to sleep, whilst others sat around the camp fires drinking rum or coffee. Beyond, in the darkness, were the pickets, who were too thinly spread to prevent infiltration by a Boer commando which had carefully noted their positions. Once past the pickets, the Boers rushed the camp and overpowered the drowsy troopers. Major McKnight realized what had happened but was too late to rally his men:

> About a quarter to eight p.m. I was lying in a bivouac which I was sharing with Captain Palmer, when firing began on the left front of the camp. I put the candles out and ran down about 20 yards and got my carbine from its bucket and my bandolier off the Cape cart. I went towards 'F' Company lines and turning to my left called out to what I thought were my own men, "Don't fire, lads, you're shooting your own comrades". These men were dressed in khaki and spoke good English. One of them turned to me and asked what I said, I told him not to fire, he then said something in a foreign language which I did not understand. I was immediately seized by three men and taken to the top of the lines.

Hazy as to friend and foe, the Australians surrendered. Their action was condemned as 'chicken hearted' by one of the Court of Enquiry, General Sir Bindon Blood, a stiff veteran of North West Frontier campaigns, who seems to have had little time for new recruits, and colonial ones at that.

On this occasion, the Boer stratagem which foxed their enemies was the wearing of khaki, for which the penalty on capture was death. The Boers protested at this on the grounds that the free-ranging commandos were often forced to don British uniforms when their own clothes wore out. There were also acrimonious exchanges over the use or misuse of the white flag by Boers, and although there were proven cases of the Boers firing after apparently having surrendered, there was also much myth written about the subject, especially in the British press. There was less myth about the Boer use of expanding or Dum Dum bullets which caused grisly wounds. Such ammunition was issued to British forces, but it was claimed that none was distributed in South Africa.[26] When faced with what were regarded as infractions of the law of war, at least as it should be conducted between Europeans, the British authorities took a severe line, and Boers who had been found guilty of deceit in the use of the white flag were executed.

In spite of the charges and counter-charges, which from the Boer side were chiefly concerned with the destruction of property and the internment of civilians, the conflict was characterized as a 'gentleman's war' by many officers since they had been able to recognize men with their own qualities amongst their adversaries. This view was to some extent upheld by the frequent occasions when the Boers treated prisoners and wounded with generosity and kindness, although one POW found that such qualities were absent from the Boer women whom he met.[27] Given the fact that so many were being placed in camps, this female curmudgeonliness was not surprising, and there was also much ill-feeling shown to troops in occupied towns. General Fuller recollected that he found the Boers an uncouth lot, many unable to read or write, a disability which some British soldiers turned to advantage by passing off elaborately printed biscuit tin labels as £5 notes![28]

Such contempt for members of the *bywoner* or poor white class was shared by some of the fighting soldiers, with results that were a long way from the world of the 'gentleman's war'. This disdain was uncompromisingly set down by an Australian, Lieutenant Witton, who served with a small scratch force of colonial volunteers and regulars called the Bushveldt Carbineers after having been commissioned in July 1901. Witton regarded the men whom he and his fellow troopers were hunting in the northern Transvaal as a 'dirty, untidy, unwashed' crew who were not soldiers but bushrangers. Such creatures needed 'a generation of purging, educating and civilising before they will be capable of taking part in national life', thought Witton. In this he was at one with his brother officers who had appointed themselves instruments of this cleansing during their patrols.

These officers' zeal and ruthlessness was not shared by some NCOs and other ranks who, alarmed by what they had witnessed during July and August 1901, appealed to the authorities for action to curb their superiors. The consequence was a Court of Enquiry at Pietersburg, the arrest of five officers and their subsequent court martial in January and February 1902. Sixteen charges of murder, all but one of Boer prisoners, appeared on the charge sheets, but investigations revealed that a further six Boers had been summarily shot as well as two troopers from the unit and an unknown number of black scouts.[29] It was a major scandal involving an active service unit, and the army, to its credit, did not obscure the details, which were made public after the execution of two of the principals, Lieutenants Morant and Handcock, and offered compensation to the near relatives of the murdered men. Yet the other principal, Captain Taylor, the Carbineers's 'native commissioner', was able to escape punishment in spite of involvement in at least eleven murders. For this reason and an unjustified suspicion that Kitchener permitted political considerations to weigh against equity for the accused, there was much subsequent fuss, most of which originated from Australia, the home of Morant and Handcock. What mattered to the army authorities was that convictions were gained on the evidence, which was, in fact, damning and not substantially denied by the accused.

The real interest of the case is the light that it sheds on the nature of the anti-guerrilla campaign and the men involved in it who did not share the discipline and traditions of the regular army. All the accused claimed that they had acted in the belief that by shooting prisoners they were fulfilling Kitchener's own orders as relayed to them by their commanding officer, Captain Hunt, formerly of the 10th Hussars, who had been killed in a skirmish with Viljoen's commando on 5 August. He had been involved in the shooting down of six unarmed Boers a month before at Spelonken and, the accused claimed, had been tortured before his death. On 9 August a Boer, Visser, was taken prisoner by a patrol, allegedly wearing items of British uniform including a jacket of Hunt's. On the following morning he was shot after a brief consultation between Morant, Handcock, Witton and Lieutenant Picton, an ex-sergeant who was dismissed for his part in this kangaroo court. There were objections from the troop's sergeant-major who was among those who later gave evidence. Morant's plea that his anger following the killing of Hunt had unhinged his judgement was disallowed, for, as the Judge Advocate in Pretoria pointed out, there was some delay between the taking of Visser and his being shot. The 'most serious crime' of the series was the shooting, at Morant and Handcock's orders, of eight surrendered Boers, then under escort to the unit's headquarters at Fort Edward, on 23 August, which was followed by the killing of another three, including an eighteen-year-old, over two weeks later. It was for these murders that Morant and Handcock were shot and Witton given a life sentence of which he served five years. Morant and Handcock were acquitted of the shooting of a German missionary,

Hesse, whose body had been found on 25 August and who it is likely had in fact been shot by Handcock.

Captain Taylor, a veteran of the Matabele campaign of 1896, was a recognizable type of brute whom the natives under his command had percipiently nicknamed 'Bulala', which meant 'to kill'. He seems to have presided over the killing not only of Boer prisoners but of two troopers, suspected native spies and other natives serving with the Carbineers. No doubt Taylor's habits had been picked up during his Rhodesian campaigning, where such behaviour was not extraordinary, but that of his colleagues is less easy to explain. One clue lies in Witton's vindicatory account of his experiences in which he recalled Morant's answer to the quite reasonable question as to why he did not bring the prisoner Visser back to headquarters to face trial: 'As to rules and sections, we had no Red Book and knew nothing about them. We were out fighting Boers . . . we got them and shot them under Rule 303.'[30]

There was no hint of sport here, save the kill, and none whatsoever of sportsmanship. This was total modern war in the most up-to-date sense, in which all that mattered was winning. Such attitudes and behaviour were exceptional, even among soldiers who had worn themselves out in otiose treks in pursuit of elusive enemies. Yet a seasoned officer, Colonel Cooper, whilst he admitted to a friend that nothing like it had ever happened before, was anxious, for, 'If the war continues much longer, it will degenerate into pure savagery in out of the way parts.'[31]

The Boer War had changed much and would, through subsequent army reforms, change much more, including the battle tactics of British soldiers. It was the British army's first experience of modern war and so taught lessons about fire and cover which prepared soldiers for the war which would start in 1914. Yet those who had thought that they had endured the full horrors of combat against the Boer riflemen were still amazed by what they experienced in 1914. As one wrote to his local paper, 'The Boer War was a picnic to this.'

III

CAMPAIGN

1. Daily Life

Feb. 22 1901 – Rain continued. River rose 4 feet in one hour. Rations finished. Troops now on ½-lb mealie flour and 3 lbs. meat per man per day. Officers' Mess affected Kaffir corn porridge and mealie flour cakes fried in melted fat of sorts. Mealie coffee tested. Feb. 23 – Soaking wet all day and night. Mealie grinding fatigues; 32 men in reliefs at work all through the 24 hours, grinding with hand-mills.

The 79th News: South African War Record

On Duty

'We have now got to rough it the Best we can, it is not like soldiering at home,' lamented Sergeant Spraggs of the Scots Guards, sweating in his red tunic and vexed by flies and heat a few days after landing in Egypt in 1882.[1] Such sentiments were widely shared by many other fighting men who found themselves serving in Africa. If they arrived there, as some did, with a simple recruiting-poster view of an exotic continent of unchanging warmth, they were soon disabused by the extremes of daytime heat and nocturnal cold and the heavy seasonal rains of South Africa. Everywhere there were long and wearisome marches over rough grassland, soft sand, shingle and rock, up hills and over rivers – marches which were too often undertaken on a diet which was sparse, irregular and made palatable only by the demands of hunger. Water was usually in short supply, and when drunk, it combined with the climate as a source of fevers and intestinal distempers. Uniforms would not be changed for months on end, became verminous and sometimes fell to pieces; some soldiers during the Boer War marched in their underpants after their trousers had been worn to shreds. In remote areas the

British soldier found himself cut off from the comforts and entertainments of his peace-time existence, often without tobacco or alcohol. In such an environment many bitterly regretted that they had ever enlisted. Private Ward of the 24th spoke for many when he wrote to his aunt in Aberdare from the borders of Zululand in 1879: 'I am now indeed sorry for it. I was under the influence of drink when I did so. I have already served fifteen months of my time, and I must go through it the best I can.'[2]

Officers suffered less. Their conditions of campaign service allowed them the help of a servant, and their officially permitted allocation of kit gave them the chance to bring with them refreshments for body and mind denied their troops. Even so, they were the victims of boredom and discomfort when on duty in inaccessible regions. Lieutenant H. Pope-Hennessy believed that, 'Every fresh bit of Africa is a new book to read', but service on lines of communication at Burao in Somaliland gave him doubts.[3] He was reduced to playing with a cricket ball until the mail arrived including 'two "Spectators" for me which in this literary wilderness are as refreshing as a cool spring in a desert!' Tedium, in a greater and lesser degree, was the common currency of campaign life for all ranks. In Africa it was made more intense by the unkind and enervating surroundings.

In this world the soldier's horizons were necessarily narrow. His object was to get through the day, attend to his duties and feed himself. He seldom had time to think much about the events in which he was involved, as Brigadier General Crozier remembered from his time as a mounted infantry trooper in Natal during the campaign of 1899–1900.

> No officer can possibly realise the lack of interest which the private soldier displays in the "big ideas" of a commander unless he has been a private himself. The cleaning of arms, ammunition and equipment, the care of the horse, the drudgery of fatigues and working parties confront him at the time, and he does them. The variation of his diet interests him at the time, and a dry bed (or a soft one, if he can get it) appeals to him much; beyond that nothing matters. He marches, counter-marches, deploys, goes into action, comes out of it and then does the hundred and one things which soldiers do collectively without question. It is the only way; if it were otherwise, battles could never be fought or wars waged.[4]

It was a fair picture and one found elsewhere in the letters and diaries of British soldiers in Egypt, the Sudan and South Africa. Sentry duty, patrols, standing by after false alarms, guarding

*Real soldiering: Men of the Rifle Brigade pass the time waiting for the
final push to Khartoum, July 1898.*

bridges, fatigues, which included mixing concrete for blockhouses, pieced out the days, weeks and months of Private Bowe
of the Border Regiment in South Africa during 1900 and 1901.
The only relief was a trip to Kroonstad races and three hours
spent in Durban where he got drunk on stout.[5] General Fuller
remembered coming across masses of listless and bored soldiers, who, in spite of gambling, drinking and smoking, were
jumpy and demoralized.[6]

Yet there was a cheery forebearance amongst some of these
men. 'Miserable, "fed up", but merry; that strange combination
one sees so much out here' was Erskine Childers's comment
after talking to some Irish regulars whom he met in July 1900.
What kept them in good heart was talk about home and the
revels they would have there, with lots of beef, bacon and stout.[7]
Something of the drift of their words can be captured from a
letter written in November 1900 from Corporal Hirst of the
Imperial Yeomanry to a fellow Mancunian who had just returned to the front.

> You ask "are you fed up"? As Tommy Atkins says, "*Well* I'm not
> (not much)". The "Yarns" one hears about going home make it
> worse dont they? I could have gone home a bit since but am going
> to 'stick it' till the finish. I dont fancy going as an invalid. You say

213

Under canvas: Tent in camp during the Mashonaland expedition of 1890, and (opposite) the well-appointed interior of an officer's campaign tent which has been tidied by his batman.

if you come out fighting again it will be on a gee gee, I'm having no more not if they gave me a blooming motor car to come on. Can you call to mind the day you and I strulled down the Stretford Rd to "volunteer"? Well I'm putting my name down for a new crush of "guards" now, Royal Fire Guards, 'Fireside Borderers' (Mothers Own) for "home service".[8]

Others were less chipper. In the gloom after Isandlwana, John Price of the 24th wrote home with a blunt warning: 'Tell Harry not to enlist for God's sake, or else he will be sorry for it.'[9]

The pattern of workaday campaign routine for soldiers and sailors varied from place to place and unit to unit. For sailors aboard HM ships in African waters, each day's duties were centred on the need to sustain a man o'war as a smart and efficient fighting machine whose crew knew how to work together, to respond instantly and unquestioningly to the commands of their officers and to keep fit for action which might well have to be undertaken in unhealthy and unwholesome places such as the river creeks of West Africa.

Cruising off the African coast, the sailor's day followed a set form dictated by tradition and necessity. On 26 November 1891, HMS *Thrush*, a newly commissioned, first-class gunboat with a crew of seventy-six, was sailing from Accra to Freetown. Her log recorded that the sea was calm and smooth, the temperature stayed at around 80°F throughout the day but there was enough wind for her auxiliary sail to be hoisted to provide an average speed of five knots. At dawn the crewmen on duty began the day by distilling water for washing, drinking and cooking. At six all hammocks were stowed away and the sailors started their daily tasks. Decks were holystoned and paintwork was cleaned, for it was imperative that the warships of the world's greatest navy always looked well. Specialists, such as sailmakers, armourers, cooks and carpenters, carried on their trades, and officers took bearings and consulted their charts. In the engine-room stokers and engineers – there were sixteen in all – worked in relays to keep the required head of steam, a grim job in the heat of the tropics. 'I will do no more work on this bloody ship,' shouted one exasperated stoker as he threw his shovel at the feet of a petty officer on board one vessel sailing in the Persian Gulf, words which secured him some respite, albeit in confinement.

At nine the captain held prayers on deck, and afterwards *Thrush*'s crew did 1½ hours' weapon drill. Cutlass men exercised with their cutlasses, and other seamen and marines practised firing their rifles and the ship's Nordenfeldt machine-guns, taking care that no brass cartridge case rolled overboard, for such clumsiness meant a small deduction from the pay of the men responsible. During this day's drill a water spout was sighted and was no doubt watched with anxious curiosity for it could have proved a hazard to such a small ship. In the afternoon time was allowed for the washing of clothes and 'making and mending', during which kit and uniform could be repaired. From 4.30 to sunset men who were off watch could smoke their pipes, which were filled with the Navy issue tobacco – it came in leaves which had to be shredded and then tightly bound with rope and canvas – hence 'Navy Cut'. A daily rum tot was issued, men danced on deck, boxed, listened to impromptu concert parties, sang or just lounged. Some, far from the eyes of authority, gambled. At Freetown stores would have to be replenished and there would be the dirty and onerous business of recharging the *Thrush*'s coal bunkers.[10] The crew were, however, fortunate in that they would have some brief shore leave, for in some cases such breaks were every three months.

For a few, characterized by the navy as 'bad hats', the discipline was the most unbearable burden of daily life; it was never absent and intruded in every area. Some chafed against it and suffered accordingly. When a marine on HMS *Pelican*, a gunboat cruising in tropical waters, was roused to duty by an acting corporal, his response, 'Go and bugger yourself', earned him ten days incarceration but his spirit remained restless. Later he dismissed himself from a quarterdeck inspection with 'I am not going to stop here'; the cunning erasure of his name from a duty roster and pointblank refusal to double at the surgeon's command finally won him six months hard labour.[11]

Grumbling, if not insubordination, its child, was endemic throughout every campaign and was heard both at sea and on land. It was an inevitable response to tedium and discomfort, and the greater part of it was directed towards food, its quality and availability. 'Food and eating' were, according to Erskine Childers, matters of 'absorbing importance in the life of the man on active service, especially when he is far from base and rations are short'.[12] What the active-service soldier ate and drank depended upon many factors, few of which were ever under his control. The fullness and edibility of his diet rested upon what he could carry on his person, the vagaries of the commissariat and its transport, what grew or grazed locally and whether it could be purchased or stolen. None of these circumstances was predictable, and there was much disappointment.

On the eve of Tel-el-Kebir, Sergeant Spraggs ate ration biscuits (square confectioneries which resembled dog-biscuits in firmness and texture) and drank water from the Sweet Water Canal alongside his line of march. He and his comrades had witnessed it sampled by the Duke of Connaught, a son of Queen Victoria, and heard him pronounce favourably on its potability, although not long after he and a few other listeners were laid low by diarrhoea. Sergeant Danby and his brothers-in-arms fought El Teb in 1884 on stomachs which had been satisfied by ships' biscuits, supplied from warships anchored off Sawakin, and a half pint of water.

Water was rationed in the Sudan desert to a quart a day for each man, but since it was carried in iron tanks slung on transport camels, it often scalded the dry lips of the drinker, for it had been heated to boiling point by the sun. Men suffered greatly from thirst. After the battle of Abu Klea, Lord Charles Beresford saw men whose 'tongues were so swollen as to cause intense pain'. Lips were black, and mouths were 'covered with white mucus' and, even though the water at the nearby wells was yellow and creamy, to such men it tasted 'cool, sweet and delicious'. Given such water and the irregularity with which it was obtained, it was hardly surprising that many officers spoke airily of a 'weeding out' process in the Sudan and South Africa by which weaker men fell out or went sick during the route marches which were intended to acclimatize them.[13]

Official protein for the fighting man came invariably from tins of bully beef. If these were exposed to the sun of the desert for too long, their contents emerged 'in a loathsome greasy mess' which could kill the appetite of even the hungriest. Hardier and probably more desperate men did eat in these conditions but some paid a heavy price, like the nine from a machine-gun detachment who had to be invalided out of the forces marching to Omdurman in 1898, a mischance their fellows blamed on bully beef. However it affected the guts, bully beef was the staple of most British soldiers throughout the African campaigns and for many years after. Its monotony was sometimes broken by another form of canned meat known as 'Maconochie' from the maker's name which appeared, together with his features, on the label. The contents were a preserved meat and vegetable stew of a 'juicy and fatty nature' but its taste was often blighted by the intrusive flavours of tin and chemical preservatives. These latter may have had something to do with the disquieting behaviour of some tins, which exploded when pierced. For

General Fuller, the memory of Maconochie was a bad one: it was 'dog's vomit', but he was no doubt used to better things.[14] Most officers were, but what of their men? The army authorities often boasted that recruits quickly put on weight and height after they had been living in barracks and eating daily rations. This was true, although it says as much for the diet of rural and urban working classes of late Victorian Britain as it does for the nutriment of standard army rations. It was not, of course, possible for peace-time rations to be brought to the front line, where there was often no means of cooking them.

The same was often true of the troopships which conveyed troops to Africa. In 1895 soldiers of the York and Lancaster Regiment bound for Cape Town were given no fresh bread or meat for the entire twenty-eight days of their voyage. A handful purchased illicit sandwiches from sympathetic sailors, transactions which had to be made covertly in the ship's latrines surrounded by what one buyer remembered as an 'awful stench'.[15] Troops shipped to South Africa during the Boer War seem to have been better provided for, with plentiful helpings of beef, potatoes, bread, pickles and puddings. Sailors too fared quite well on the Africa station, for stocks of biscuits, tinned meat, rice, raisins and flour were stored at the Cape, Sierra Leone, Luanda and Ascension Island. On Ascension there were herds of cattle and flocks of sheep which provided fresh meat; vegetables were also grown, and there was a bakery.[16]

There could not be any such luxuries for the men in the front line. Here the regimen was based upon the tinned meats and biscuits, and facilities for cooking were scarce. On the South African veldt mounted troopers scavenged for firewood, stripping doors and window frames from deserted Boer farmhouses or else tearing up the stakes which held the barbed wire originally intended to contain guerrilla bands. Once gained, such wood was valuable, and one trooper slept with his stake beside him for fear that it might be filched by one less lucky. Firewood meant hot coffee for breakfast, which was a treasured luxury; troopers guarded their kettles of boiling water jealously and grieved bitterly if they were knocked over by a restless horse or the fire burnt out. One observed, 'A long drink of hot coffee first thing has a marvellous effect; you will probably have to go without drink and with very little food all day quite comfortably, whereas without coffee you will be both hungry and thirsty.'[17] Firewood and coffee were freely available for the troopers who mustered with Jameson at Pitsani in 1895 but an administrative

Daily staple: Mounted infantrymen brew up a pot of coffee on the veldt; the emaciated horses (background, right) suggest that they, like their riders, are on short commons.

oversight left them short of kettles and saucepans so they had to boil up mutton and beef in buckets filled with the repellent 'thick and horrible' local water.[18]

Some found this rigorous life much to their liking. Tracking the spoor of the Matabele in 1896, Baden-Powell found himself and his fellow troopers infected with a cheery manly spirit and cared little for dietary deficiencies: 'We have now got only a pound of bread left for each man, a little tea, a spoonful of rice, and plenty of horseflesh; no salt, sugar or coffee – these luxuries are past; and we expect nothing more for the next three days. Yet the men are singing and chaffing away as cheerfully as possible while they scoop the muddy water from the man-hole for their tea.'[19] Everyone on the patrol was 'thin, but very healthy and hungry', and for Baden-Powell this Spartan, purposeful life was a heaven which he would soon offer to his young fellow-countrymen through the Boy Scout movement.

The self-discipline, comradeship and manly heartiness of the bush campaign were the roots of scouting, and with it Baden-Powell's hope for the moral and physical regeneration of the youth of Edwardian Britain. His ideas filtered back to Africa a generation later, for one new officer of the Somaliland Camel

219

Clean in body: Major Baden-Powell has a quick bath during the march to Kumasi, 1895.

Corps remembered how he and his fellows played polo and other games 'all out' to keep themselves fit and hard. Baden-Powell would have approved but he might have been less happy about the lacklustre attitude of one cavalry trooper, a public school man at that, during the Boer War, for whom the austerity of campaign on the veldt was far from invigorating. He had risen at 5.30 and spent a frenzied hour attending to the needs of his horse and consuming a breakfast of cold left-overs from the night before. At half past seven his column moved off:

> This is the time when the monotony becomes so terrible. In twos, or fours, or in troop, as the case may be, you plod, plod, plod, on till about 12 o'clock, with perhaps two or three short halts of a few minutes, during which you dismount and lie down in the shade of your horse, and, if he will only stand, go to sleep at once, only to be wakened in a minute or two by that dreaded cry "Stand t'yer 'orses". Then "Prepare to mount", "Mount", and plod, plod, plod on again. At about 12 you off-saddle for an hour or so, feed up, collect fuel, finish the remnants of biscuit and bully, and on-saddle, to plod, plod, plod on till 5 or 6 at night. While on the march there is no change or excitement, no nothing to while away the weary hours but one's pipe, and how fond one grows of that![20]

Resisting the instinct to ferret about for wood, the trooper had then to look to the wants of his horse, discover whether he had

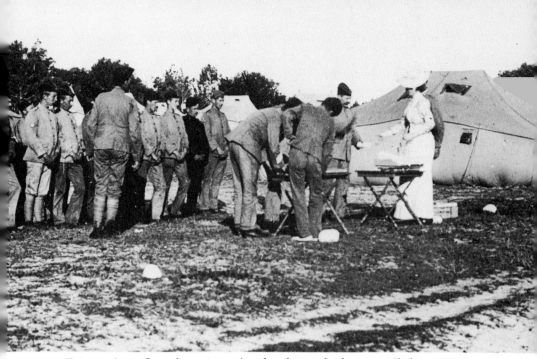

Extra rations: Convalescents receive chocolate and tobacco, a gift from Queen Victoria, at the Portland Hospital, South Africa, 1900.

been chosen for picket or sentry duty and then prepare his meal. The mind was dulled and conversation revolved around daily trivia such as the likelihood of wet blankets drying out and speculation about the scope of the following day's rations.

There was, at least, some improvement for the soldier serving in Africa in the years after the Boer War. In 1904 men of the Hampshire Regiment found that the inhospitality of Somaliland was in part offset by daily rations which were generous, at least by the standards of front-line soldiers in the Boer War. Each man had a pound of flour with which to make chapatis, a pound of meat, a quarter of a pound of onions or potatoes and smaller measures of sugar, tea, rice, coffee and occasionally Worcester sauce. For cooking, a four-pound allocation of firewood was issued daily. Native troops were given different rations, composed with an eye to local tastes and diet. King's African Riflemen serving in Somaliland were allowed daily rations of a pound of rice, half a pound of dates, a quarter of a pound of onions and smaller helpings of *ghi* (clear butter), potatoes and salt. Native porters got much less. In 1874 1½ pints of uncooked rice was the allocation for carriers, but during 1893–4 this daily staple was augmented by four ounces of dried fish upon which men had to carry loads of up to sixty pounds for as many as a dozen miles. In West Africa riverine transport made a varied campaign diet possible, and in 1894 men of the West India regiment, marines and bluejackets in the Gambia received fresh bread, biscuits, vegetables and meat which were brought from Bathurst by the steamer *Countess of Derby*. Nevertheless, native rations appear to have been of a quality inferior to those handed out to British troops. In the Sudan in 1898 some ravenous infantrymen cadged some Egyptian army issue bread from Sudanese troops even though it was 'very black in colour' and smelled 'evil'. Those bold enough to taste it soon threw up, and there was no further sampling.[21]

A soldier on campaign was expected to spend some of his pay on buying additional food, just as he did in Britain. What he could purchase depended on where he was and how much he had. Sailing down the Nile in 1898, Sergeant Skinner of the RAMC was able to boost an already ample shipboard regime with eggs (fourteen for 2½d) and six chickens (4s.2d) bought from local traders at Luxor. Sir Charles Warren, when a junior officer surveying Griqualand in the 1870s, stocked his small expedition with bread, rusks, biltong (dried meat) and tinned lobster, herrings and salmon, which he shopped for in Kimberley. Prices were high in the mining town since there was, as yet, no railway and so all food came from the Cape by ox-wagon. A cabbage, rather wretched after its long trek, was as much as 2s.6d.

During the Boer War, shops and hotels cashed in on the passing trade from soldiers, many of whom found that the prices were beyond their means. These upward adjustments were a direct response to the spending-power of officers, yeomanry-men from Britain and mounted colonials, some of whom were paid four or five times as much as the private soldier. The presence of men with a greater spending power naturally aroused the resentment of the other ranks, who could not afford bottles of infant food at 2s.6d each or 6d loaves for the same amount. The CIV (City Imperial Volunteers) amateur enthu-siasts, many of whom were from London's business and profes-sional communities, were specially singled out for envious ridicule, with nicknames like 'Covered in Vermin', 'Called in Vein' and more nastily, 'Cunts in Velvet'.[22] One of them, Erskine Childers, went with some friends to the Grand Hotel in Pretoria where high living was exclusively and officially for officers and sergeant-majors. Childers and his party had no trouble in getting a table, for whilst they did not have the badges

Marching on their stomachs: King's African Rifles infantry share a common pot during the Somaliland campaign of 1903–4. On the other side of the continent a West Africa Frontier private has a cooking pot of his own (below).

Taking time off: Governor Carter of Yorubaland and two of his staff during a stroll in Yorubaland in 1893; the bloodless expedition gave its European members the chance to collect plants and insects during their spare time.

of rank, they were very clearly gentlemen. Elsewhere officers could benefit from their social and economic position. A subaltern on a tour of duty with the King's African Rifles in Uganda in 1906 was able to cash a cheque for £7 at the stores at Masindi and buy cigarettes, soap, sparklets for a soda siphon, whisky, lime juice, potatoes, mustard and salt. Commercial penetration and the presence of a growing number of European businessmen, missionaries and administrators meant that such serendipity could be found increasingly in other distant areas. Most remarkable, perhaps as a token of the code by which all officers were expected to cash cheques which would be honoured automatically, was the fact that some who were POWs in Boer hands drew cheques on their London banks at stores in Pretoria.[23]

Private soldiers relied heavily on regimental canteens which were managed by NCOs and were established near regimental lines. One set up for the Scots Guards in Cairo in 1882 offered tinned jam, salmon and potted lobster, although the main selling line came from seven barrels of Younger's Edinburgh Ale. Within a day of opening, the takings were over £50. The canteen attached to the Hampshire Regiment in Somaliland in

1904 sold Oxford pork sausages and such campaign necessities as carbolic toothpowder and lavatory paper, this last setting the fastidious back 6 annas (6d) a packet. This was all very well for those with money or close to such facilities, but many had to do without. Hungry soldiers in South Africa turned to barter with natives, whom they found shared their distaste for ration biscuits and were unwilling to accept them in return for something more palatable. Others, more desperate, baked biscuits made with insect powder and were very sick.[24]

One such wretched man, a trooper of Dragoons hunting guerrillas on the borders of Zululand in May 1901, disdainfully examined his daily ration of 'a bit of meat' and 1½ biscuits and thought back to happier times at the 'biginning of the war', when, 'we could do a bit of looting'.[25] The plundering of food was an unavoidable necessity for both men and officers during the campaigns in Africa. What could be taken obviously depended on where the soldiers were, and certain regions had very few attractions. In Zululand soldiers took, killed and ate cattle, sheep and goats but in Egypt and the Sudan the poverty of local agriculture made for scanty pickings. In the advance along the Nile after the fight at Toski at the end of 1885, it was discovered that the dried dates stocked in many villages made good eating for men and horses. The well-stocked grazing lands and farms of South Africa were a very different matter and offered fruitful opportunities for the pillaging of food and other necessities. As they moved towards the Tugela river in January 1900, the Connaught Rangers 'pillaged the neighbouring kraals and got pigs, potatoes, chickens and raw hides which we used as blankets'. Their officers endorsed this behaviour, for, like the men, they relished the warmth of the hide blankets during the cold night.

There was much official plundering which was part of the policy by which the farms of Boers who continued to fight on were razed and their livestock confiscated. On one farm, close by the Natal Transvaal border, a medical officer, who had been called to attend to a couple of seemingly unwell girls, found two Mausers hidden in their blankets. Under the bed were two guerrillas. The farmhouse was immediately set alight, and its livestock was seized by the delighted soldiers. Everyone joined in, noted Private Rutland of the Middlesex Regiment, who shared a roasted pig with his colleagues that night. A young yeomanryman claimed that, 'It would be impossible to name all the items I have seen taken. Fruit, vegetables, eggs, poultry,

pigs, milk, butter, forage, clothes and cooking utensils, anything and everything in fact which might possibly come in
useful. His haul was a straw mattress which provided him with a
good night's sleep and fleas the following morning. But then, as
an officer noted, Boer living habits were very squalid. There
were drawbacks, especially if the looters had been used to a
sparse diet, like the mounted colonials who dined off a fat lamb,
slaughtered with a bayonet by an officer's batman, stewed with
newly dug potatoes. It was a rich stew, too rich in fact, for all the
diners were sick during the night.[26]

Looting placed senior officers in a very awkward position.
Some were distressed not so much that property was stolen but
by the fact that, unchecked, looting led to a break-down of
discipline. In the words of one general who saw its effects during
the chase after de Wet, 'Once private gain, in other words loot
and looting is recognised, goodbye to discipline, and goodbye to
fighting.'[27] In January 1900 Lord Roberts had cautioned all
officers in command of columns to take care in such matters, in
particular to pay for all goods and restrain their men from
housebreaking. His order had no real effect, for a very fine line
separated private looting from the official policy of the army
which aimed to deny supplies to commandos then at large. In
theory all beasts impounded as part of these operations were
rounded up, taken to depots and slaughtered to provide fresh
meat for soldiers. The soldiers, who received little of this meat,
suspected that the whole business was fraud. One camp rumour
alleged that the captured herds and flocks were sold to the
commissariat at one place but stampeded by their captors who
then drove them elsewhere, where they were sold for a second
time. The crooked process continued until at last the creatures
died of exhaustion. General Younghusband blamed the shame-
ful business on 'certain scallywags, masquerading under various Colonial Corps cognomens', and whilst it was natural that
a stiff-necked regular should think the worst of colonial
amateurs, there was some substance in his charge.[28]

Few culprits were ever caught, nor does there seem to have
been much effort to catch them. A native chief, whose contingent was under Colonel Byng's command, was sentenced to
eighteen months imprisonment for stealing 110 head of cattle,
deceitfully taking cash for them and evading discovery by a vain
effort to bribe another officer.[29] More formidable seem to have
been the enterprises of Major F. V. Steinaecker's Horse which
operated in the region of the borders of Swaziland, Mozambique

and the Transvaal. Complaints were made by a Mr Forbes in December 1900 that Steinaecker's irregulars were a gang of plunderers who exaggerated their own military value.[30] There is not a single man among them of any social standing', and, he alleged, they were known to the Royal Scots stationed at Komati Port as 'Steinaecker's forty thieves'. They had done much to enrage local settlers, including Forbes, not only by their robberies but by arming natives with rifles and paying them up to £6 monthly, far beyond what colonists ever offered. On one occasion armed native scouts had ambushed a small Boer camp six miles inside Portuguese territory, wounded one Boer and captured four others, who were tied to their wagons, looted the camp and returned to their white colleagues with £500 in cash and 530 head of cattle. For men like this the war was an opportunity for profit, and Major Congreve, Kitchener's secretary, was quite happy for them to make it. 'No one thinks Steinaeker an angel,' he observed, 'but he has his uses.' At the onset of the 1893 Matabele War the British South Africa Company had openly promised a share of the expected plunder to volunteers, and a year later one, Lieutenant Tyndale-Briscoe, was calculating how much he had made. If the three hundred head of Lobengula's cattle were sold at £5 each, he and his fellows stood to gain £20 apiece, which was heartening.[31]

Public disasters, like war, always offer a rash of opportunities for profit and advancement. Many sharks found the Boer War a chance to prosper, and there were plenty of minnows also willing to try their hand in the same game. But, as Swift rightly noted, laws were nets which tended to catch the petty villains and let the larger rogues escape, and so it was in South Africa. There were many ordinary soldiers who could or would not distinguish morally between those Boers who had submitted to the Crown and were no longer foes and those who had not and were enemies. The official policy of looting may well have confused their judgement in the matter, and it took the consequences of courts martial to bring them to their right senses. In November 1899 a private of the Dublin Fusiliers received one year's hard labour after having been found guilty of housebreaking at Escourt in Natal, the first of many to be so punished during this war. Another private, from the Inniskillings, received a week's field punishment for entering a native kraal with an eye to loot, and a private of the Worcesters suffered similarly for stealing eggs from a native. The shortages during the siege of Ladysmith encouraged a spate of looting, including the theft of a bottle of gin from a hotel, which earned the culprit a fortnight's field punishment. A less promising source of plunder was the guardhouse itself, but a driver of the Royal Artillery strangely thought otherwise and was caught breaking into one. In towns civilian dwellings were more tempting, and there were many convictions for housebreaking during the South African campaign, some involving assault. Even after the end of the war, garrison duties offered opportunities for the soldier-burglar, as they did at home, and in 1903 three artillerymen were sentenced to three years each for housebreaking and the possession of burglary tools at Bloemfontein. Not all such men were after food or valuables. A Gordon Highlander was found guilty of forcible entry and intimidating the householder in order to procure a woman for immoral ends.[32]

It is impossible to know whether such offenders were driven by plain greed, hunger or a belief that their culpability was lessened by the army's official policy of sequestration of Boer property. It is, of course, very likely that some would have behaved in the same way wherever they happened to be serving. Amongst the many bad soldiers discharged as incorrigible in 1870 were a private serving a gaol sentence for highway robbery in New South Wales and another finishing a two-year sentence for burglary in Springfield prison, Essex.

Natives troops also succumbed to the temptation to loot. The emir of Bida's palace was rifled by carriers and soldiers serving with the Royal Niger Company's forces during the 1897 expedition, and their behaviour earned them no reproof. Amongst the goods carried off were silks, cloth and brass basins. A native serving with the West Africa Frontier Force was shot by Maxim-gun fire in 1903 after he had been sentenced for the robbery of a Kano merchant and for murdering another man in the market there. The carrying out of the sentence was made the occasion for a display of the impartiality of the new imperial government's justice, for local dignitaries were invited to watch, along with the murdered man's kinsfolk. A similar public show was made of the flogging of a company of WAFF infantrymen who had broken their march by looting a native village in 1903. They were flogged in the village they had violated and given long prison sentences, while their back pay was handed out to the villagers in compensation.

Off duty

When food was short, and at any other time, servicemen in Africa were always willing to turn to alcohol and tobacco for comfort and the appeasement of an unfed stomach. When he arrived in the Cape in the mid-1870s, Sir Charles Warren was soon introduced to the local lore which insisted that 'alcohol was good for the system' and its devotees who drank as much and as often as they could. G. A. Henty, who must have been influenced by what he had seen as a newspaperman during the 1874 Ashante campaign, later cautioned his young readers against drink, which he feared would sap 'the vigour and enterprize' of the imperial breed. This warning was unheeded by those sons of the breed who served in Nigeria, 'where excessive drinking was notorious' in the early 1900s. For the veteran colonial warrior, alcohol became a necessity. 'I, from budding youth to early manhood, had been accustomed to see men, not women, "doing themselves well" daily, year in and year out, and when I went into the world alone, I really thought that plenty of good beer, good port, good whisky, good liqueurs and good champagne, if I could get it, was quite "the thing", and as necessary as food or sleep!'[33] On arrival in Northern Nigeria this twenty-two-year-old subaltern was, in his own words, 'a good full seed thrown on to very fertile ground' although one of his colleagues later left the region to save himself from 'the drink habit'.

There were, however, good reasons for the reliance on alcohol, since the alternative, water, was a source of enteric fever and dysentery. An army's water supply was often contaminated by all forms of human activity, as one soldier serving in the Boer War noted: 'It is in all probability drawn from the dam where the horses were watered last night, and where, if you reached the camp early enough, you and your fellow Tommies, and the nigger drivers washed yourselves, and possibly also your clothes, and where you washed your mess tin and bathed your horse.' There were, of course, alternatives. In the Sudan men sat in temperatures of 100°F (in tents) and 120°F outside and daydreamed about cold drinks whilst making do with gallons of sugared, milkless tea drunk from porridge bowls. On the banks of the Niger, whose water was rightly feared to be polluted, Captain Abadie plumped for Schweppes soda water, brought up from the coast by steamers. Each big bottle cost 5d, and in a month he got through a gross.[34]

Cooling off: British soldiers bathe, wash, swim, drink and do their laundry in the Modder river, off-duty pastimes which some will soon pay for with enteric fever or dysentery.

For many fighting men, strong drink was essential, as both services knew. Sailors and soldiers were issued with rum, and drink was often available from field canteens. During the Boer War soldiers could buy whisky for 6 shillings a bottle, and in 1904 the field canteen in Somaliland offered whisky for 2s.8d a bottle and brandy for 5s.5d, which does much to support many soldiers' contention that South African prices were extortionately high. For nearly all men on service in Africa drinking was the extension of a habit begun in the barrack towns of Britain. There was, as a consequence, a marked preference for British beer, but in its absence substitutes were found quite acceptable. One sergeant serving in the Sudan in 1898 survived on clandestine whisky and lager but was only truly satisfied when he returned to Cairo and drank a pint of British beer. Likewise a happy private who discovered bottled Bass on sale in Pietermaritzburg whose taste evoked warm memories of home. Local brews could, however, be quite bearable, and a yeomanry trooper stationed at Deelfontein confided in a friend that he could get 'absolutely "beautiful" on well under 3 pints' of a local beer.[35]

In Africa, as in Britain, strong drink was a narcotic which could help the soldier lose contact with his surroundings and situation, and a prophylactic which offered resistance to local

Serious drinkers: Officers from a regiment with a hard drinking reputation, the West Africa Frontier Force, contemplate the papers and a nearly empty whisky bottle, Northern Nigeria, 1904.

Picnic: British officers pause before cheese and biscuits (already laid out on the Huntley & Palmer's tin) whilst their bottled 'Export' ale cools in the stream, Yorubaland, Nigeria, 1893.

diseases. The search for such release was a permanent headache for the army authorities, for drunkenness lay at the root of indiscipline and inefficiency. Punishment for drunkenness was therefore severe, particularly when the drunkard was on active service. An artilleryman who broke into a Pretoria brewery in December 1880, perhaps as part of his Christmas celebrations, and drank some of the ale he found there was given a dozen lashes, one of the last British soldiers to be so punished.[36] After the abolition of flogging a year later, heavy sentences of imprisonment were given for men who were drunk on sentry duty; one, at Alexandria in 1882 received two years hard labour. Later, punishments diminished in severity: a private of the West Yorkshires who was drunk during the Ashante campaign of 1895 and who used threatening language to his sergeant received a fine of £1 and twenty-eight days field punishment, which, given the humidity and heat of the Gold Coast, must have been very unpleasant.[37]

Drink led to crime, committed either in pursuit of it or under its influence. Sentries fell asleep, prisoners escaped, officers and NCOs were sworn at, threatened and sometimes hit, and local people were abused and terrified. At Kajbar during the Sudan campaign in 1885 two privates from the South Staffordshires got drunk, broke from their camp, attacked a native and murdered him.[38] One was sentenced to be shot (which was commuted to penal servitude for life), and the other received ten years. During the Boer War the court martial registers offer a baleful testimony of the consequences of heavy drinking. A sergeant of the Gordons (which had a hard drinking reputation) took drinks from civilians and lost his stripes; two NCOs of the Donegal artillery distributed drinks to men under arrest, their guards and patients convalescing in a field hospital and then struck an officer who was no doubt trying to limit their generosity. Elsewhere soldiers swore obscenely, brawled, assaulted patrols and damaged guardrooms. Documents were faked to secure medicinal brandy, medical stores were broken into, regimental beer rations were siphoned and officers' messes forcibly entered in pursuit of whisky. Even the gamekeepers were tempted and turned poachers, like a patrol which was seeking out the army topers of Barkley West and, at their sergeant's instigation, had a few drinks themselves. When arrested, all were unconscious on their backs in the street. In excuse the sergeant pleaded that he had behaved so recklessly so as to rid himself of his stripes, for he hated his rank – 'A privit is a gintleman compared.'[39]

For all this, it is unlikely that campaign or garrison service in Africa substantially added to the ordinary soldier's consumption of alcohol, although, when a man had spent a long time in the field, the temptation to over-indulge when he returned was very great. Scenes in which legless soldiers scuffled with patrols and each other must have been much the same in Pretoria or Cairo as they were in Colchester or Dublin.

Officers too had many chances to indulge themselves. Indeed, when in 1898 the rather perverse and eccentric General Gatacre told other ranks that he planned a 'dry' campaign, the disconsolate noted sourly that his prohibition did not extend to officers.[40] Champagne seems to have been abundant during most campaigns; it was drunk widely in and around Sawakin in 1885, and Churchill was given a bottle by Lieutenant Beatty on the eve of Omdurman. Other, luckier officers on that campaign were given not only vintage champagne by Lord Rothschild but also some 1812 brandy. The recipients found many guests drawn to their mess.

Whatever they did consume, the code of conduct for officers demanded that they never displayed their intoxication in public. To do so was to invite disgrace and dismissal if it led to neglect of duty or loutishness. A drunk yeomanry officer in command of a picket was dismissed after he had shoved his way into a railway carriage reserved for ladies and resisted efforts of the local police to dissuade him. The same fate awaited another drunk subaltern who shouted, 'You are a bloody whore' to a soldier in the lines of Kitchener's Horse. A captain of the Leinsters out on a spree drank too deeply at the Queen's Hotel, Kimberley, in November 1901 and was urged by a military policeman to get a cab home. He rounded on his helper and shouted, 'Oh, you go to hell – damn you, you bloody Lance Corporal of the Provost!' – words which cost him his commission.[41]

There were other ways in which officers were brought low by drink. In January 1901 a subaltern of the yeomanry scouts was found guilty of selling forty-eight cases of duty-free whisky to a civilian, but since he was ignorant 'of the obligations of an officer' – that is to say, not a gentleman – the court martial recommended leniency. A yeomanry quartermaster, who held the ex-officio rank of lieutenant, who was also running a whisky racket, was likewise excused on the grounds of unawareness of the responsibilities of his position.[42] If and when they drank, officers did so in their own company, and in 1904 one was discharged for being drunk and drinking in the sergeant's mess.[43] This rule remained for many years, and in 1917 an Australian officer of engineers was reprimanded for offering to share his whisky with a sergeant and some privates. Off duty, whether sober or intoxicated, the army insisted that the social proprieties were observed. The navy was less rigid, and on Christmas Day officers were chaired and carried through the ship's divisions, where they were offered shares in the sailor's rum. The unpopular dreaded such celebrations for they could be the targets for bags of flour or orange peelings.[44]

Sailors and soldiers both smoked heavily on campaign. The navy made a daily issue of tobacco, and soldiers could buy a pound of tobacco from their canteens for 2 shillings. Men leaving Britain and disembarking in South Africa during the Boer War were given pipes, tobacco and cigarettes paid for by patriotic funds or handed out by local patriots. Still supplies were often spent up during long marches, and letters home commonly contained pleas for more. The well-meaning family of Lieutenant Grubb of the Balloon Section of the Royal Engineers sent tobacco for him to give to his men, then serving at Bloemfontein, but he asked them to send no more since 'mild baccy . . . is not appreciated as much as the foul stuff they buy at home'.[45] Such strong plug and twist, smoked by private soldiers, was too pungent for the palate of one officer, who was sick after smoking a pipeful. Compared to Erskine Childers and his fellow troopers, this man was lucky, for they were so short of tobacco that they were forced to empty the dopple from their pipes, let it dry in the sun and then smoke it again. Rather than face this, one officer turned to dried peach leaves, which he found not too disagreeable. All smokers concurred that their pipes relieved the tedium of long marches or rides, so much so that a corporal and four troopers of the 5th Dragoons disregarded regulations and lit up during a night march in the Transvaal in 1901. Such carelessness, which endangered their column, got them seven days hard labour apiece from a court martial.

A soldier's off-duty entertainment depended upon the nearness of urban life, which, for most soldiers, townsmen themselves, possessed sources of diversion with which they were familiar. Regulations as to bounds and the presence of police patrols limited pleasure, but not to a great degree. Officers did better, as a private of the Middlesex regiment noted, enviously, after a visit to Pietermaritzburg: 'One would not think there were Boers a few miles from here. Officers playing Polo, Tennis, with Ladies and plenty of Dinners and Tea parties, there is also

Civilizing influence: Lord and Lady Airlie and Miss Roberts, the Field Marshal's daughter, talk with officers and ambulance drivers, the Portland Hospital, 1900.

plenty of Balls, but not for Thomas Atkins.'[46] Elsewhere colonial society had much to offer officers, even Old Calabar on the febriferous coast of Nigeria in the late 1890s. 'There is generally a cricket match every Sunday, when the band plays, tea is dispensed, and ladies from the mission and hospital come and keep the rude man from forgetting his manners and politeness. In addition, the hard-working and weary official can generally get a game of lawn tennis or quoits every evening; while the magic game of golf has not failed to make its appearance.'[47] The style of such occasions was made even more British by the band of the native constabulary, which, after two years of training and rehearsal, was sufficiently versatile to render pieces from *Gaiety Girl*.

For the private soldier the main urban attractions in South Africa or Egypt were more basic: music halls (that at Pietermaritzburg was passable by London standards) drinking places and prostitutes.

In Egypt, which had had a British garrison of at least four thousand since 1882, whores were abundant, as one British soldier discovered when he arrived at Alexandria in 1914: 'It is a most immoral place is this. The people we got to know, regulars

&c. say there is only one worse in the world and that's Cairo. Port Said is reckoned to be bad but they say it is a fool to this place. You can get down street after street with women at every door and window, shouting each other down to get your custom. All sorts and practically every nationality, some not more than children to fat Arabs and coal black Soudanese.'[48] Their sisters in Cape Town were quick to adapt to the growing market created by the Boer War, and when troopships docked, soldiers were showered with yellow discs, like sovereigns, each with the name and address of a local prostitute. At Stellenbosch pickets patrolled on the lookout for soldiers flirting with native girls, behaviour which, it was feared, might lower the standing of the British army in the eyes of the local Boer population.

Boer women of the *bywoner* class also appear to have been willing to offer sexual pleasures to soldiers, one of whom commented that, 'They don't wear drawers.' He had no doubt found this out for himself.[49] The Boer women in refugee camps also offered opportunities, and in September 1901 a private of the Devons received fifty-six days hard labour for entering a railway wagon containing Boer women for an allegedly immoral purpose. A corporal in the King's Own Lancashire Regiment was reduced to the ranks for twice entering a refugee camp and indecent behaviour with one of its inmates. This was a rather light sentence which may reflect that the woman concerned was not in any way reluctant.[50]

Soldiers who forced their attentions on local women received weightier sentences, and rightly so. After the battle of Tel-el-Kebir two soldiers of the Royal Irish raped a native woman and were given seven years penal servitude each. The crime was reported to Colonel Tulloch by an Arab sheikh, and General Wolseley, when informed of the matter, expressed willingness to confirm a death sentence had one been passed.[51] In South Africa rapists received between two and five years, and one, whose offence involved a child, was sentenced to death, but this was commuted to penal servitude for life by Lord Kitchener. The death sentence was, however, carried out on two rapists from a native scout unit in 1902.[52] Unnatural offences between men were uncommon, but when discovered and brought before a court martial, punishment was often condign. One soldier found guilty of sodomy in Egypt in 1885 received ten years, although a pair involved in an offence with a native in Natal in 1900 received eighty-four days hard labour each.[53] Such incidents were rare, and the late Victorian and Edwardian army appears to have been heterosexual, often aggressively so to judge from the numbers of men who suffered from venereal diseases contracted on home and Indian service.[54]

There were, of course, many ways in which the off-duty soldier could be both entertained and rescued from the temptation to seek out women and drink. From the middle years of the century the proven drinking and whoring capacities of soldiers and sailors had aroused the concern and compassion of philanthropists of all kinds. The motive power for moral reformation amongst servicemen came from the Churches and their offshoot, the Temperance Movement. There was much resistance, for, like many of the Victorian working class, servicemen were often either indifferent to religion or openly hostile. When he steadfastly rejected the drunken and blasphemous *milieu* of the barrackroom of the Royal Welch Regiment in the late 1870s, Edward Goodall endured persecution. 'They called me holy Joe & threw pillows at me when I was at prayer,' he remembered.[55] In South Africa in 1881 he preached before two hundred civilians and soldiers in a mission church, which aroused much scorn from his fellow sergeants. Men like Goodall were already the servants of good habits, but for those who were not there were branches of the Soldiers' Christian Association, one of which was set up in 1892 for the men of the Cape Town garrison. Here the soldier could find a sanctuary which offered food, non-alcoholic drinks, newspapers, books and writing materials.

There were, of course, already many men in the army whose background embraced Sunday School, church, chapel and Temperance lodges, like the Good Templars, and on campaign they gave strength to others and offered assistance to the chaplains of their battalions. One serving chaplain remembered warmly a service on the veldt in 1900 which possessed all the fervour and passion of a revivalist meeting: 'Two soldiers led in prayer – short and very earnest – then we sang and prayed. Two addresses which had a deep effect upon all. . . . Kneeling on the veldt, man after man broke down. Many openly confessed their sin, others rejoiced in true Methodist style.'[56] There was also the 'official' religion of the church parade. In June 1902 one such, on a large scale, with men from many regiments, was held in Pretoria as a thanksgiving for the end of the war. It was preluded by Lord Kitchener giving decorations, including VCs, to officers and men, and on everything there was an unmistakably clear imperial stamp. The hymns sung included the Old Hundredth, 'O God, our help in ages past', 'Nearer, my God, to thee', the

An army mourns: Church parade for a memorial service for Queen Victoria, Harrismith, 1901.

National Anthem and Kipling's 'Recessional', which was sung to the tune of 'For Those in Peril on the Sea'.

Like religion, organized sport helped to interest and raise the morale of off-duty soldiers. Company and regimental football matches were becoming more and more common in the army of the 1890s, a reflection in part of the game's popularity with the working classes as a whole. Cricket had been played by men of the 24th in Natal in 1879, and the York and Lancaster Regiment was given a welcome week's leave on their arrival in Cape Town in 1895 to watch the matches played against local teams by Lord Hawke's XI. Boxing was also popular and, like football, was organized on regimental lines. In May 1902 a series of bouts between men in Colonel Kekewich's force was held, in which the highlight was a contest between J. D. Erasmus, a guide and middle-weight champion of South Africa, and Private Alfred Smith of the Cameron Highlanders. The South African was a fit and burly fellow, and most punters laid their cash on him, but he was beaten in a bout of 'muscle and weight *v.* science'. Smith lacked the former, since, in the words of a spectator and fellow soldier, 'Those who have campaigned in South Africa know how impossible it is to keep up even an ordinary amount of nerve and strength on a soldier's "field rations".' Erasmus was a true sportsman who congratulated the winner during the celebrations afterwards.[57]

If Africa offered limited amusements for the private, it was a paradise for the officer whose sporting enthusiasms were those of the chase. Campaign and sporting life merged conveniently for a fashionable Hussar officer stationed in Northern Nigeria in 1902. 'Bertie Porter is off again. As there are no more slave-raiders to kill or ponies to pinch he is off to Porter's Flats (called after him) to bring in some "beef" for the pot.' The beef in this fellow officer's letter was antelope. Colonel Meinertzhagen's diary of Kenyan service between 1902 and 1906 is an unending obituary of lions, leopards, rhinoceroses, zebras and elands, all the victims of his gun. Sometimes the victim would be eaten, but as often as not its skull or skin would become a trophy which would in the course of time be inscribed with the date and place of its death. Like the medieval knight, the British officer held to the belief that skill in hunting improved skill on the battlefield. It was argued that exploits in the field raised the prestige of British officers and of their race in the eyes of askaris and natives alike. So thought a District Resident in Nyasaland, who wrote in 1908 that: 'The Germans never move off the roads, they don't care for sport, and have no idea of the word as used by the Britisher. There are very few officials that shoot at all, but those who do, always take a band of Askaris with them, who fire with them at such game as elephant, rhino and buffalo.'[58] By contrast the British officer knew that fair play was the quintessence of sportsmanship. Alone, or with a single native servant, he offered his prey a chance and stalked and shot it as he would have done on a Scottish hillside, relying on skill rather than firepower.

When not out on the trail of game, officers relaxed in their mess. Such places were not for the cultured or intelligent, thought Esmé Howard, then serving with the Imperial Yeomanry, when he wrote to his wife in October 1900:

> They loll about in easy chairs and smoke cigarettes. Military questions are never discussed at mess. That would be "bad form" and they only wake up from a state of bodily lethargy in the afternoon when they play polo, and mental lethargy after dinner when they sing music hall songs out of tune to the accompaniment of a gramophone, the "bones" and an ocarina. . . . I must say it is an awful thing to think that the most serious of all professions, war, is entrusted to men who – with rare exceptions – train themselves by their mode of life never to think – it would

be "bad form" – and whose brain therefore must become more or less atrophied in course of time. They are brave enough and go to their deaths with as little thought as they have gone through life.[59]

What these cavalrymen thought of Howard, with his conversation more suited to a college high table, is not known. His predicament, that of an educated man, faced with others of his class who were not, was like that of Erskine Childers, who discovered that he needed an officer's approval before he sent a telegram home. He approached an officer of the Staffords for his signature but found the situation rather strange: 'We were, I suppose, about equal in social station, but I suddenly – I don't know why – felt what a gulf the service had put between us. He was sleek and clean, and talking about the hour of his dinner, to another one, just as if he were at a club. I was dirty, unshaven, out at knees, and was carrying half a sack of fuel – a mission like this has to serve subsidiary purposes – and felt like an abject rag-and-bone picking ruffian.'[60] Poor Childers, social barriers, attitudes and behaviour from Britain were as much a part of the army's campaign baggage as were its uniforms, guns and mules. The same truth was discovered more alarmingly by another middle-class ranker who found to his dismay that his unit's water ration was unavailable after a long march in Natal for it had been used up by officers for washing.

This gross but uncharacteristic thoughtlessness was recorded by the victim in a letter to his public school magazine. Like others, throughout Britain, the schoolboys were anxious to know all they could about the reality of campaign life. Many soldiers were more than willing to supply this knowledge, and from the 1879 Zulu campaign onwards there was a flood of letters out of Africa from fighting men in which they described what they were doing and what they had seen. Families who received such accounts sometimes forwarded them to local papers, and in some cases the soldiers wrote direct to the papers. The *Evening News* paid a guinea to the author of the best letter from the front line during the Boer War and drew an often vivid response from soldiers. The army was sympathetic, although in May 1901 a private of the Royal Lancashire Regiment was given a six-month prison sentence for sending a letter to the press in which he censured his officers. Another private, in the RAMC, who used the same means to air personal grudges a few months later got thirty-five days.[61] Still the tradition continued until the first months of the First World War, after which military censorship intervened.

Together the first-hand campaign literature of Africa is no more than a huge collection of individual responses to hardship in a strange land. There are, however, some threads which run through the whole. Discomfort and boredom are perhaps the most obvious, but beyond them are fortitude, a willingness to accept misfortune and privation, humour, courage and a dogged adherence to duty.

2. Men, Machines and Medicine

The next job was to get carriers for the kit and ammunition, and it was only then that I realised what kind of pagan we were going to deal with. They had a tremendous reputation for fighting, they had 'strong juju', which made the white man's bullets turn into water when they left the barrel. They eat all prisoners after torturing them for a week, and altogether they were desirable enemies. The result was that no carriers were forthcoming. I got the Company Sergeant Major to go into the town and tell the people that I was 'a little devil at fighting', and that the Company had a better 'juju' than our pagan friends, namely the Maxim.

Anonymous British officer, 'A Little Show in West Africa',
Hampshire Regiment Journal, I, no. 5 (1906)

British regular servicemen

The nineteenth- and early twentieth-century serviceman was a creature who occupied a pedestal or a pit, according to the prejudice or mood of the public. In the widest social terms, the ranker fell well below the accepted standards of respectable behaviour which were set by the middle classes and aspired to by many of the working.

When a newly enlisted young man of sixteen, from what would have been considered a decent working class background, arrived at Pontefract barracks and was asked to hand his watch and other valuables to the duty corporal, he was shaken. 'This gave me a turn and my spirits fell and it seemed to me that rumour was true regarding the social lowering on becoming a soldier.'[1] Worse was in store for another young recruit in the 1890s. After a daily torment at the hands of impatient drill instructors and those professional bullies, army

242

Soldiers of the Queen: Grenadier guardsmen board a felucca on the Nile, 1898.

gymnastics instructors, he had to endure the 'utter callousness and shamelessness' of his fellow soldiers' talk, most of which consisted of boasts about their exploits with local whores. Sleep, in beds just eighteen inches apart, was fitful. Drunkards threw up and others sprawled 'full-dressed on the beds in a semi-drunken stupor occasionally muttering curses, others smoking and some snoring'.[2] Of course it would have been little different in a doss-house for casual workers or the jobless.

Such falls from grace were forgotten or ignored when the soldiers went to fight for the empire, and the fighting man became the hero of the patriot muses, newspapermen and their readers. The bruiser and drunkard of the beerhouses then became Kipling's 'gentleman in khaki' who would stand and die bravely for his country. The tenor of such sentiment may be judged from a poster of 1899, drawn up for the Duke of Corn-wall's Light Infantry in which the regiment was represented as 'guarding the interests and dignity of its country, a duty which has often called forth the utmost exertion of the brave fellows who have ever been ready to follow its colours'.

The 'brave fellows' who had protected and pushed forward Britain's interests in Africa came from many backgrounds and countries. There were regular soldiers and sailors, volunteers like the Imperial Yeomanrymen from Britain, Canada, New Zealand, Australia, Rhodesia and South Africa who enlisted to fight the Boers in 1900. West Indians fought in West Africa, Indian regulars served in Egypt and the Sudan, East Africa and Somaliland, and everywhere there were local natives in units commanded by British officers.

Soldiers and sailors from Britain were volunteers drawn mainly from the urban labouring classes, whilst their officers came from the upper-middle, professional and landed classes. Before 1870 soldiers signed on for twenty-one years, but after the reforms of Edward Cardwell, the Liberal Secretary for War, the period of enlistment fell to twelve years, with the option of half this time in the reserves. Diehard officers regretted the change for they were often sentimentally attached to the old long-service soldier, trained, tried and toughened by years of duty and discipline, who had shown his fighting mettle in the Crimea and the Indian Mutiny. It was wondered whether setbacks in Zululand and South Africa were the consequence of the younger, short-service soldiers but in fact there were plenty of the other kind on the battlefields of Zululand, Egypt and the Sudan, all of whom had taken the Queen's shilling before 1870.

Then and later the armed services appeared to offer little to attract men. Pay was mean (7s.7d weekly for privates) and there were deductions, as much as £7 a year, for necessities such as kit and for misdemeanours. After 1873 sufferers from venereal diseases had their pay cut, although some avoided detection by self-medication, often making their condition worse. If a soldier was ambitious and secured the appropriate educational certificates, he could obtain promotion and with it more money – corporals received 14 shillings a week and sergeants up to 35 shillings. These were not high wages but they brought their recipients in line with the skilled working class, and they had the advantage of a secure income. By contrast the industrial worker lay at the mercy of trade recessions with their inevitable lay-offs and unemployment. There was a natural relation between the state of trade and enlistment, and in lean times more and more men beat a path to the recruiting sergeants. In 1880 and 1885, both bad years, the rush meant that two out of every five had been rejected on medical grounds, no doubt poorly fed casual workers, always the first victims of a slump.

Once in the army, it was possible for a sober man to advance himself and make a career which would bring rewards which might not have been found in civilian life. Edward Pegley, the son of a soldier, enlisted in the South Staffordshires in 1862, re-entered the regiment in 1885 and retired six years later with a weekly pension of 17s.6d, as well as a two-year posting as an NCO in the Grenada police force. Later, like many other pensioner NCOs, he got himself a place as a manager of a regimental canteen. William Sherlock, a York plumber, transferred from his local militia to the Royal Irish Fusiliers in 1869 when he was eighteen and spent the next fourteen years in India, where he made sergeant and had enough income to marry. He later fought in the battles of El Teb and Tamai, returned to Britain and left the army with a good record and a reputation for temperance.[3] This was a success story of the type of sober and educated recruit which the army always hoped to tempt.

There were plenty of exceptions to this rule of diligent soldiering, an unblemished record and their reward, promotion. Private Charles Bruce of the Durham Light Infantry, who had joined in 1884, was tried by court martial in 1889 for going absent without leave for fifteen days, a lapse he excused with the lame plea, 'I got into bad company and was led away.'[4] An examination of his previous record showed ten charges of drunkenness, twelve for absences, six for kit deficiencies and one for threatening a sergeant ('I'll do for you') and punching a member of his escort, all in five years. The army did not like such men but it had to make the best of them. For their part such soldiers, officially described as 'incorrigible and worthless', had a bizarre affection for the army, even though they regularly suffered at its hands. It was a haven in an otherwise unkind world to which circumstances forced them to return, even after expulsion. John Smith [*sic*] enlisted in the Royal Scots Fusiliers in October 1884, stayed three weeks and then deserted, but shortage of cash and the lure of the bounty money drew him to the Inniskillings within two weeks. He stayed longer there but after two years was discharged with ignominy. In 1890 he tried the Durham Light Infantry, deserted and was only caught up with five years later when he foolishly presented himself again to the Royal Scots Fusiliers.[5] There were others like Smith, and before 1870 they had been sent on their way with official tattoo marks on their thumbs, a 'B' for bad character or a 'D' for deserter. Many were also said to have had the marks of corporal punishment on their backs. Flogging, thought by many to be the only sure means of imposing order on such wayward spirits, was abolished in 1881 in the army and 'suspended' for the Royal Navy, along with the pressgang. After 1870 men were flogged only whilst on active service, the last severe sentence of fifty lashes carried out in Zululand in 1879 on a private who had stabbed a corporal.[6] The spirit of salutary public punishment survived, for in 1905 a private of the Lincolnshire Regiment was publicly hanged at Trimalgherry in India for the murder of a warrant officer. Like Kipling's Danny Deever, his death was made an example to others, for men from his own and other regiments were paraded to watch the spectacle.[7]

This display, a relic of the army of Wellington, was watched by soldiers whose conditions and way of life had slowly changed over the past thirty years. Thanks to the spread of education in the 1870s and 1880s and army schools, nearly all soldiers could read and write, although old prejudices died hard. In 1899 a well-meaning young girl at Durban offered to write letters for illiterate soldiers, rushing up to them as they disembarked and making her first approach to a major![8] After 1904 daily pay was 1s.6d, and the burden of stoppages was removed, save when they were imposed for indiscipline. The stodgy, monotonous barrack diet was improved, and this, together with exposure to regular medical attention, made the soldier healthier than the poorer classes from which he had often come.

When he went to war, the soldier did so because it was his duty. Loyalty, carefully nurtured by his officers and NCOs, was to his regiment. The 16th Lancers had, in the 1890s, the advantage of being able to pick and choose recruits (drawn no doubt by the handsome uniform and dashing reputation of the regiment), and great pains were taken to instil in them a sense of corporate pride. They were an elite united by a common bond of tradition and mutual dependence. Elsewhere such regimental loyalties were strong, and in the pubs and beerhouses of barrack towns regimental pride was a common source of quarrels and brawls. Frank Richards remembered, how, in order to needle Highlanders, his fellow Welshmen would ask for a pint of broken square. Hallowed rumour had it that a Highland square had once broken under the charge of the Dervishes, and it was the duty of the Highlander to stand by his regiment with his fists, which he usually did.[9]

Patriotism and its new offspring, imperialism, meant less than regimental pride. When the soldier was forced to carry its principles into action on the battlefield, he had little thought for anything beyond survival, and the daily chores of campaign life did not inspire lofty thoughts of national destiny. As schoolchildren in the Board Schools, soldiers would have been exposed to

Africa bound: British infantrymen on board a troopship bound for the Cape, c. 1890.

such ideas, and on one troopship bound for South Africa troops were given lectures by their officers which were compiled to explain the rightness of Britain's cause against the Boers. They do not seem to have made much impression.[10] Sometimes Irish soldiers, who made up about one in five of recruits, felt more attached to their own local nationalism, like a private of the Irish Rifles in 1900 who spoke grossly and disloyally about the Queen and called for cheers for the Boers.[11] His foul tongue caused a quandary for the army authorities, for, in the words of the Judge Advocate, 'The words used as regards the Queen are of a character that could not be laid before Her Majesty' when the time came for her to read the trial evidence and confirm the sentence.

When the private soldier fought, he did so for his regiment and for his mates, with whom he had shared much of his life. For this reason an extraordinary number of gallantry awards were given to men who had shown their courage in rescuing comrades who were endangered and wounded, like the men of the 21st Lancers who had ridden back to the Dervish line to pick up unhorsed brothers-in-arms. For officers, imperialism was a creed which they both understood and sympathized with, and they had no misgivings about its application in Africa. There

247

were exceptions, like Lieutenant Meinertzhagen, who discountenanced guests at the governor of Kenya's dinner party by outspoken comments about the rights of Africans to their own country. More common was the plain imperialism of Lieutenant Crozier, who believed that the virtues of the British, in particular their sense of equity, made them natural and worthy rulers: 'I had seen Zulus, Basutos, Cape Boys, Hottentots and Swazis obeying the white man and respecting the flag, and I had seen that this had only been achieved by fair dealing.' As with many military men of his generation, Crozier's political views were a *pot pourri* of bucolic Toryism and what might collectively have been called practical soldierly common sense. When confronted with a strike by a handful of carpenters from Lagos, Crozier gave a flogging to each of them, which ended the strike and created a rumpus. Crozier's seniors were, however, sympathetic and he avoided censure.[12] Sir Garnet Wolseley had no truck whatsoever with Liberals or Radicals and confided to his wife that he would have liked to have been another Cromwell so as to overthrow 'the licence of democracy and socialism'.[13]

What angered soldiers most was the apparent inability of politicians to see things their way, especially when it came to fighting wars against natives. In 1885 there was much railing against Gladstone for his decision to evacuate the Sudan. General Lyttleton, a friend and admirer of Gladstone, found that nearly all his fellow officers were 'Military Tories' in the 1870s but they distrusted Disraeli, probably because of his flash cleverness. Whatever their other political opinions, there can be no doubt that the officer class endorsed imperialism and welcomed the chances, it offered them, of both serving their country and advancing their own careers.

In spite of the abolition of purchase of commissions in 1870, officers' messes remained the more or less exclusive preserve of the sons of upper-middle and upper classes, who were all the products of public schools. All would therefore have been exposed to a moral education which embraced Christianity, an almost mystical adherence to duty and honour which was close to that of the knightly code of chivalry, sportsmanship and a sense of national destiny, which made them easy converts to the ideals of empire. Empire meant something more than the obligation of Britain to conquer and rule in the name of civilization: it opened roads to promotion and professional recognition. Soon after his graduation from Sandhurst in the 1880s, Aylmer Haldane hoped that as time went by he would not stay 'bald chested' – that is, without campaign medals. The quest for medals, campaign bars and mentions in despatches was obsessive amongst all officers who hoped to forward their careers. Kitchener quibbled over his right to get the 'Bombardment of Alexandria' bar for his Egypt medal, and others moaned about the War Office's slowness in issuing campaign medals.[14] As well as the handsome imperial token to wear (the medals' iconography was a true image of imperial conquest: that for the Matabele Wars showed a raging lion running over scattered spears and shields), the officer could hope for 'brevet' promotion on campaign – that is, a higher rank for the duration of the conflict.

Imperial wars in Africa offered further opportunities for the officer through the creation of locally recruited native forces which required British officers. Many leaped at these chances which brought with them added pay as well as the likelihood of field service. General Younghusband, when a subaltern in 1880, found that his father could no longer afford him his £50 annual allowance and so, unable to maintain the spending levels required in an infantry mess, sought and gained a transfer to an Indian regiment. In the same way other officers, the impecunious, adventurous or ambitious, offered their services to the Royal Niger Company, the British South Africa Company, the British Imperial East Africa Company or the regular colonial forces in East and West Africa. Service in these forces was also attractive to the small numbers of officers who had been promoted from the ranks (never more than 150 a year and often less) for whom the social unease and financial burdens of the mess could be oppressive. Lieutenant James Arnold, who had enlisted in the 3rd Hussars in 1886 and who was commissioned eight years later, almost immediately took leave from his regiment for service with the Royal Niger Company. Like many other officers in charge of small punitive expeditions in Africa, he received the DSO for his part in the 1897 Bida-Illorin campaign, during which he held the local rank of major.[15] The terms of such service were generous. A subaltern in the West Africa Frontier Force received £350 a year and a daily, local allowance of 7s.6d, although for some this was quickly swallowed up by large mess bills, all too common in a unit celebrated for its serious whisky-drinking.[16]

This type of service also provided a convenient means of disposing of regular officers whose *mores* made them unwelcome in British or Indian messes. The army, like the public schools in Evelyn Waugh's novel *Decline and Fall*, took care of its

Captain Grimeses. An ex-officer who had left his regiment after gambling losses which he could not make good turned up in South Africa with his mistress and thanks to a good word from the War Office was appointed as a magistrate in the Eastern Cape in the 1870s. He commanded a force of Fingo levies in 1878, by which time he had fallen to a new vice, for he was 'almost always under the influence of drink and looked very bad'. To pay for his liquor he plundered government money, was sacked and finally died. His fellow magistrate, Frank Streatfeild, was perplexed by the business but thought that it would not have ended badly had the man kept his fingers out of the till, for 'The Government didn't appear to me to care twopence whether their Frontier Magistrates were drunk or sober.'[17] Men of the same lack of fibre were found elsewhere. When he arrived in the King's African Rifles mess in Nairobi in 1902, Lieutenant Meinertzhagen found that his brother officers were a crew of degenerates:

> Mackay [the Adjutant] is a ranker, keen, of the sergeant-major type, but most anxious to get efficiency; I like him. He won his commission at Omdurman; he is both helpful and considerate. My brother officers are mainly regimental rejects and heavily in debt; one drinks like a fish, one prefers boys to women and is not ashamed. On arrival here I was amazed and shocked to find that they all brought their native women into the mess; the talk centres around sex and money and is always connected with some type of pornography.[18]

Kindred spirits had gathered on the other side of the continent in the mess of the West Africa Frontier Force in Calabar on the Nigerian coast. When Major Hugh Trenchard went down for his first breakfast, he found a soiled collection of unshaven officers sitting around in their pyjamas. Their conversational staples were sexual prowess, gambling and drink, and when the irate Trenchard complained to the commanding officer, he was told what he had already discovered, that on the coast mess conduct was different from that in England.[19]

Whilst for some African service was clearly an opportunity for incessant drinking and sexual exercise which would have been frowned upon at home, there were others who found in African service a vehicle for remarkable preferment. The most famous were Wolseley, Kitchener and Lugard, all professional soldiers whose careers progressed alongside the expansion of the African empire.

Wolseley, who from the 1870s made for himself a reputation as a 'professional' and clear-headed soldier who planned his campaigns with diligence, got £25,000 from Parliament after the 1874 Ashante campaign and went on to command in Egypt and Sudan. Kitchener, whose knowledge of Arabic paid dividends during the Sudan campaigns of 1884–5, bypassed the traditional promotion structure of the British army by ascending through the ranks of the Egyptian army, an experience which secured him command of the Sudan invasion army in 1896. After Omdurman he received £30,000 from Parliament and a further £50,000 at the end of the Boer War. Both men from unmoneyed and uninfluential backgrounds, they gained peerages and the most senior posts in the British army – Wolseley was made Commander-in-Chief in 1894 and Kitchener Secretary for War in 1914.

Lugard, a professional soldier with campaign medals and £48 in his pocket, chose in 1888 to become a *condotierre*. He considered service with the Italian army in Eritrea, professional game-hunting in Somaliland and service in the Emin Pasha relief force before taking his chances with the Lakes Company forces. He then offered his skills to the East Africa Company and the Royal Niger Company and, after many campaigns, was appointed Commissioner for Northern Nigeria. His career ended with a peerage and the governorship of Nigeria. He was not just a freelance, for his experiences fighting and overcoming slavery convinced him that he was advancing the frontiers of civilization and bringing order and peace to peoples who lacked them. He was a soldier transformed into a proconsul, a process which was common, for in many newly conquered areas of Africa the only men sufficiently experienced to be able to take up the reins of government were those who had taken part in the conquest. Gilbert Carter, a junior naval officer and paymaster of the Sierra Leone government steamer in 1864, served in the Ashante campaign and then moved into the colonial service. In 1888 he was administrator of the Gambia, in 1890 governor of Lagos, and after his successes there he was knighted. His career ended with the governorships of the Bahamas and Barbados.

Native forces

Many officers, like Kitchener, who had won names for themselves in African campaigns had done so in command of native

Afternoon tea in the Gambia, 1888: The chief administrator, Gilbert Carter, his wife and daughter. A former junior naval officer, Carter transferred to the colonial service where he had a successful career, first in West Africa and then in the West Indies.

troops. These were of two kinds: the first were regular forces, trained along British lines and under British officers and sometimes NCOs, and secondly there was what were loosely called tribal levies, irregulars drafted or cajoled into service for the duration of a campaign. For the greater part such bodies were a military liability, and their behaviour vexed British commanders. Typical were the exasperated remarks of a commander in Rhodesia who had secured the help of a local chief for an attack on Mashona rebels. When ambushed, the natives, armed with spears and a few muskets, 'behaved badly and could not be got to the front'.[20] Wolseley was a little more generous about the Haussas who fought with his forces against the Ashante in 1874.[21] They 'behaved bravely but wildly as might have been expected'. During the Irryeni expedition in Kenya in 1904, Masai levies mistook British service for a licence to kill as they wished, and Meinertzhagen found them spearing women and children and was forced to shoot several.[22]

If there was an official view of natives as soldiers, it was contained in the regulations for native forces published in 1878

African warrior: Captain W. H. Milligan who served with West African units in the 1890s and with Rimington's Scouts during the Boer War before returning to regimental duties in Britain. He spoke Hausa well and entertained his nieces with Hausa tales, learnt from his men.

during the operations in the eastern Cape. The native possessed the physical strength of a man but the mind of a child and was therefore to be treated with kindness but firmness and always required supervision. Natives who attempted to show independence of action or mind were viewed with either mistrust or contempt. Officers who visited the only black republic, Liberia, during this period regarded it and its people with amused condescension.[23] In its extreme form, this general sense that the African needed discipline was expressed by one experienced officer who warned, in 1917, that in Africa, 'The "liberal idea" at bottom spells rape and loot in the negroid tribes.'[24] Yet at the same time the African, under British training, could emerge as a good soldier and behave in battle as well as his British counterpart. The creation of units of such soldiers was imperative from the 1880s in areas where the climate prevented the frequent use of British troops and where permanent garrisons were required. In 1914 these forces, from West, Central and East Africa, were used to fight German-trained askaris in Togo, the Cameroons and Tanganyika, but Britain, unlike France, never saw its African colonies as '*un immense resevoir d'hommes*' which could be tapped to provide armies to fight in Europe.[25] Between 1914 and 1918 157,000 black Africans from the French empire were drafted to fight in Europe, and their conscription caused much unrest.

253

Learning their trade: King's African Rifles infantrymen oil their Martini Rifles under the eye of their British officer, Somaliland, 1903.

Standing easy: Native soldiers of the Sultan of Zanzibar wait for inspection by their British officers, 1896.

Britain's main African forces were the West Africa Frontier Force, which incorporated units from all the West African colonies and the King's African Rifles. In 1914 this consisted of three battalions, each with just over a thousand men and thirty-five British officers, and were recruited from Kenya, Uganda and Nyasaland. In contrast to British battalions, which each possessed two machine-guns, each company of the KAR had one, making five per battalion, a proportion which reflected their continuing use in small-scale policing operations.[26] Pay was much less than that of British troops: a private received 18s.6d a month and a senior NCO 37s.4d. Until recently flogging had been common, in both West and East Africa, for often quite trivial offences. In 1902 Meinertzhagen witnessed a Sudanese private receive twenty-five lashes for insubordination – he had called his sergeant the offspring of a hyena and a crocodile.[27] He was also horrified at the general laxness of the Kenya battalion, after having found that many of his company had rifles which were rusted or unworkable. It was just as bad in Somaliland, where Lieutenant Pope-Hennessy found men recruited locally 'not worth a damn – no discipline or anything else'.[28] He was cautioned against drilling them too fiercely or giving them fatigues for punishment, since they might desert to the Mullah or would lose face in front of their womenfolk. During one parade, a native lance-corporal dismissed himself to perform his devotions to Mecca, leaving Pope-Hennessy to conclude that only through years of drill and rigorous punishment would such men become real soldiers. In West Africa, where Moslem soldiers had to fight their co-religionists, it had been common for Moslem 'chaplains' to accompany the forces, and in Uganda Sudanese troops had been permitted to deck themselves with charms and amulets which they believed offered them supernatural protection. Even British officers had, at times, to bow to local customs.

Whereas the pre-1914 British army consisted largely of unmarried men, African forces contained a high proportion of married soldiers. They often expected to bring their wives and families with them on campaigns, and one cause of the 1897 Uganda mutiny was the ill-considered official insistence that each soldier could bring only one of his wives. The Sierra Leone contingent of the West Africa Frontier Force, stationed at Kumasi after the 1900 campaign, had been promised a brief tour of duty after which they could return to Freetown and their families. In 1901 they mutinied, seizing and locking up their British officers and NCOs before marching to the coast, led by a senior NCO. They had planned to return home, by way of Liberia, but were intercepted by other local forces. Two NCOs were sentenced to death, and ten others to long terms in prison, but these sentences were reduced to penal servitude for life and five years.[29] The common view among officers of the regiment was that their own commanders had failed to keep faith. It was a matter of accepted principle that the British officer's word was inviolate. Just as in India, he was a father to his men, ruling and guiding them like a father, although it is hard to imagine some of the officers uncovered by Meinertzhagen and Trenchard fulfilling this paternal role with any conviction. Still, in battle these troops did behave admirably even by the demanding yardstick applied to them by their officers, which was, naturally, the conduct of British regulars. During the operations against Benin in 1897, a black junior officer of the Oil Rivers Protectorate constabulary was observed by his commander, Captain Boisragon, to be 'as plucky as any white man'.[30]

Volunteers and Colonials

The largest force of volunteers to fight in Africa was the Imperial Yeomanry, of whom over thirty thousand served in the Boer War as mounted infantrymen. The lack of vital mounted troops, the shortage of regulars (one in three recruits was turned down as medically unfit in 1899) and the national response to the disasters of 'Black Week' in December 1899 led to public demands for a new volunteer force. A north-country squire wrote to his local paper on 18 December to put the case for forming units of 'young men (my son one of them) who can shoot and ride'. This and many similar appeals to the sons of the gentry fell on fertile ground, seasoned and watered by the moral teaching of the public schools and the tales of G. A. Henty and others. Not only were the young of the landed and professional classes willing to give their services but there were volunteers from the lower-middle and working classes, where many young men were keen for adventure in a foreign war against the enemies of the empire. The fires which lit up the youth of England also singed the middle-aged, who reached for their pocketbooks and pledged cash for uniforms, kit and horses. Steamship companies promised a free passage for the yeomanrymen, and they were included in the Prudential Assurance's special war offer which gave life cover of £100 for a single man, £250 for a married.

The army welcomed this outburst and the men who followed it, providing each with a rifle and a bayonet. Officers were found, often from the yeomanry's own ranks, like an eighteen-year-old Etonian who was an adjutant for one unit. There was a spirit of public school manliness abroad, and what the volunteers lacked in training and discipline was more than made up for by their enthusiasm, even in the face of drudgery and poor victuals of campaigning. 'We are all longing to have a good go in at the brutes,' wrote one in March 1900 as his detachment was moved up to the fighting line.[31] All this was something new for the army, whose rank and file were marked with doggedness and laconicism. A cavalry commander, Major General Brabazon, considered that the new men represented 'the intelligence of the English nation' but in spite of that they did what they were told.[32] He regretted that they were not proper cavalry and since, in his mind, the Anglo-Saxon liked to use a chopping weapon, he wondered, in a magnificent flight of fantasy, whether they should be armed with battle-axes or tomahawks. The suggestion was passed over.

There were other volunteers in South Africa, drawn from the white dominions, Canada, New Zealand and Australia. For them and their services, the army's welcome was often qualified, for senior officers soon noticed that the strapping young pioneers looked askance at the deference and slavish discipline demanded from British soldiers. This was understandable, since the fathers and grandfathers of these men had left Britain to escape from a social hierarchy in which the limits of a man's advancement were dictated by his birth. There were no such handicaps for pioneers in countries where there was a freer and easier relationship between the classes and where authority did not inspire the same deference and awe as in Britain. The elected colonial governments and their peoples were often, in terms of loyalty to the British Crown and empire, more royalist than the king and for this reason were anxious to send volunteers to fight in colonial campaigns. In 1885 volunteers from New South Wales had been sent to the Sudan, all smart in red tunics and white helmets and well able, in spite of this, to rough it in a hot climate. 'Fine fellows, and as keen as mustard' when it came to fighting, they were not, in the mind of one officer, inured to discipline. On a route march they took off their jackets and belts and hung their rifles on transport camels, to the horror of their colonel, a Crimea veteran.[33] Another, more sympathetic officer, realized that in the outback the division between master and man did not exist; each worked with and helped the other, a workaday condition which made it hard for the mounted men of the volunteers to accept a rigid chain of command on campaign. Likewise the freedom of speech of the outback raised the eyebrows and blood pressure of British officers, who found the Australian soldiers' camaraderie distasteful.[34] No British officer would have contemplated the example of the colonel of a Canadian unit, Strathcona's Horse, who was challenged to a stand-up fight after a dispute with one of his troopers. An ex-Mountie, the colonel obliged and laid the man out before he had time to get out of his jacket, catching him unawares and vulnerable the moment his arms were pinioned by the sleeves.[35]

For their part, colonials had little time for the traditional British officer. General Carrington was bluntly told by settler volunteers in Matabeleland in 1896, 'We will consider it an honour to stand under you, Sir, but object to eye glasses and kid gloves otherwise.'[36] Hide- and book-bound officers of the stiff and officious kind got short shrift from such fighting men, although Baden-Powell, whom they seem to have adored, was

Brave colonial boys: Volunteer troopers of Major Wilson's column, Matabeleland, 1893. All were killed in a heroic engagement on the banks of the Shangani River.

full of their praises. From his experience he knew that southern Africa 'teems with good material for forming a fighting force at a moment's notice'. In Rhodesia he found an ex-scout from the United States army who had fought in the Indian wars, a Cambridge graduate with a pince-nez, an ex-Royal Navy able seaman, 'a fine young fellow, full of pluck, who will press on where devils fear to tread' and many like them serving with the British South Africa Company. Some of these were members of the Company police, and the *Times* correspondent encouraged young colonists to join this force to help find their feet in the colony: 'The troopers are a good lot, as a rule, a remarkable proportion of them being gentlemen, men who had her Majesty's Commission, public schoolboys, University men and others.'[37] One, Mark Brown, a young man from Berkshire, who joined the Bulawayo police in May 1895, quickly got into the spirit of his new life and wrote breezily home the following October: 'Active service won't be much of a picnic though I reckon the maxims will make short work of the niggers if they show themselves.'[38] Such work was well paid: the rates during the Matabele rebellion were 10 shillings a day, and half that amount under regular army rather than company discipline.

The latter was little liked, for it meant not only punctilious officers but also army punishment, and during the 1896 operations a fair number of volunteer troopers endured field punishments for drinking on patrol and sleeping on sentry duty.[39] Still, as Baden-Powell observed, they were ardent, quick to adapt to new methods of fighting and, as good frontiersmen, fine riders and crack shots. For all this, 'colonials' made other British officers uneasy, since despite their fighting skills they were considered brash, insubordinate (Australians in South Africa tended not to salute British officers and saw no reason why they should) and uncomfortably egalitarian. Ironically, an Australian officer, trying to rally a detachment of the Victoria Rifles, shouted at his men, 'Get up, you lumps, and behave like Englishmen.'[40]

Weaponry

Whilst the valour and pertinacity of Britain's fighting men played their part in the conquest of Africa, the frequency and totality of their victories owed much to the overwhelming firepower which they possessed. The European inruption into Africa in the late 1870s and 1880s had coincided with an arms revolution. In less than twenty years a quick succession of technical advances increased the range and rate of fire of European firearms and directly sealed the fate of Africa. There were three outstanding features of this revolution. The first was the development of the machine-gun in the United States during the early 1860s; the second the invention of reliable mechanisms for efficient breech-loading rifles, and the third an advance in industrial engineering which made possible the mass production of these weapons and their ammunition with unprecedented precision. Both the Admiralty and the War Office kept abreast of these innovations and were quick to exploit them.

In 1867 the British army adopted the Snider-Enfield breech-loader which, in its carbine form, was used by mounted colonials in the Kaffir war of 1878. Its range and rate of fire enabled seventy-five dismounted men to break a force of fifteen hundred, many armed with smooth-bore muzzle-loaders, and kill fifty-eight before they scattered.[41] The way ahead was clear. In 1871 the army replaced the Snider with the .450 Martini-Henry breech-loader which fired a soft-nosed bullet a thousand yards; it remained in use, particularly with native regulars, until 1914.

The Gatling gun: Used by the British army and navy in the 1870s and 1880s; this model is being manned by the British South Africa Company police to defend Bulawayo in 1896.

Its place as the standard British infantry weapon was taken by the Lee Metford rifle in 1888, which, after some alterations to its design and mechanism, became the .303 Lee Enfield. First issued in 1895, the Lee Enfield, like its immediate predecessor, was a bolt-action rifle with a magazine which held nine rounds. Its range was 2,800 yards, and in the hands of a skilled man it could fire up to nine or ten rounds a minute.

The Royal Navy adopted the crank-operated, multi-barrelled Gatling machine-gun in 1871 and the army followed suit a few years later, using the new weapon in Zululand and Afghanistan. In 1884 the army turned to the five-barrelled Nordenfedlt .450 machine gun and the lighter, single-barrelled Gardner. Each of these guns suffered from jamming, through the fault of brass Boxer cartridges, but both the Gatling and Nordenfeldt could manage up to three hundred rounds a minute, and their value against massed charges was obvious. Whilst they remained in use for many years (a Gatling was employed in 1915 during the suppression of a mutiny in Singapore), these crank-turned machine-guns were superseded by the Maxim, which had been first tested in 1885. It was a single-barrelled, water-cooled machine-gun which fired six hundred rounds a minute thanks

Imperial arsenal: This party of British South Africa Company troopers stand with the whole apparatus of imperial firepower. From left to right, a Maxim, a Nordenfeldt, a seven-pounder, another Nordenfeldt, whose five barrels can be clearly seen, and a war-rocket launcher.

to a gas recoil mechanism. It was light and, unlike the others, could be fired from a concealed position. One was taken by Stanley to Equatoria in 1887, and in the same year another was employed against Yonni tribesmen by colonial forces in Sierra Leone. Two years later it became the British army's standard machine-gun.

This novel weaponry changed irreversibly the balance of military power in Africa. Before, when both European and African forces had been equipped with smooth-bore muzzle loaders, the Africans stood some chance of success. An Ashante army had, in 1824, proved this by inflicting a signal defeat on the forces of the governor of Cape Coast. Naturally many African rulers made efforts to acquire the new arms, but with disappointing results. Cetshwayo's predecessors had imported great stocks of muskets (at 7s.6d each) into Zululand and had asked for help in their maintenance from local missionaries. Others tried to buy new rifles or encouraged black troops to desert their European officers and bring weapons with them. The Dervishes were, perhaps, the most successful, for in 1891 the Khalifah possessed an armoury of four Krupp cannon, three rocket tubes and six machine-guns, all of which were cared for by an ex-Egyptian officer and his staff of former Egyptian gunners.[42] An Austrian prisoner, Neufeld, was coerced into making ammunition for these and the Khalifah's arsenal of Remington rifles, which, like his other modern weapons, were spoils from the 1883–4 campaign. Yet in 1896–8 none of these weapons seem to have been used against the Anglo-Egyptian forces, nor even earlier against the Ethiopians. It is of course possible that their mechanisms had deteriorated or that the Khalifah, faced with much domestic restlessness, wanted to keep them under his close control at Omdurman. Any hope which he or any other African ruler may have had of getting more of such arms was squashed when the European powers signed the Brussels Act of 1892 by which they jointly promised to ban and suppress any importation of modern arms into sub-Saharan Africa.

If African armies possessed few modern weapons, their enemies had them in abundance. As a matter of military principle, European forces always went on campaign with a high proportion of machine-guns to each unit. In 1897 six Maxim guns travelled with the 539 men of Royal Niger Company's expedition to Bida and Illorin, and there was one machine-gun to 130 men in the German forces engaged in the suppression of the 1905 uprising in Tanganyika.[43] Theory and its practise were simple: the enemy was overwhelmed with firepower. It was observed in West Africa that, even when the enemy was hidden by bush or jungle foliage, the noise of the bursts of Maxim gun fire was sufficient to scare them off. This had been the case during the fighting around Bida and Illorin in 1897. Two of the brawniest native porters carried the Maxim tripod and barrel on their heads, and when the bugler sounded the note 'G', they brought them forward and the gun was set up. A European officer always fired it, with four constables to feed the ammunition belt and change the water. Since the .450 cartridges used black powder, the gun was quickly enshrouded in thick black smoke, so a constable would be sent forward to shout back the directions of the targets. It was very haphazard, but what really mattered was that the sharp, short bursts of fire created a real or potential killing zone or scattered groups of natives. In each battle just over a thousand rounds were fired by each gun, the equivalent of two minutes firing, but this was all that was needed to unnerve the Nupe tribesmen. There had been some jamming, in spite of careful supervision of the guns' manufacture, but this

The Maxim gun.

was the consequence of faulty cartridges. Jameson's eight Maxims also suffered problems and in the fight near Johannesburg were *hors de combat* because water supplies ran out.[44]

Where logistic evidence exists for an African battlefield, it suggests that the key to success was to swamp the enemy with fire of every kind. At Toski in 1885 115,815 rounds of Martini-Henry ammunition were fired from rifles and cavalry carbines, and the eight artillery pieces fired 161 explosive shells, 169 rounds of shrapnel and five of case (grapeshot). Together shells and bullets killed an estimated fifteen hundred, one in ten of the Dervish army, and another three thousand surrendered, shattered by the weight and rapidity of the fire which hit them as they rushed over eight hundred yards of open ground. None seems to have got to grips with the Anglo-Egyptian forces who pursued them after the battle. At Jidbali in Somaliland in 1904, thirty thousand rifle and machine-gun rounds were fired in forty-five minutes at targets which were skirmishing in the bush between four and six hundred yards from the square. The enemy's dead was thought to be about five to six hundred, which suggests that one in six hundred rounds found their mark. There were no figures for Somali wounded, who were carried off, but the fact that expanding bullets were used during these campaigns indicates that many more may have died later from their injuries.[45] At Toski each infantryman had fired between twenty and fifty rounds, depending on his unit's whereabouts in the battle. These would have been fired in volleys. One tenth of the rounds fired at Jidbali came from the barrels of three Maxim guns which would no doubt have 'sprayed' the bush, whilst the British and Indian troops fired on average eighty rounds from their bolt-action rifles. In sum, what machine-guns and rifles created were concentrated waves of fire which both caused casualties and broke up formations, forcing men to keep their distance and making advance impossible. Other weapons created other kinds of terror.

> The 7-pounders are most excellent guns, as they are made to stand any amount of knocking about, and also to be mounted and dismounted in a very short space of time. They are much disliked by the natives of the country, who call them 'the gun that shoot twice', referring to the explosion of the shells, which they consider distinctly unfair, taking place as it does so far away from the gun and most unpleasantly close to themselves, when they are, they fondly imagine, out of range. Another thing they object to strongly is the war rocket, which they look on as an invention of the devil, and cannot understand how the wretched thing keeps on working its way through the thickest of forest, looking for them everywhere, as it were.[46]

In moral terms such demonstrations of firepower and explosive technology must have created, as their users intended, a sense of hopelessness which, for many, turned to despair. Explanations for such phenomena were made in terms in magic, which, for Dervishes, West Africans and Matabele, sometimes offered a vain defence in the form of spells, charms and potions which gave, as it was said, invulnerability.

Transport

The arms revolution of the later nineteenth century underwrote British superiority on the battlefields of Africa, but there was the constant problem of how to get armies to the battlefield and to keep them supplied with ammunition, food and medicine. It was of course easier where railways existed, as in South Africa in 1899 or where they were built as part of military operations, as in

New lines of conquest: African navvies work by day and night (thanks to the arc lights) to build a military railway, South West Africa (Namibia), 1915.

the Sudan in 1885 and again in 1896–8. This was the only way in which large British contingents could operate without falling into the snare which had destroyed Hicks in 1883, foodless, waterless and cut off in the desert. At Sawakin the army had to build its own railway, and since the local Dervishes were unwilling to undertake the track-laying, navvies were shipped in from Britain. They made a strange sight in billycock hats, corduroy trousers and fustian jackets; they drank too much beer and consequently many fell sick. They were, however, better paid and fed than the regular soldiers and sailors, for whom they quickly developed some compassion.

Where there were no railways, the forces had to make do with what transport could be commandeered or hired locally. The Zulu campaign of 1879 highlighted many of the hitches which occurred elsewhere at other times. The standard army wagon was soon found to be useless in a land where there were no roads, but the American 'buckwagon' and local forms of transport were quickly brought in. These were drawn by oxen, and both beasts and wagons had to be bought or hired from the Cape

Mules for Maxims: Indian transport troops lead ammunition mules across a pontoon bridge, South Africa, 1901.

Essential transport: Native labourers loading a standard army service wagon, South Africa, 1900.

and Natal, where there were plenty of *entrepreneurs* who were anxious to make as much money as they could from the army's misfortunes, honestly and crookedly.[47] With the means of transport came the men to look after it, but they soon found that a military regime was unbearable. The conductors, who overlooked the wagon-trains, were, in one officer's judgement, 'independent, lazy and not over civil' and were often ignorant of native languages, which caused all sorts of difficulties when giving orders to the Africans who did the chores. They were, like their white masters, dissatisfied with their conditions, often deserted back to their homes and plundered the goods carried by wagons which had broken down, of which there were plenty.

Much the same sort of snags faced transport officers during the Boer War, where even more horse- or ox-drawn transport was needed. Once supplies and ammunition left the station sidings, they had to be moved by cart to the front line. Over a hundred thousand Africans were locally recruited for this work and paid wages of between £1.10.0. and £4.10.0. a month, rates which were better than those earned in the mines. Discipline was strict. Two native drivers who got drunk and hit a conductor were given five lashes each at De Aar in November 1899, and in Worcester, which was under martial law, a labourer who refused to shift burnt dung at a remount depot and hit the overseer got twelve lashes.[48] Indian labourers and Indian soldiers from service battalions were also drafted in to assist the transport departments.

In malarial regions, like West Africa, horses and oxen died. Columns which moved through the bush and jungle therefore relied on native porters, either recruited locally, like the 'loafers' dragooned from the streets of Freetown and shipped to the Gold Coast in 1874, or through friendly chiefs who would hire out men from their tribe for cash. Given that columns had to carry all their food and ammunition, the numbers of porters needed were often large. 825 were needed to support the 538 men who marched on Bida in 1897, where the commander thought that the additional porterage would help make life easier for the British officers who would thereby be assured of a better diet. The loads carried were up to eighty pounds, but it was widely agreed that forty pounds was the most convenient burden (this represented 250 rounds of ammunition) to be carried on the porter's head, and cases of bully beef and the like were accordingly packaged. In Somaliland camels were used, and in 1903–4 the army required over thirteen thousand of them, together

Black man's burden: Porters for a military column, East Africa, 1916.

Punishment: Flogging of an African labourer, bound to an army water tank, South Africa, 1900.

Women at war: Somali women carry out their traditional tasks loading camels, Somaliland, 1903.

with their attendants. This type of drudgery was not liked by Somali men, who by tradition left it to women, and so hundreds of women had to be enlisted. Those men who served in this menial capacity had to be given a fez and a spear, tokens which enabled them to boast that they were, in fact, warriors.[49] There were other drawbacks in the local recruitment of carrying-labour, for many tribesmen, living on the thin rations desig-nated to them, deserted and went back to their villages in spite of the coercion of boot and whip. Some, like the four thousand recruited in Natal and the Cape in 1879, were justifiably alarmed by thoughts of what their fate might be if they fell into the hands of the Zulus. In general, the military authorities preferred to bring porters in from other countries, to where they could not run off.

In South Africa steam-traction engines were imported to haul supply carts, and they managed quite well, and by 1914 motor vehicles were being considered as a means of moving troops and supplies quickly across desert areas. Other devices of late Victo-rian and Edwardian inventiveness also found their way to remote campaigns. The heliograph, transmitting messages by flashing sunlight on mirrors, was particularly suitable for Africa, and in 1893 the Matabele, perplexed by its behaviour, concluded

270

*Technology fails: One of Colonel Templer's steam-engines comes adrift,
South Africa, 1900.*

that the white men were speaking to the gods in the sky.[50]
Equally awed were the Dervishes around Sawakin who, in
March 1885, watched the slow inflation and ascent of an
observation balloon which then hung over them for seven hours
whilst a junior officer, suspended in a wicker basket, spied out
the land. The balloon was the brainchild of Colonel James
Templer of the King's Royal Rifle Corps whose private enthusiasm for ballooning had enabled him to persuade the War
Office of their military value. The balloons were made from the
guts of oxen (74,000 were needed for one) and they were made
by the wives and daughters of soldiers stationed at Aldershot
under conditions of tight security. In action, the balloons were
blown up with gas, contained in zinc cylinders, and secured by
wire rope. The 'aeronaut' was given a parachute and a telephone
with which to inform the men on the ground of what he saw.
During the battle of Paardeburg in 1900 one remained up for
thirteen days in spite of the efforts of the Boer artillery to shoot it
down. When Templer retired from the army in 1906, he was
enthusiastically considering the possibilities of aeroplanes for
army reconnaissance. Of course there were some who were
unimpressed, and Templer's steam-engines were mistrusted by
many officers who insisted that the horse was still essential in
war. Anyway, for those in more fashionable regiments, the
Army Service Corps remained the 'muck train'.

Medical services

Contrary to what is sometimes argued, the introduction and use
of quinine in the 1850s did not make the febriferous regions of
Africa safe for Europeans. The death rate from fever, which for
the most part meant malaria, remained high throughout this
period; it was five per cent on the Niger Coast in 1894–5, a
mortality rate which one British officer attributed to the excessive drinking of the British community, whom he characterized
as 'counter-jumpers of the worst type and the biggest bounders
into the bargain'.[51] To prevent being invalided home or falling
victim to fever or dysentery, the soldier was strongly advised to
take precautions.

Most of the preventive measures recommended by service
physicians were concerned with personal hygiene and the
maintenance, where possible, of temperate habits. Although
some troops fought in tight red tunics until 1885 (the battle of

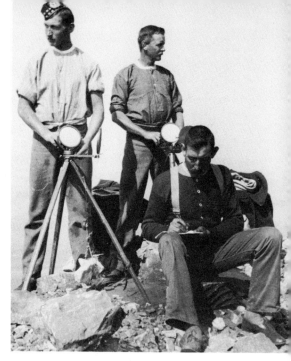

Messages from the sun: Heliograph unit of a Highland Regiment on duty, South Africa, 1901.

Ginnis was the last time red coats were seen on the battlefield), from 1874 onwards there were attempts to introduce a uniform more suited to African conditions. During the Ashante campaign British soldiers wore grey serge Norfolk jackets, flannel shirts, loose pantaloons and 'drawers according to taste'.[52] In the Sudan in 1884 grey corduroy jackets were worn with Bedford cord breeches and, as a measure against sun-blindness, tinted glasses. Later additions included quilted neck-flaps to prevent sunstroke, and spine-pads which were thought to reduce the risks of the backbone becoming over-heated. At all times the sun helmet was essential. Cholera belts of flannel were worn under their white serge uniforms by sailors during the 1886–7 Niger expedition, and they were also issued with mosquito nets.

As well as dressing in a way which, it was imagined, might lessen the effect on the body of extremes of heat, servicemen were ordered to forestall tropical distempers by common sense and regular habits. All British officers who served with the 1897 Bida-Ilorin expeditionary force were ordered to drink alcohol sparingly, take tepid baths, never swim in pools or streams and close crop their hair, while at all times 'the bowells should be kept open'. Water was crucial and it was insisted that supplies for European drinking and cooking, for native use and for horses were to be kept separate. For the British officers all water was to be filtered and boiled. At each camp latrines were dug a distance away and were to be of three kinds: for Europeans (which were

273

Looking for the Boers: Balloon detachment of the Royal Engineers near Pretoria; the horses are pulling waggons which carry the gas cylinders.

Lift-off: Observation balloon prepares to ascend, Pretoria, 1900.

screened), native constables and porters. A constable stood guard and another shovelled earth over the excrement at regular intervals. Despite all this the casualty rate was high: four out of twenty-three British officers suffered from fever and dysentery, and one died and one in five of the native troops were taken sick with diarrhoea, bronchitis and pneumonia in the course of a two-week campaign.[53]

When men were taken sick, it was imperative that they were given speedy medical treatment, but this was an area where arrangements were often woefully haphazard. In the Gold Coast in 1874 and 1895 a reserve of porters with hammocks were kept in readiness to carry sick British soldiers back to the coast, and in the Sudan the wounded were carried in panniers slung on the side of camels. This, in terms of jolting, was bad enough, but the victims of sickness or wounds in the Boer War suffered even more in horse-drawn ambulances whose suspension was so poor that many cried out to be killed rather than endure being bumped back to the field hospitals. Often the chances of being picked up at all were slim. Private Bowe of the Border Regiment contracted pneumonia after exposure whilst sleeping in the open in June 1900 and spent an eight-hour journey in an ambulance without food or drink.[54] Lieutenant Fuller, taken ill with a high fever and abdominal spasms, was treated first with peppermint juice, then castor oil and finally abandoned by the Medical Officer, who wandered off, leaving him on his back. He managed to gather up a dozen other invalids and malingerers and got a soldier to stop a train, which took them to a siding not far from a hospital. Only through the help of another officer did he get to Wynberg hospital, where, in the nick of time, his appendix was taken out.[55]

Such experiences give weight to the contemporary arguments that during the Boer War the army's medical facilities were not up to the mark, even when they were helped out by volunteer units. Dr Richard Tooth, bravely serving in the Portland Hospital, which had been financed by private subscriptions, found four to five thousand sick men, many crawling with lice and 'in every stage of misery and desolation'.[56] As more and more enteric cases were admitted, he found that, not far from the sick men's tents, dead horses were being left to rot by the local military authorities. Unreadiness was one excuse, and the other was the shortage of army doctors, but this was not surprising, as the Royal College of Surgeons pointed out.[57] Pay was low, the opportunities for study were curtailed and promotion was based

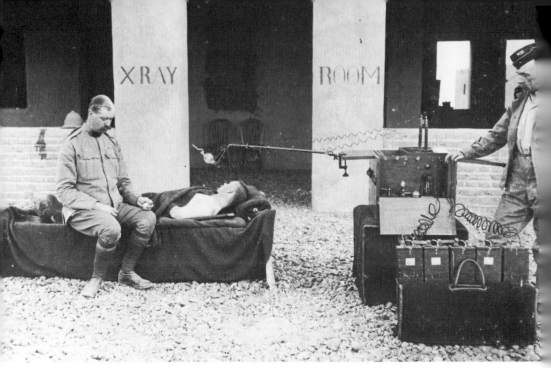

Looking for bullets: An X-ray unit accompanied British forces to Khartoum in 1898 where this picture was taken. During the Boer War such machines were invaluable for helping surgeons find and extract bullets.

(bottom left) Battlefield dentist: A quick extraction by an army officer on the veldt, South Africa, 1900.

(bottom right) Field ambulance: 'A vehicle designed to cause the greatest amount of suffering to its inmates' – J. F. C. Fuller

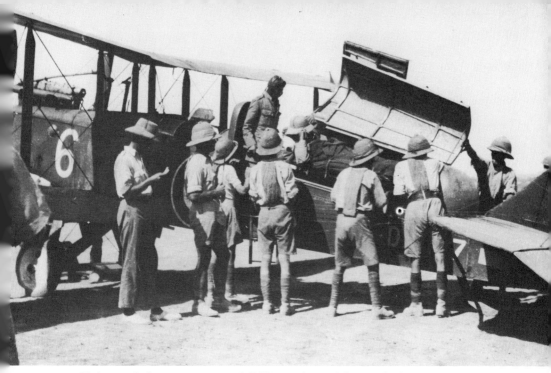

Flying ambulance: a converted DH9 carries a sick man back to base, Somaliland, 1920. Over three quarters of the RAF unit involved in operations became victims of exhaustion and disease in spite of their spine pads.

Beating enteric: Steam pump, sterilizing unit and newly laid pipes at the Portland hospital, all part of the army's answer to the high death rate during the Boer War.

Nurses: The Boer War revealed their value in field hospitals and that there were not enough of them – the ladies here are volunteers from a London hospital.

upon seniority and not talent. In the field, doctors had to make do with unsuitable tents and bad ambulances and had to get necessary requisitions through the Army Service Corps.

The answers were found, but late. Bacteriology, hygiene and sanitation were added to the exam requirements for the Royal Army Medical Corps, where conditions of pay and service were made more enticing. Still old obsessions fought their way to the surface, and the Royal Commission investigating ways of reform insisted on single doctors, for married ones might have 'wives . . . obtained whilst students, and who are not fitted socially for the position of an officer's wife'.[58]

Meanwhile, in South Africa, where there had been over thirteen thousand cases of typhoid in nine months, remedies were in hand. Correct procedures were adopted for the treatment of water and sewage, and the sickness rate dropped accordingly. In May 1901 the daily sick rate stood at 850, with 152 cases of dysentery, and two months later this had fallen to 224 and 59 respectively. Those who did find their way to hospital were, on the whole, well-treated or at least found that its dietary regime was better than they had been used to. But the RAMC orderlies seem to have got a bad name, a forerunner of the 'Rob all my comrades' of the 1914–18 war. Dr Tooth found some who were ignorant of how to make a bed, and Lieutenant Fuller was horrified when one strolled through his ward holding an amputated limb by the toe; another was pointed out to Erskine Childers as 'the _____ who stole the _____ boots off the _____ corpse in the _____ dead 'ouse'.[59]

Afterword

There had been no pattern to Britain's imperial wars in Africa. The largest had been fought to secure strategic advantages such as control of the Nile and the domination of southern Africa. Others had their roots in the need to secure local political advantage, which invariably meant teaching the natives an iron lesson on the hopelessness of resistance. The time span of conquest and pacification was short, stretching from the late 1870s to 1914, by which date all but a few Africans had submitted to British governance. Other colonial powers were less lucky: Italy, Spain and France were faced with campaigns in North Africa and Ethiopia which lasted until the mid-1930s. For the British army and navy the wars in Africa were an extension of their traditional roles as imperial police which had first been undertaken over a hundred years before the partition of Africa and which they continued to play until the final dissolution of the Empire in the 1960s. Wellington's campaigns in India in the 1790s, wars in Afghanistan, the Maori Wars, the bombardment of Alexandria, the Boer War, the overthrow of the Mad Mullah, the struggles in Palestine, Malaya, Cyprus and Brunei were all part of the same process by which Britain's armed forces underpinned Britain's global and imperial pretensions.

In Africa, as elsewhere, such campaigns were the ladders by which officers climbed to preferment. Kitchener, Haig, French, Plumer and Hamilton were all veterans of African campaigns in which they had embellished their reputations and advanced careers which culminated in high command during the First World War. Few such officers would have been so foolish as to have imagined that battle experience against ill-armed tribesmen was a testing ground for war in Europe, although some may have concurred with the commonplace assertion that the machine-gun was a weapon whose greatest value was in fighting natives. Still, what was learnt in the Boer War paved the way for reorganization and reform of the army in the years before 1914 and therefore helped improve the efficiency and effectiveness of the British soldier in the battles of that year and later.

For the British public, imperial wars in Africa were a source of excitement and pride. They placed no heavy burdens on the taxpayer and were fought by professionals trained for the purpose. Only during the Boer War were there any hints of misgiving, largely as a result of the high cost of war in money and lives and doubts about some of the measures taken against civilians. As to the treatment which was sometimes handed out to natives, this aroused little concern, save of those who were implacably opposed to empire-building on moral grounds. In 1920 and after, the British voter was little troubled by imperial issues. For him the Empire, in Africa and elsewhere, was a national responsibility, a burden which had to be shouldered and which, in an indirect way, offered some benefits to Britain. Even the Labour Party concurred in this view, although its paternalistic attitude was, in part, shaped by a belief that it was Britain's duty to do all that was possible to bring colonial peoples forward to a state where they could support and govern themselves. The inter-war period also saw 'policing' problems created by tribal disorder and nationalist agitation, but these created few difficulties for the armed forces, whose armoury now included the aeroplane.

It was the Second World War which highlighted the weaknesses and contradictions of the British Empire. Its peoples, including many Africans, fought a war for the 'four freedoms' and the Atlantic Charter, concepts which seemed at odds with an imperial system which balanced a benevolent paternalism with the threat of intimidation by force. In 1945, at the end of a struggle in which Britain's success had been dependent on the United States (an ex-colony), British claims to global power were in doubt. Britain possessed neither the will nor the wherewithal to support her claims or resist the pressure for the relaxing of imperial rule. Colonial peoples or those who had been educated in British traditions demanded what seemed to them British political rights. A new pattern emerged in Africa and elsewhere by which political resistance grew, to be met with force and then political compromise. In 1956 the Gold Coast became independent, as Ghana, and just less than twenty-four years later Rhodesia, after a settler revolt and a civil war, bowed to the pressure of black nationalism. But as Britain's African empire was dissolved, the newly independent countries discovered that British rule had created not only a civil elite but a military one. British-trained officers of the local forces, the successors of those which had first been the instruments of imperial conquest, stepped forward to prove that, just as ultimate power had once come from the Maxim, it now flowed from the Kalashnikov.

Sources

Official Records

Public Record Office, London.
Admiralty: Adm. 1, Adm. 53, Adm. 123.
Air Ministry: Air 8 (reports and memoranda relating to aerial policing).
Cabinet Office: Cab. 7 (minutes of the Imperial Defence Committee, 1885–99).
Colonial Office: Co. 291.
Director of Public Prosecutions: DPP 1/2, 1–2 (witnesses' depositions and letters for the Jameson prosecution).
War Office: WO 18, WO 32, WO 33, WO 76, WO 81, WO 83, WO 86, WO 91, WO 92, WO 97, WO 106, WO 107, WO 108, WO 148.

National Army Museum, London.
Headquarters Diary, Somaliland Field Force, 1963–4 (6,503–30).

Private and secondary sources

* denotes unpublished; NAM: National Army Museum; IWM: Imperial War Museum.
*Abadie, Capt. G., Diary, Rhodes House, Oxford
Anon. (A. Dickson), *Six Months in the Ranks* (1883)
*Anon., An autobiographical account of an army recruit, 1891 (NAM 7008-12)
*Anon., Letter from Natal, March 1900 (NAM 7907-135)
Anon., Letter from an Imperial Yeomanryman, *Sedberghian*, 14 (1902)
Anon., *The Non-Commissioned Officers Guide to Promotion* (1913)

Army Lists, 1860–1920
Austin, H. H., *With MacDonald in Uganda* (rpt., 1973)

Baden-Powell, R. S. S., *The Matabele Campaign, 1896* (1897)
Bagot, Mrs D., *The Shadows of War* (1900)
Bayham, H., *Men from the Dreadnoughts* (1976)
Beresford, C., *The Memoirs of Admiral Lord Charles Beresford* (2 vols, 1914)
Birdwood, Lord, *Khaki and Gown* (1941)
Blythe, R., *Akenfield* (Harmondsworth, 1969)
Boisragon, A., *The Benin Massacre* (1897)
*Bowe, L. (Private, Border Regt), Diary, Southern Africa Collection, Borthwick Institute, York
Boyle, A., *Trenchard, Man of Vision* (1962)
Brereton, F. S., *One of our Fighting Scouts* (1903)
—— *In the Grip of the Mullah* (1904)
*Burrough, Lieut., S., Diary 1905–6, Author's collection

Cameron, V. L., *Across Africa* (1877)
Champion de Crespigny, C., *Forty Years of a Sportsman's Life* (1925)
*Charles, Lieut. R., Letters and Papers (NAM 6706-66)
Childers, E., *In the Ranks of the CIV* (1901)
*Churcher, Lieut. D. W., Omdurman Diary (NAM 7804-53)
Clowes, W. L., *The Royal Navy* (7 vols, 1903)
*Cooper, Col. H., Letters and Papers (NAM 6112-190-18)
Cromer, Lord, *Modern Egypt* (2 vols, 1908)
Crowder, M., *The Story of Nigeria* (1962)
—— *Revolt in Bussa* (1973)
Crozier, F. P., *Impressions and Recollections* (1930)

*Danby, Sergt. W. (10th Hussars), Letters (NAM 7003-2)
*Daniels, J. (Trooper, 6th Dragoon Guards), Letter (NAM 8102-5-7)
*Davies, I. W. O. (Private, York and Lancaster Regt.), Papers (NAM 8201-13)
Donovan, C. H. W., *With Wilson in Matabeleland* (1894)

*Eastwood, Capt. H. de C. (King's Dragoon Guards), Letters (NAM 7111-16)
*Eden, Brig. General A. J. F., West Africa Diary (NAM Microfilm)
Emery, F., *The Red Soldier* (1977)

Fieldhouse, D. K., *The Economics of Empire* (1973)

Firm (the magazine of the Worcester Regt.), April 1934
Flint, J., *Cecil Rhodes* (1976)
Fuller, J. F. C., *The Last of the Gentlemen's Wars* (1937)
Furse, R., *Acuparius* (Oxford, 1962)

Gann, L. H. and Duignan, P., ed., *Colonialism in Africa, 1870–1960* (Cambridge, 1969)
Gardiner, A. G., *The Life of Sir William Harcourt* (2 vols, 1923)
Geary, W. M., *Nigeria under British Rule* (1927)
Glass, S., *The Matabele War* (1968)
Gleichen, Count, *With Camel Corps up the Nile* (rpt, 1975)
*Goodall, Colour Sergt., E., Letters and Papers (NAM 7403-70-1 to 7)
Gough, H., *Soldiering On* (1954)
Guy, J. J., 'A note on firearms in the Zulu kingdom', *Journal of African History*, 72 (1971)
—— *The Destruction of the Zulu Kingdom* (1979)
Gwynn, C. W., *Imperial Policing* (1936)

Haldane, A., *A Soldier's Saga* (1948)
Hamer, W. S., *The British Army; Civil Military Relations, 1885–1905* (Oxford, 1970)
Hamilton, I., *The Happy Warrior; a life of Sir Ian Hamilton* (1966)
Hansard, 4th Series
Henty, G. A., *By Sheer Pluck* (n.d.)
—— *Through the Sikh War* (n.d.)
—— *With Buller in Natal* (c. 1902)
*Hopwood, Sergeant H. (Manchester Regiment), Letters and Papers (NAM)
*Howard, Sir Esmé, Papers (Carlisle Record Office)
Huttenback, R. A., 'G. A. Henty and the vision of Empire', *Encounter*, July 1970
Hynes, W. G., *The Economics of Empire* (1979)

Ikime, O., *The Fall of Nigeria* (1977)

*Jelf, Captain R., Letters (NAM 6903-6-1)
Johnson, D. H., 'The Death of General Gordon: a Victorian Myth', *Journal of Imperial and Commonwealth History* (1982)
*Jourdain, Lieut., H., Letters and Papers (NAM 5603)

Kennedy, P., *The Rise and Fall of British Naval Mastery* (1976)
—— *The Rise of Anglo-German Antagonism* (1980)
Kiernan, V. G., 'Colonial Africa and its armies', *War and Society*, 2 (1977), ed. B. Bond and I. Roger

—— *European Empires from Conquest to Collapse* (1982)
Knight, E. F., *Rhodesia Today* (1895)
Kruger, R., *Goodbye Dolly Grey* (1983 ed.)

Langer, W. L., *The Diplomacy of Imperialism* (New York, 1956)
Lehmann, J. H., *All Sir Garnet* (1964)
Lloyd, A., *The Drums of Kumasi* (1964)
*Lucas, R. H. (Trooper, Imperial Yeomanry), Author's collection
Lyttleton, N., *Eighty Years* (1925)

McCalmont, H., *Memoirs* (ed. C. E. Callwell, 1924)
*Mackie, Lieut. McD., Papers (IWM)
Magnus, P., *Kitchener; Portrait of an Imperialist* (1958)
May, E., *Changes and Chances in a Soldier's Life* (1925)
Meinertzhagen, R., *Kenya Diary, 1902–1906* (1983 ed.)
Miers, S., 'Notes on the Arms Trade and government policy in Southern Africa between 1870 and 1890', *Journal of African History*, 12 (1971)
Miller, C., *Lunatic Express* (1978).
Missionary Year Book (1889)
Moneypenny, W. E. and Buckle, G. E., *The Life of Disraeli* (6 vols, 1920 ed)
Morris, D. R., *The Washing of the Spears* (1965)

Niger Coast Protectorate, Reports and Correspondence, 1889–1899 (Shannon, 1971)

Pakenham, T., *The Boer War* (1979)
Pease, H., ed., *The History of the Northumberland (Hussars) Yeomanry* (1924)
Perham, M., Lugard, *The Years of Adventure, 1858–1898* (1956)
Plaatje, S., *The Boer War Diary of*, ed., J. L. Comaroff (1976)
*Pope-Hennessy, Capt. H., Papers (NAM 7610-7)
Porter, B., *Critics of Empire* (1968)
Prevost-Battersby, H. F., *Robin Corfield of Somaliland* (1914)

Reitz, D., *Commando* (1982 ed.)
Richards, F., *Old Soldier Sahib* (1956)
Robinson, R. and Gallagher, J., *Africa and the Victorians* (1981 ed.)
Rosebery, Lord, *Miscellanies, Literary and Historical* (2 vols, 1921)
*Russell, Major A. B. (Somaliland Camel Corps), Papers (IWM)
*Rutland (Private 2nd Middlesex), Papers (NAM 8107-18)

Sellers, Revd., W. E., *From Aldershot to Pretoria* (n.d.)
Selous, F. C., *Sunshine and Storm in Rhodesia* (1896)

Seventy Ninth News, South African War Record, 1900–2 (Inverness, 1903)

Shibeika, M., *British Policy in the Sudan, 1882–1906* (Oxford, 1952)

Skelley, A. R., *The Victorian Army at Home* (1977)

*Skinner, Sergt. G. (RAMC), Papers (NAM 7909-15)

*Skoulding, Air Commodore F. A., Papers (IWM)

Slatin, R. C. von, *With Fire and Sword in the Sudan* (1897)

Smith-Dorrien, H., *Memories of Forty Eight Years Service* (1925)

Speirs, E. M., *The Army and Society, 1815–1914* (1980)

*Spraggs, Sergeant C. (Scots Guards), Diary (NAM 7706-14-6)

*Stackwood, W. (New Zealand contingent), Papers, Southern Africa Collection, Borthwick Institute, York

*Steele, Capt. M. (Army Service Corps), Diary of the Gambia Expedition, 1894 (Public Record Office, WO 107/10)

Steevens, G. W., *With Kitchener to Khartoum* (1898)

—— *From Cape Town to Ladysmith* (1900)

Streatfeild, F. N., *Reminiscences of an Old 'Un* (1911)

*Templer, Col. J. L. B., Papers (NAM 7404-59-1)

Thornton, A. P., *For the File on Empire* (1968)

*Tooth, Dr R., Diary (Private possession)

Trevelyan, *The Life of John Bright* (1913)

Tulloch, A. B., *Recollections of Forty Years Service* (1903)

*Tyndale-Briscoe, Lieut., W. E., Letters, Southern Africa Collection, Borthwick Institute, York

Vandeleur, S., *Campaigning on the Upper Nile and Niger* (1898)

Warner, D., *Dervish* (1973)

Warwick P., ed., *The South African War* (1980)

Webb, A. B., *Principles of Missions* (1896)

Wellesley, Lady Diana, *Sir George Goldie; Founder of Nigeria* (1934)

Wilkinson-Latham, R. and C., *Infantry Uniforms, 1855–1939* (1970)

Williams, W. W., *The Life of General Sir Charles Warren* (1941)

Wingate, F. R., *Ten Years Captivity in the Mahdi's Camp (Account of Father Ohrwalder)* (1898)

Winton, J., *Hurrah for the Life of a Sailor* (1977)

Witton, G., *Scapegoats of Empire* (rpt, 1982)

Wood, E., *From Midshipman to Field Marshal* (1907 ed.)

Woods, F., ed., *Young Winston's Wars* (1972)

Wylde, A. B., *'83 to '87 in the Soudan* (2 vols, 1888)

Younghusband, G., *Forty Years a Soldier* (1922)

Notes

THE NEW ROME: Imperial Visions, 1870–1914

1. Richards, p. 19
2. Blythe, p. 35
3. Furse, pp. 10–11
4. Webb, p. 10
5. Slatin, p. 402
6. Knight, p. 45
7. Prevost-Battersby, p. 68
8. Cameron, p. 374
9. *Hansard*, 76, 518
10. Langer, p. 123

Frontiers and Wars: Southern Africa, 1870–1902

1. WO 32/8329–31
2. Guy, p. 47
3. Emery, pp. 63–4
4. Lehmann, p. 246
5. WO 32/7786
6. Flint, pp. 248–52
7. I owe this information to Dr John MacKenzie of Lancaster University, who interviewed the man concerned.
8. Glass, pp. 41–2 and note
9. Flint, p. 205
10. WO 32/8551
11. DPP 1/2/2 fos. 833–4
12. Birdwood, p. 103
13. Reitz, p. 256
14. WO 32/8029-1
15. WO 32/8029-2
16. WO 32/8029-1

Egypt and the Sudan, 1882–1920
1. Lehmann, p. 300
2. Wingate, pp. 27–32 and WO 106/221
3. WO 106/221
4. Warner, p. 92, and WO 106/221
5. D. H. Johnson, *passim*
6. WO 106/222
7. WO 106/15
8. Steevens, *With Kitchener &c.*, p. 49
9. WO 32/256
10. WO 32/8385
11. WO 106/41
12. Ibid
13. For further details, *Times History of Great War* (1920) IX, 281–319
14. WO 106/259
15. Ibid
16. Kiernan, *European Empires &c.*, p. 198
17. Mackie
18. Kiernan, *European Empires &c.*, p. 199 and Gwynn, pp. 150–78
19. Air 8/40
20. Air 8/72

West Africa, 1870–1914
1. Adm. 123/126 fo. 152
2. Boyle, p. 89
3. Boisragon, p. 58
4. Adm. 123/126 fos. 3ᵈ–4ᵈ
5. *Niger Coast &c.*, p. 296
6. WO 32/7622
7. Abadie, fo. 8
8. Crozier, p. 108
9. Crowder, *Revolt in Bussa*, p. 119
10. Cab. 7/7 (memos of 17.11.87 and 8.3.92)

East and Central Africa, 1880–1920
1. WO 106/259.
2. Miller, p. 208
3. Meinertzhagen, p. 39
4. Ibid, pp. 39–40
5. Austin, p. 35
6. Ibid and WO 32/8417

7. WO 18/106
8. Somaliland HQ Diary
9. WO 32/5932
10. Ibid
11. WO 106/259
12. Ibid

BATTLE: **The Savage Foes**
1. Fuller, pp. 7–8 and Jelf
2. Donovan, pp. 265 and 283 and Champion de Crespigny, p. 248
3. Wylde, II, 109–110
4. Smith-Dorrien, p. 67
5. Danby
6. Smith-Dorrien, pp. 24–5
7. Tulloch, pp. 336–7
8. Wood, p. 401
9. Emery, pp. 200–201
10. WO 92/4
11. Emery, pp. 49–50
12. Ibid, p. 233
13. Lyttleton, pp. 191–2
14. Gleichen, pp. 131–2
15. Wylde, I, 153
16. WO 92/4
17. Danby
18. WO 32/8380
19. Smith-Dorrien, p. 19
20. Hansard, 42, 720, 840 and 1420, Selous, p. 31
21. Guy, p. 62
22. McCalmont, p. 175
23. WO 32/7622 and Vandeleur, p. 273
24. WO 32/7620
25. Steele
26. WO 32/6818
27. WO 32/8385
28. Selous, p. 130
29. Baden-Powell, pp. 150–152
30. Adm. 123/128
31. Air 8/40
32. Austin, pp. x and 107
33. Meinertzhagen, pp. 51–2
34. Mackie

35. Skoulding, Russell, WO 106/272, WO 32/5809, 5828 and 5932 have been used to compile this account of operations in 1920.
36. Skoulding
37. Air 8/40
38. Air 8/45
39. Air 8/40

The White Man's War
 1. H. Bailes, The Military Aspects of the War, in ed. Warwick, p. 84
 2. Younghusband, p. 226
 3. Lyttleton, p. 141
 4. WO 32/7827
 5. Hamer, p. 175
 6. May, p. 192
 7. Gough, p. 33
 8. May, p. 172
 9. Anon. (NAM 7907-135)
10. Stackwood
11. Jourdain
12. Rutland
13. Jourdain (quoted in W. Nasson, Tommy Atkins in South Africa, in ed. Warwick, p. 125 where the events are wrongly set at Colenso)
14. WO 90/51
15. Reitz, p. 28
16. WO 32/8045
17. May, p. 258 and Younghusband, p. 226
18. WO 32/8006
19. WO 91/51
20. WO 92/4, 8 and 9
21. Pakenham, p. 140
22. *Firm*, p. 33
23. Quoted in Warwick, p. 134, where 'sangar' is oddly said to be 'stomach'
24. Pease, pp. 33 and 36
25. WO 32/8007
26. May, p. 210
27. Howard
28. Fuller, p. 42
29. This account is drawn from Witton, *passim*, the letters of the Judge Advocate at Pretoria (WO 93/41 fos. 43–4, 69.81 and

123–40[d]), Witton's petition (WO 32/9116) and WO 90/6; I am indebted to Professor Davy, who drew my attention to material in the Transvaal archives (CS 1092)
30. Witton, p. 84
31. Cooper

CAMPAIGN: **Daily Life**
1. Spraggs
2. Emery, pp. 101–2
3. Pope-Hennessy
4. Crozier, p. 25
5. Bowe
6. Fuller, pp. 111–12
7. Childers, p. 129
8. Hopwood
9. Emery, p. 99
10. Adm. 53/14399 (Log, HMS *Thrush*)
11. Adm. 1/6788
12. Childers, p. 145
13. Beresford, II, 1 and Spraggs
14. Fuller, p. 44
15. I. W. O. Davies
16. Adm. 123/10
17. Anon., *Sedberghian*
18. DPP 1/2
19. Baden-Powell, p. 333
20. Anon, *Sedberghian*
21. Skinner
22. Hopwood
23. Burrough
24. Spraggs
25. Daniels
26. Crozier, p. 40
27. Younghusband, p. 225
28. Ibid and Stackwood
29. WO 92/9
30. CO 291/27/4357 fos 117–32
31. Tyndale-Briscoe
32. Cases cited in WO 90/51, WO 86/61 and WO 92/4, 8 and 9
33. Crozier, pp. 112–3
34. Abadie, fo. 64
35. Hopwood
36. WO 92/4

37. Ibid
38. Ibid
39. Younghusband, p. 227
40. Rutland
41. WO91/51 and 90/6
42. WO 91/51
43. WO 90/6
44. Bayham, p. 23
45. Charles (Letter of Lieut. Grubbe)
46. Rutland
47. Boisragon, pp. 37–8
48. Hopwood
49. Warwick, p. 133
50. WO 92/8
51. Tulloch, p. 321 and WO 92/4
52. WO 90/6
53. WO 92/4
54. Skelley, pp. 54–5
55. Goodall
56. Sellers, *passim* but especially pp. 54–5
57. *Seventy Ninth News*, pp. 166–7
58. WO 106/342/8/1/3
59. Howard
60. Childers, p. 181
61. WO 86/61

Men, Machines and Medicine

1. Davies
2. Anon. (NAM 7008-12)
3. WO 25/3893
4. Court Martial file (NAM 6012/238)
5. WO 81/134B
6. WO 92/4
7. WO 32/9117
8. Jourdain
9. Richards, pp. 39–41
10. Warwick, p. 124
11. WO 81/134B
12. Crozier, p. 82
13. Speirs, p. 227
14. Lyttleton, p. 100 and Haldane, p. 61
15. WO 32/7622
16. Crozier, pp. 73 and 128

17. Streatfeild, pp. 184–5
18. Meinertzhagen, pp. 9–10
19. Boyle, pp. 71–3
20. WO 32/8551
21. WO 106/276
22. Meinertzhagen, pp. 143–4
23. Eden and Crozier, p. 66
24. WO 106/259
25. Kiernan, *War and Society*, pp. 28–9
26. WO 106/276
27. Meinertzhagen, p. 11
28. Pope-Hennessy
29. WO 92/4 and Crozier, p. 93
30. Boisragon, p. 171
31. Lucas
32. WO 108/263
33. Younghusband, pp. 56–7
34. Stackwood
35. Birdwood, p. 113
36. Baden-Powell, p. 86
37. Knight, p. 42
38. DPP 1/1/1 fo. 685
39. WO 92/4
40. WO 32/8007
41. Williams, pp. 106–7
42. WO 106/15, 257 and 278
43. WO 106/242
44. DPP 1/2/2 fos. 975–6
45. WO 106/15, 194
46. Boisragon, pp. 26–7
47. WO 107/10
48. WO 148/48
49. WO 106/238
50. Donovan, pp. 26–7
51. Eden
52. WO 106/285
53. WO 32/7222
54. Bowe
55. Fuller, pp. 50–53
56. Tooth
57. WO 30/114
58. Ibid
59. Childers, pp. 231–2 and Fuller, p. 55

Index